Itch

A Life Well Lived

By

Randy and Ellen Hasness

Dedication

This book is dedicated to our wonderful children and grandchildren, to encourage them to live life to the fullest. We want them to know they are part of this book and Mom and FSD, *favorite step-dad*, Papa Randy and Grandma Ellen cherish them all.

Kevin, Traci, Lacey, Skip and Kim, and Rick.
Amanda, Val, Steven, Wyatt, Katie, Abby, Austin, Ella, Kai, and Sloane.

Noah, Ava, Autumn, and Matthieu.

Acknowledgment

To Ellen's brother George and sister-in-law Sara.

To Sara for her encouragement and proofreading skills.

To George for making the best martinis for Ellen and ensuring my whisky glass was always full.

Table of Contents

Chapter 1

The Beginning

A life story, a love story, a sailing story
...always an adventure

Some people are born with the need for the comfort of the familiar. There's a lot to be said for that; it's just not me. Somehow, I was born with itchy feet.

My beautiful stepdaughter, Lacey, gave my wife, Ellen, and me an amazingly fitting sign that hangs in a place of honor in our home, wherever and whatever that home might be. The sign, designed to hang upside down, is now in our current home in the desert. Before that, it hung in our beautiful sailboat, *Kwanesum*.

Years later, it hung in our home in the house we purchased in California, and then in our Airstream, Drifter, that we took three years to drift in. Always itchy feet. Always in our home. The sign states, *"Why be Normal?"* I'd say that's my life, before Ellen and after, and continues to this day. I don't know if I was actually born with itchy feet, or I just developed it along the way. It seems to stay. The encompassing comfort of the familiar is just not me.

I decided to write this story for our children and grandchildren, friends, and fellow sailors, in the hope it will show the many choices available to them throughout their lives. To me, adventure and travel are the spice of life, and keeping a sense of humor is the most important item to pack in your personal kit.

My story begins growing up in Beaverton, Oregon, with my mom and brother; my mom and dad were divorced when I was about 5 or 6. This was a time in Beaverton, during the '50s and early '60s, that were halcyon days; days I wish we could all turn the clock back to, now and then. Those were days where you hopped on your bike with your best friend and rode all day long, not always sure of where you were headed but knew you had to be home by the time the street lights came on for supper. Carefree days of building things in Grandma's basement with the hammers, nails, and spare blocks of wood she always had. Days of Boy Scout campouts telling ghost stories. Walking to town to the movies and then running fast to get home because that was a scary one with 3D glasses, and the monster might be running behind you! Days of making the Ouija board fly around, spelling out the next scary thing that might happen that night. Halcyon Days.

My mom worked for the Portland Police Department. Can you imagine that... your mom working for the Police Department? That could be a good thing or could be a bad thing. When you're younger, there were lots of good reasons for having a mom that worked in a police department. When we got older, not so much. We grew up having been taught to have great respect for the police. While Mom worked there in Portland, that department showed great respect for her. Mom was a character, loved people, respected people, and was damn good at her job. They all knew it and loved her.

2

Mom was in charge of the data processing center, a fairly new area at that time. Computers were just making the scene in large police departments, and she was a whiz at running the whole thing. It was a really big deal in those days for a woman, in a mainly all-male dominated police department, to be in charge of such a major portion of the office. Mom, in her feisty, strong-willed manner, did not have a lot of sympathy for the Feminist Movement of the time. She did not have patience for those damsels in distress who became victims at the whim of any small discrepancy. She could handle herself just fine with her male counterparts. "A good pair of spike heels was all you needed for defense." She didn't cringe at the language or sexism.

Mom had a wonderful friend named Audrey who worked for her and was gay. In those days, it was not something you really talked about openly. Some of the policemen (the word *"cops"* was not considered respectful in those days) began making disparaging remarks about Audrey, which, as you can imagine, made for an uncomfortable work environment.

Well, when Mom found out about these remarks, she immediately marched into the office of the Chief of Police and raised holy hell! Mom told him that Audrey was the best damn worker and employee she ever had, and her sexual orientation didn't make a God damned bit of difference! "If the harassing doesn't stop and it causes Audrey to leave, well, I'm going to leave right behind her!" The harassment stopped.

I must say my Mom was a fantastic friend to my brother and me. As you can imagine, a woman raising two boys by herself, keeping a roof over our heads and food in our bellies, did not have a lot of extra spending money to go around. We shopped at the Salvation Army Stores, canned vegetables, and if my brother and I were lucky enough to shoot a deer, the meat was cut and wrapped and stored in our freezer for later consumption. Mom cooked the best venison steaks ever.

Our house was in bad need of painting, and Mom must have mentioned that at work at some point. Well, low and behold, one day a bus pulled up in front of our house with a bunch of trustees from the Portland Police Department! They piled out of the bus and promptly started painting our house! What a testament to the integrity and thoughtfulness of my mom's workplace. A sorely needed project was completed.

The Portland Police Department was a tight-knit community. One final example of this great organization happened when I came home from school one day during Christmas and wanted to show my best friend Terry our Christmas tree with lights. In my excitement, I plugged the tree lights in and instantly, flames shot up the back of the tree and caught our curtains on fire! Oh my gosh! Terry ran to get his mom next door and I threw a cup of water on the tree. Terry's mom came quickly and bravely grabbed the tree and pulled it outside. Soon, the fire department arrived and extinguished what was left of the fire. I was devastated, scared out of my mind—a horrible, crazy, scary experience. The next morning, Mom, my brother Rollie, and I woke up to see a brand new, flocked Christmas tree in our front yard, compliments of the Portland Police Department.

There were better, bonus, cream of the crop plusses to where Mom worked. My brother and I practically grew up in that building in downtown Portland.

We were there often because... Mom. The biggest plus I remember, the biggest one for me, other than the new Christmas tree, was always getting the best seats for parades in Portland! You see, that was important to this young boy. Getting a superior seat to view the prestigious Portland Rose

4

Parade was monumental in my eyes at the time. Parades were magical. This parade always passed in front of the Police Department building, so my brother and I would perch in awe out the open windows upstairs to watch. Definitely a magical memory.

In the '50s, the elevators in the police department, and most department stores, had elevator operators. People were assigned only to work the elevator up and down to whatever floor they wanted. The door opened, you got in and, "Floor, please," they would say. The Elevator Operator would pull a lever and point it to the correct floor number, and up we'd go in the clanging elevator. The Elevator Operator in the Portland Police Department took a liking to my brother and me, as we were there often. He would sneak us up to watch the police lineups. He would bump the elevator up slowly to the floor where the lineups took place, just high enough so that we could peek in. In those days, there was a glass front on the elevator; pretty exciting for two little guys, and a bit scary and thrilling seeing those bad guys. We were there often in the summers as Rollie and I would climb aboard a Greyhound Bus in Beaverton and ride to Portland by ourselves to either meet Mom at the Police Department or go to the YMCA nearby.

We never had a problem traveling by ourselves. We felt quite grown up having that privilege.

When I reflect back on my life, I realize what a great neighborhood we lived in. Wonderful families lived next door, across the street and down the street. Since my mom was divorced, the dads in those homes embraced my brother and me like their own. They taught us to hunt, took us camping and hunting, were our Boy Scout leaders, had barbecues…just the type of neighborhood you'd see on TV. Mom took us camping, too, and taught us how to fish, and gave us the pleasure of tasting that fresh fish cooked that night or fried with eggs the next day for breakfast.

The cast of characters in my life growing up was the best. Roberta, one of my mom's best friends, had a farm where I worked during haying seasons, and where I also hid out when I was mad at Mom and ran away from home. Oh, yes. That did happen. My mom always knew where she could find me, though, when that happened. Roberta's farm was magical. She and her husband raised both Welsh and Hackney ponies that we showed at various competitions. They even had a grand champion pony named *"Kerr's Candy Kid"*. I loved life on the farm, and when I got my first pair of cowboy boots, I refused to take them off, even when I slept. I was a hardcase kid when I got older, always getting in trouble, and I never did very well at school. Roberta and Mom decided to get me a horse to teach me some responsibility. *Randy's Renegade* was their hope to give me purpose. I loved that horse. Halter and saddle breaking him gave me great pleasure, but soon enough, I lost interest and went back to my wayward ways.

Beaverton High School was the alma mater for my brother and I and where we practiced spreading our wings and figuring out life, like all young people. I'm sure every young person finds their high school years challenging, exhilarating, and somewhat painful, yet full of discovery. Doing so in the '60s was a challenge of its own, but the music was great. I played the drums in the Beaverton High School Band. I loved marching bands, and still do today. I also played in a two-man band with my friend John Walters. We thought we were the grooviest. We actually won first place in a parade in a little town outside of Portland, riding and playing on a float my mom's friend Ray entered. He was advertising his outboard engine repair business. Now, we were even more groovy. Mom actually ended up marrying Ray after I'd left home and joined the Navy. He was a great guy. I wish he had entered my life earlier.

I was not, as you probably surmised, enamored with school and found myself getting into trouble; too much trouble. In 1964, I thought maybe I should just quit school, join the Navy, and get on my own. I was 16 years old and a sophomore in high school. I got myself down to the nearest Navy recruiter and he said I would be able to join when I turned 17 that summer, but I would need to pass an exam and get my mom's permission. Well, I took the paperwork home and showed it to my mom. She looked at it and signed that thing so fast it almost hurt my feelings! Later on, my mom said it was one of the hardest things she'd ever done, but she knew it was a sink or swim time for me.

Chapter 2
Navy

Can't Wait to Get That Uniform On!

So, off I go, on a plane to San Diego. I'll never forget getting off that plane and seeing a young sailor in uniform with a big liplock on a beautiful girl. "Wow", I thought, "I can't wait to get that uniform on!"

The first few weeks of boot camp were... paperwork... yelling... learning the Navy 11 general orders that you must recite when ordered by your drill instructor or any non-commissioned officer... "Sir, the second general order is, I will walk my post in a military manner"... etc. Yelling, marching... yelling, and more... yelling. At barely 17 years old, I was homesick but determined to put up with whatever was dealt.

One day, a Non-Commissioned Officer came into the barracks and asked if anyone played a musical instrument. I stood up and told him I played the drums. He gave me a set of drumsticks and immediately tested my knowledge. Of course, I passed and was told to pack up my gear and report to the barracks of the Naval Drum and Bugle Corps! OK! How great is that?!

That stint in the Corps was, and still is, one of my greatest memories. We played at all the boot camp graduations, LA County parades and fairs and Disneyland. The Navy Choir lived on the top floor of our barracks, with the Drum and Bugle Corp on the first floor. Every evening, the Navy Choir would come down to the first floor and we'd all gather around a large center pole in the barracks and sing the Lord's Prayer and listen to Taps. It's a memory that warms my heart every time I think about it.

After boot camp, I was assigned to Point Magu Naval Air Station in Ventura County for some on-the-job training in Radio Communications. Next was scheduled 6 months of Radio "A" School back in San Diego. I'm sure I was mainly assigned as a Radio Operator because I learned Morse Code while in the Boy Scouts for a merit badge. I'm not kidding. I actually think that gave me a head start on the Dah Dit Dahs a Radio Operator needs to know. Big shout out to the Boy Scouts!

I received my first security clearance there in Point Magu and had "Crypto" (cryptography) Training.

After 3 or 4 months of training in crypto, I headed back down to San Diego to start 6 months of Radioman School. Radio School consisted of electronics training and learning to copy and send in Morse code. We'd sit in class for hours with headsets on while looking at a screen depiction of a typewriter keyboard that had keys that lit up. In the headsets, we'd hear Di Dah and the "A" key on the typewriter would light up.

We would all yell, "Di Dah!...! ALPHA!" and then strike the "A" key on our typewriters.

These specific typewriters were called "*Mills*" and had no lowercase letters. The process consisted of going through the whole alphabet, numbers and punctuations mentioned above. We practiced yelling the Morse Code with the letter or number it corresponded to over and over. It was drilled into us so much that at night in the barracks, you hear guys yelling in their sleep saying, "Di Dah, Alpha".

There are a lot of things that really perplex me in my life. Chief among these is racism and antisemitism. I cannot for the life of me understand how anyone could hate someone because of their skin color or religious belief. Or, for that matter, sexual orientation or any other label society sticks to you. As mentioned earlier, I was raised in Beaverton, Oregon. By today's standards, it was definitely not a diverse community.

To my knowledge, there was no racism, mainly because I never grew up hearing bad things about anyone, no matter what they looked like. I didn't know any black people at the time, not because I didn't want to, but because there just weren't any around to know when I was growing up. I learned about racism when I went into the Navy. In our barracks, a natural segregation of sorts, took place in the barracks. The African American guys all bunked together in one area. They were not told to do that, it's just that they wanted to stay together. That's natural. But I noticed. And it's the first time I noticed a separation of people based on their color. I loved them. You know how much I love music and they loved playing their music. And their music was great. And we all loved it when they played their music! To this day, I can still hear it, the Temptations, *"The Way You Do the Things You Do"*, and it always takes me back. Good memories. They were great guys and we all got along.

As life would have it, one of my Navy classmates, for some reason, took a disliking to me and wanted to fight. Now, in high school, I got in a scuffle now and then but no big fights. I wasn't expecting to do that here... in the Navy. I have no idea why this guy didn't like me and wanted to fight. I only weighed about 155 pounds at the time, and he was taller and bigger than me! I never really liked confrontation and tried to avoid it as much as possible.

As a matter of fact, to jump forward to later on, when I went to work for the CIA, I had a class called "Risk of Capture and How to Avoid It." Well, that was right up my alley! Avoid trouble as much as you can but don't back down when confronted. Anyway, this guy wanted to fight, so off we went one night into the barracks "*head*" to have it out. I knew I only had one shot and prayed I wouldn't piss my pants in front of the whole barracks that came to watch. I knew I'd have to hit him first, and fast. And that's what I did as soon as we walked through the door. Boom!! He fell down and immediately backed off.

He ended up being one of my best friends for the rest of the time we were in Radio Operator School. Life lessons are great.

From Radio School in San Diego, I was assigned to the USS *Pitkin County* LST-1082, a tank landing ship that was being recommissioned at the Bethlehem Steel Yard in Long Beach, CA. To familiarize you with an LST, it is a *"Landing Ship, Tank"* (LST), or *"Tank Landing Ship"*, the Naval designation for ships first developed during World War II (1939-1945) to support amphibious operations by carrying tanks, vehicles, cargo, and landing troops directly onto shore with no docks or piers. This enabled amphibious assaults on almost any beach. These ships had a highly specialized design that worked for ocean crossings as well as shore groundings. The LST had a large door on the bow that could open, deploy a ramp and unload vehicles. It had a flat keel that allowed the ship to be beached and stay upright.

As crew, we stayed in barracks in the steel yard while commissioning work was being completed on the ship. When Liberty was allowed, we'd all pile in the Liberty Bus at the yard and go to Long Beach to The Pike, an amusement park on Ocean Boulevard. The Pike was famous for a huge wooden roller coaster that everyone loved to ride. It was called the Cyclone Racer and was built in 1930 on pilings that extended out over the ocean! Once in a while, we would even spot members of the Hells Angels there: the Long Beach Chapter. We thought that was pretty great, having never seen anything like a motorcycle gang in our small hometowns. All a part of my life training, I guess.

The USS *Pitkin County* was recommissioned on 9 July 1966 and immediately became the flagship for Landing Ship Squadron 3. We packed out of the barracks and loaded on the ship, found our bunks and foot lockers, and the ship headed to San Diego to start what was called Underway Training— another new southern California town to experience. Since I left high school early to join the Navy, I never completed high school and received my diploma. So, while we were stationed in San Diego, I was able to take and pass the GED exam. A good accomplishment for me.

San Diego was a neat town to explore. I discovered Mexican food! There were no Mexican food restaurants in Beaverton, Oregon, at that time. Oh, man, I loved the tostadas. I couldn't get enough tostadas to quench this new taste I discovered. At only 155 pounds, tall and skinny, I was able to down a lot of tostadas and not worry a thing about it. And...I learned about the Mexican culture in Tijuana, Mexico! Drinking in bars at 17 and sampling various other delights, it seemed to me that life couldn't get much better.

Underway Training was interesting and tiring. As I noted before, an LST (*Landing Ship, Tank*) has a flat bottom and is made to go up on the beach, open it's front doors, and allow the Marines to charge out with all their equipment, including Jeeps and Amtraks (personnel carriers) directly onto shore with no docks or piers needed. As the ship made way up on the beach, a stern anchor was dropped, and the anchor chain was released as it went ashore. That maneuver took place while we, on the ship, backed off the beach. In a real-life situation, we were leaving the Marines on the beach to fend for themselves. It was pretty exciting if you weren't a Marine charging up the beach and getting shot at. All of these maneuvers we practiced on the shores of San Diego.

Finally, the day came when all the training and practice was over and we cast off the lines for South Vietnam. Before we got underway for the long voyage to Vietnam, I managed to get off the ship an hour or so before we cast off to call my mom to say goodbye. I think she cried and I tried not to.

While underway, I sat on the stern under the 40mm cannon and watched the US coast slide under the horizon. I was not scared or worried, just excited about the adventure… itchy feet. We had a Marine Amtrak division with us. They were the toughest guys I ever knew, before or since, but the "Gunny" Sargent was an SOB. I say that because he always picked the Marine that had the worst case of seasickness and put him in the galley to scrape dinner trays and take care of the garbage. Most of the Marines and the crew were seasick for the first few days at sea, including me. As I said before, an LST is flat-bottomed and has no keel which makes it ride really rough.

The first stop was to be Hawaii. This leg of our journey took a little longer than it should have as we blew an engine about halfway over and had to limp into Pearl Harbor. The whole crew donned their dress uniforms, manned the rail, and saluted as we passed by the USS *Arizona* Memorial. That was an awesome moment. We were only in Hawaii about a week when a bunch of us guys on Liberty heard loudspeakers from the street calling for all Naval personnel to report to their ships immediately due to a tidal wave warning. In retrospect, we all curiously thought it might have been a sneaky ruse to get us all back on the ship quickly. Turns out we immediately pulled out and never came back. Next stop … Okinawa, Japan.

I never thought of myself as gullible, but after weeks and weeks of the old salts telling me about Japan and that everything there was on a slant, I started to believe it. HA! A few days of shore leave in Okinawa set me straight. (That may not be understood by some, and maybe some will get it.) Along with my fun time in Tijuana, Okinawa was one of the only places I could walk in a bar and order a drink at my age! To be able to do that at e ag18 was quite the deal. I think I ordered every drink possible and paid for it dearly over the golden throne, the lessons of youth. And I definitely wasn't the only one.

We departed Okinawa for Da Nang, Viet Nam and ended up heading directly into hurricane Carla. The following is a quote from the USS *Pitkin County* plan of the day for Wednesday, 18 October 1967: *"We intend to turn back toward Da Nang this morning and should arrive on the morning of 22 October. Carla passed to the south of us yesterday morning at a distance of 180 miles to her eye. The worst weather we encountered consisted of about 65 to 70-knot winds with gusts up to 90 knots, and 40-foot seas, with an occasional swell up to 50 to 55 feet. We didn't lose any cargo, and about the most serious damage to the ship occurred when the high winds stripped the gears in our radar antenna, putting the radar out of commission."*

With these big winds and swells the ship was doing all ahead flank speed and barely making headway. Flank speed is maximum speed. Flank speed is reserved for situations in which a ship finds itself in imminent danger. And we were. The captain tried to turn the ship so we could go back to Okinawa but the danger of being flipped over was evident, so we continued heading into the storm and waited for the winds and seas to calm down enough for us to turn back on course to

Danang. You must remember that an LST is flat-bottomed with no keel, making it a really, really rough ride. Quite the harrowing experience for young sailors.

On 29 November, we finally reached Da Nang, Vietnam and started shuttle operations between Da Nang and Chu Lai. That operation was what I described during training: disembarking our brave Marines and their onboard Amtraks and equipment into very dangerous situations on shore. We'd naturally become friends with a lot of the Marines aboard and were sorry to see them go. And we were worried for them. I later heard only a few of them made it out alive.

We left Da Nang on 21 December and headed to Guam, arriving on 2 January 67. Guam was to be our home port. During this stay in Guam, we had a very fast change of command. Our captain, Captain Quarles, had a very bad temper and, when mad, he'd knock his officer about, though he never hit an enlisted man that I know of. I did have an encounter of my own with Captain Quarles. I was lucky, though. One time at sea, in a storm, I received an immediate message on the ship's radio and had to run it up to Captain Quarles' sea quarters. When I knocked on the door and the Captain opened it, I immediately removed my cap, which was full of water from the storm, and the water hit the captain in the face. I thought I was dead, but the Captain just said, "*son, you need a haircut*". Phew! In another incident, he got so mad at an Ensign on the Bridge that he knocked him about, made the Ensign dip his hands in green and red paint to distinguish port and starboard, and sent him to the bow of the ship in bad weather to be the ship's "reindeer watch" on Christmas Eve. We were later all called in to see the Admiral to testify regarding these incidents. We don't know what all that entailed but he was definitely taken off duty as Captain on our ship.

Our new Captain was a stand-up guy who was what we called a Mustang Officer (someone who came all the way through the ranks from enlisted to captain). While on "Market Time" duty off the Vietnam coast ("Market Time" is explained later) as a morale builder, the new Captain dropped an LCVP, Landing Craft Vehicle, Personnel, a small boat, over the side and loaded it with ice cold beer and allowed the crew to take turns climbing down cargo nets to the boat and indulging in a cold one. It's against Navy regulations to drink on a US Ship but not in a small boat tied to the side. This was a great Captain.

Guam was a SCUBA diving mecca and several of us took lessons and got certified to dive, and then spent as much of our liberty time in the water as we could. Because we were docked at a Naval base, we were able to transfer our communications messages to the shore base, which was much easier than having to stand watches just to keep our equipment on, like we had to when at sea. Much easier on shore.

At the base, we just had to take the ship's truck over to the communications center 4 or 5 times a day to pick up our communication cables. The only problem with this was ...I didn't know how to drive! Before going into the Navy, I never had time to learn to drive. So the other two *"Comm"* guys had to take all the duty. Our Communications Chief told me he'd remedy this at some future time. That time came a few months later when we were sailing through the San Bernardino Straights on the way to the Philippines and the weather was calm. The Chief took me down to the empty tank deck, unlatched the ship's pickup, and taught me how to shift and drive back and forth on the 300-foot tank deck on the ship. I'm probably the only person ever to learn to drive a car in the middle of the ocean.

At the end of January, we got underway for a survey cruise, taking us to the Marianas, Volcano Islands, Bonins, and

Ryukyus. We stopped at the various islands and provided medical help while completing a census of the population. When visiting these islands, we often got what we called '*dungaree liberty*,' which meant we could go ashore and explore. We found caves and discovered gun emplacements used by the Japanese during WW2. These were concrete slabs that contained bolted-down huge guns, big WW2 cannons and armaments. That was an exciting discovery for us. This survey cruise to the islands fueled my dream of someday sailing my own boat to tropical islands.

We now headed back to Chu Lai, Vietnam, via Okinawa.

Our next assignment was Operation Market Time. This was a coastal surveillance operation used to stop the flow of troops, war material and supplies by sea, coast, and rivers from North Vietnam into South Vietnam. Small boats were sent from the ship to patrol up and down the coast to support the PBRs (Patrol Boat, River), inspecting the Vietnamese boats along the way. This assignment became very monotonous at times. We were just cruising up and down the coast, supporting the guys on the PBRs who actually searched the Vietnamese vessels. We were allowed to volunteer for duty on the PBRs, which we did as often as we could. This broke up the monotony and was always exciting, allowing us to get up close and personal with the Vietnamese. After searching a boat, the Vietnamese crew would make a brushing movement with their fingers over their mouth, which meant they wanted toothpaste. We had toothpaste and most always gave it to them. I think they ate the toothpaste like candy. Because we had a great Captain now, and because it was so hot and humid and boring, the Captain would stop the ship, open the bow doors and drop the ramp, put sharpshooters up on the bow watching for sharks, and have an "all hands swim". That was much appreciated and great for morale.

From Operation Market Time, we sailed to Vung Tau on Christmas Eve to support the Riverine Assault Force on the Mekong Delta. The Riverines were a joint US Army and US Navy force that comprised a substantial part of the brown-water Navy in order to deny the Viet Cong any access to these areas.

While in Vung Tau Harbor, our ship answered a distress call received from the merchant tug Makah, which was ablaze. We were able to pull alongside the tug and get hoses to the stricken vessel to extinguish the fires, ultimately saving the ship.

The Mekong Delta was very interesting during this time, in 1967/68. Our main deck became a helicopter-landing pad and supported the Swift Boats and other boats on patrol on the river. Our 50 caliber machine guns were in constant operation, shooting debris floating down the river towards us in case there were explosive devices attached.

On 1 July 1968, I received orders to return home. The Navy asked if I would re-enlist, and I said I would if they would guarantee me orders out of the *"Gator Navy"* (brown water sailing/Swift Boats). The amphibious fleet, or *"Gator Navy"* as it's known inside the service, was key to the Marine Corps' strategy to bring their forces back to the shoreline. They couldn't guarantee it, so I said goodbye. My Captain called me up to his cabin to say goodbye and thank me for my service. He said he'd never seen anybody with a bigger smile on his face than mine.

My fellow USA-bound mates and I traveled to Saigon to catch a plane back to the real world. While in Saigon, Vietnam had one more *"gotcha"*. We were in the transit barracks and bullets started rattling through the walls and windows, and sirens were going off. We high-tailed it out to a bunker and jumped into about 3 feet of water. We waited for the all-clear and went back to the barracks, sopping wet, where we discovered that most of our gear had been stolen. Well, at least we were alive, that's more than we could say for a lot of our friends.

Landing at the San Francisco Airport was surreal; many kissed the ground, but others like me spotted their first mini skirt and forgot all about Vietnam! We were taken to Treasure Island Naval base for processing and eventual discharge. While waiting for the long-awaited discharge, some days in the future, we were assigned various duties to keep us busy. My duty assignment was to report to the Brig to escort prisoners to various locations on the base. My first prisoner was the biggest, tallest, muscular man I'd ever seen. And I weighed maybe all of 155 pounds. The Marine Guard gave me a measly nightstick and told me to escort the prisoner to the personnel office. Oh, man. Well, I knew where that nightstick might end up if the prisoner decided to overtake me and escape, so I said to him,

"I just got back from Vietnam and, as you can see, I survived, and I'd sure hate to break my lucky streak of survival here at Treasure Island!" My prisoner stood at attention and shouted, "Brig Chaser Hasness, sir, I'll follow your orders and will not run!" He turned out to be a great guy who, like me, just wanted out of the Navy.

I finally got home to Salem, Oregon, where Mom and my now stepdad, Ray, lived. Ray immediately took me down to a local bar and introduced me to his friends, telling them I'd just returned from 'Nam. The owner looked at me and said, "Son, you'll never pay for a drink in this bar." What a great welcome that was. I was so lucky to receive a lot of support while I was away in the form of many wonderful letters from the people of Oregon. It was overwhelming. There were not enough thanks for all that I received. Letters from students in school were so heartfelt. It meant a great deal to all of us over there so far away to get those letters.

Thank you, thank you. I never felt, and still don't feel, I did anything great in Vietnam except to stay alive and do my time. But I'll never forget the thanks I got coming home. Unfortunately, there were many others returning from 'Nam that got pretty nasty treatment during that time, so I felt very grateful that my homecoming was not like that.

Chapter 3
CIA

Psychological Tests/Polygraph Tests

I'm back in Oregon, back from the service. I wasn't sure exactly what I was going to do, so I worked various jobs in canneries and such. Then I decided I should go back to school. I registered at Multnomah College in Portland and moved in with my best friend Terry's family to be closer to school. My college stint didn't last long, though. I soon got a letter from the Central Intelligence Agency asking if I would come back to Washington, D.C., to interview for a job. Well, that would be interesting! I had never been to D.C. before, so I thought this might be a good opportunity to see the other side of the country.

Itchy feet.

I interviewed with the CIA and took lots of psychological tests, and polygraph tests, and medical tests. (Because of the clearances I would hold for the rest of my career, with both the Agency and Lockheed Martin, I continued from then on to be polygraphed every two years until my retirement in 2008.) Polygraphs were of two types: CI, which were Counter

Intelligence Polygraphs that consisted of questions about foreign contacts and Lifestyle Polygraphs, which were exactly as the name implies; questions about friends, finances, etc. After my interview and exhaustive test taking, I was sent home, not knowing if I got the job or not. Well, I figured I at least got to see the District of Columbia.

I was having fun in Portland, going to school and partying with my buddy Terry, and just enjoying life. Two weeks later, I got a call. The CIA was offering me a job. It would start at a GS6 pay scale, just above an entry-level Government General Services pay grade. An average pay scale as those jobs go. As I said, I was having lots of fun in Portland, so I said no to the job offer, and Terry and I went out to another bar. The next day, they called again and offered me a GS7 pay grade. That was a surprise, and a better offer for sure. So I said, "Yes!" and headed back to Washington, DC.

A curious thing …when I reported to Headquarters in Langley, VA, after receiving numerous correspondence at my home from the company (CIA), with Central Intelligence Agency letterhead and such, I was now told not to tell anyone about my employment. HUH?? How in the world am I now to erase all my friends' and relatives' memories of me excitedly telling them about my new employment while I was in Oregon? I'd already advertised this fact to many! Yikes!

We *'freshmen'*, neophytes, CIA personnel, were awaiting our training classes to begin and the completion of the FBI investigations into our backgrounds for our security clearances. At that time, we also received our covers, cover stories and pseudonyms.

We would be undercover agents when we got in the field. In the meantime, we were given different mundane odd jobs around Headquarters; collecting newspaper articles on specific

22

subjects, working in the Lock Shop, etc. In the big CIA Compound of Langley, VA, there seemed to be numerous safes in every room. And invariably at least one of those safes needed someone to help open the lock. That was one of my jobs. Safe cracking.

In the meantime…I lived in Georgetown, Washington D.C., for a bit, bought bell bottom pants, and paisley shirts, and rocked out to the disco music in Georgetown. What a great time that was! A great time to be young. This was during the 70s, so you can imagine the fun. Soon, though, I was sent to a site near a small Northern Virginia town to go through training on Communications Systems and electronics and learn to Code and Decode One-Time Pad (OTP) messages. One-Time Pad messaging was the method we were taught, and used from then on, to do the coding and decoding of emergency encrypted messages. It was a lot of difficult memory work. All of this while using Morse code, or CW (Continuous Wave communication) that I was taught in the Navy, and remember… in the Boy Scouts, too! This was the lowest-order basic communication that was taught. We were also taught the highest level of sophisticated communications as part of our training. The whole gamut.

There I am in Georgetown, D.C., living the life. So, it's only natural that I got the notion to buy a brand new MG Midget, British Racing Green, with the then-new concept no one had heard of before… RADIAL tires! Why not?! I was making what I thought was a lot of money at the time. It was quite a luxury that I indulged in. But then, after purchasing my prize possession, I actually worried if I was going to be able to make the payments. I think the total cost was about $2,000. At the time, it felt like I had 'made it' in life.

I was making as much money just starting with the Agency as my mother was making after working many years for the Portland Police Department.

Our training lasted for 6 months. During that time, some of my classmates and I became involved in skydiving during our downtime. My first time up in the plane was just to observe. I was with Karen Roach and Martha Huddleston, two members of the US Skydiving Team. They were two of the nicest ladies you'd ever meet. They convinced me to try it, so I signed up for lessons. In those days, you had to pack your own chute and jump with it. Training sessions were conducted at Ft. Myers in Arlington, VA, where we students learned to pack our chute and land properly.

My first jump was with a couple of girls who were also taking lessons. On this first jump, we were attached to the plane via a static line that would pull tight after jumping and automatically open our parachute. I was to be the first one out. The Jump Master said, "When I put my hand on your knee, step out the door and, stand on the strut, and look straight at me." Well, I kept looking at the girls and thinking, "I'm scared shitless." But I was not going to crawl back in and make a fool of myself. I'd rather die. So when the Jump Master said, *"Jump!"* I jumped, knowing I was going to die, but looking cool. From then on, we jumped a lot all over Virginia and Maryland. The name of our group was St Michael's Angels. I really enjoyed it.

After our Agency communications training was completed, I received orders, along with another guy from my class, to head to Asmara, Ethiopia. We remained in Asmara for the next two years, working in a communications site called a relay station. Haile Selassie was the Emperor at the time and was still in charge. A liberation army called the ELF (Ethiopian Liberation Force) was also active in the area. My roommate "Rat", Michael Ratlif, and I shared a large house together. We hired a maid whose name is pronounced. *"Head-ah-grew"*, but I don't have a clue how to spell it, and we settled into life in Ethiopia. Our maid was the best thing that happened to us while there. She was amazing. She made the best lasagna in the world but could only make it in one size, LARGE, so we'd be eating lasagna for days. That's the only thing she ever cooked for us. She did our laundry on an old-fashioned ringer washing machine that smashed all the buttons on our shirts and ruined the zippers on our pants. Our house kind of turned into the local party palace for everyone. It was perfect.

One year, our organization in Asmara asked if we'd host the New Year's Eve party. Well, Rat and I did it up big with a parachute hanging from the ceiling, decorations, and, of course, "Head-ah-grew" agreed to help. We paid her extra and even took her to the base beauty salon to have her hair done (I don't think she'd ever been to a beauty salon before). The party turned out great and *"Head-ah-grew"* was even dancing on the bar by the end of the night. Before we left Asmara, Rat and I asked her if she'd come with us. She said, "No way!" We were too much trouble. We loved that lady.

I was big into hunting in those days and had the opportunity to join a group that was headed to Central Ethiopia to hunt kudu, oryx, and gazelle. We had the use of a military transport, so we loaded up several 55-gallon barrels of gasoline. We headed out for the first half of our journey on good roads. A day later, the Army truck broke down. We, of course, were now in need of parts, so I agreed to take one of the other vehicles back to Asmara and obtain the parts we needed. On the way back, it was pitch black. All of a sudden, machine gun fire opened up on the road in front of us. I immediately told my interpreter, who was riding with me, not to go for his gun, but we would just raise our hands, which we did. It turns out these were Ethiopian Military Personnel who were looking for the ELF, the Ethiopian Liberation Force. "What in the hell are you doing out here?! Didn't you see the road bock?!" We explained what we were doing and, "No, we didn't see a roadblock!" We were escorted to a small village where we were told to remain until the next day when we could then continue to our friends and fix the truck.

We repaired the truck and finally made it to our destination. We ended up living with Danakil tribesmen for most of our stay in northeastern Ethiopia, the Afar Region. The Danakil were very primitive and mostly all naked. They were beautiful people who were fascinated by our equipment. They loved our beer cans and always wanted us to cut the tops off for them for their use for various things. One of our guys got tired of the repetition of the request and said, "Fuck it" when they asked. Well, that now became the Danakil word for "Please take the top off". We figured National Geographic would come there someday and pop open a beer and a tribesman would ask him to *"Fuck it"*. This probably never got published in any of their magazines.

During my time in Ethiopia, I would occasionally get sent to the Embassy in Addis Ababa to help out or relieve someone who had to leave for some reason, such as medical reasons or on vacation. During one of these trips, I got called into the Embassy late one night to set up communications with the Khartoum Embassy, which was right in the middle of a coup! The only communications the Embassy had at that time was CW, Continuous Wave, or Morse Code. My counterpart in Khartoum could look out the Embassy window and see tanks pointing right at the embassy! My job was to receive the message, and decode and format it to be sent back to D.C. as *"Flash Traffic"* for dissemination. *"Flash Traffic"* is the highest-priority traffic. That was quite a night that I will never forget, being the sole contact between Sudan and Washington, D.C., as the coup continued. Sudan's neighbors, Gaddafi in Libya (who was staunchly anti-Communist at the time), and Egypt's Anwar Sadat, both stationed troops on the border. The coup was short-lived; tanks and troops removed. The coup brought major changes to Sudan's foreign and domestic policies, in the aftermath. Leading members of the Sudanese Communist party were executed.

On another memorable night, I was called into the Embassy to receive *"Immediate Traffic"* (priority just below *"Flash"*) because Vice President Agnew was visiting. When I walked into the Embassy, the Marine guard had his hands over his face and kept saying, "Please, Mr. Hasness, don't tell the Gunny!" I opened up the Communications Vault (a safe room) and went back out to find out what was going on with the guard. Apparently, the guard was bored and shot himself in the face with tear gas just to see what it was like. After I stopped laughing, I promised not to tell the Gunny. Soon after I met Agnew and shook his hand. Then I checked to make sure I still had my watch.

Itchy feet.

After two years, I received orders from CIA Headquarters for a one-year tour in Iran, at a location up in the mountains next to the Russian border. We were spying on the Russians. I was to be undercover there. My cover was an Air Traffic Control teacher, teaching Iranian Military Cadets. I knew nothing about Air Traffic Control.

This was a time when the Shah and Empress Farah were in charge before Jimmy Carter destroyed the country. We had an Upper Camp and a Lower Camp that we rotated to, depending on requirements. The Upper Camp was the main area where we had our permanent quarters consisting of a bed and a desk. We worked 12 hours on/12 hours off, 7 days a week. But as you must know by now, we managed to have fun. Having a bunch of engineers around who are bored can be a wonderful thing.

The engineers all got involved launching Estes Rockets. They started launching toward the Russian border! They would rig them up with telemetry that we could track using the same equipment we'd use to track Russian rocket launches. But, after a while, this became boring. We needed to up the game somehow. We needed a payload, a live payload. "How about catching some mice and sending them to Russia?" "Great idea!" "How will we recruit our Astro Mouses?" The engineers decided to devise the perfect mousetrap that would capture them alive. The mouse trap was built, and we now needed a system to monitor the activity. They rigged up a closed-circuit TV system to watch the action with the monitor at our bar. Our bar just happened to be *"hosted"* by a plastic blow-up porn goddess who agreed that this was a great idea. Well, we'd be sitting at our bar, talking to our *"hostess"*, watching a mouse come on the screen, sniff around, and fall into the trap. Immediately the mouse was taken to the Astro Mouse crew quarters and fitted out in his flight gear, which consisted of a specially engineered parachute. One of our engineers built a capsule. We put the mouse in this Astro Outfit in the capsule and launched him over the Russian border. Now, not every launch was successful, and some of our Astro Mice didn't make it but we did get better. I can't prove it, but I'm pretty sure a couple of the mice came back to be captured again for the thrill of the ride.

One of the great perks we had at this location was being able to order almost any kind of food to be flown in on our specially modified Caribou plane piloted by US Air Force pilots. One of the extremely bad memories from this location will always stick in my mind. This was a Muslim country. We were unfortunately present when a young girl from the local village was stoned to death because the powers-that-be in the village accused her of having a relationship with one of the students we had at our base. We hurriedly left the premises. The grim reality of Iran.

The Caribou Aircraft in Iran, with Air Force pilots that flew our provisions in, would, at times, take us out. I was on one of these trips when the pilot asked me to sit in the copilot seat and fly the plane while he took a break! Huh?? He told me, "Just keep it straight, as we are right next to the Russian border." Huh?? I guess I did okay since we didn't get shot down or crash.

About the time my tour was over, I got into an altercation with our Chief. Our camp dog had puppies that he didn't want in the compound, so he shot them. This pissed me off, and we got into an argument. I told him he could take this job and shove it. I sent my resignation to headquarters. Headquarters came back, asking me to finish my tour and then return straight back to DC. Well, that was not happening. Three of the guys and I left at the same time, none of us too happy with the way things worked out on the mountain. We decided to ignore the order to return immediately and headed to Munich to the Oktoberfest with two kilos of Caspian Sea caviar. What a great time we had. Since we were already in trouble, we thought we might as well see some of Europe. We rented a car and drove from Munich to Paris, stopping at all the sights. In Paris we stayed in the apartment of my friend's sister. She fixed us up with dates, and we all went to the Moulin Rouge and drank champagne. Life continues to be great. From Paris, we went to Amsterdam for a week or so, being tourists. We then caught a plane to London and decided we should call the U.S. Embassy and let them know where we were. The Embassy said, "Everyone in Europe is looking for you guys! You need to report to the Embassy immediately!" We said, "Screw it!" and headed to the airport to catch the next plane to Washington, D.C.

I reported to headquarters and was told to immediately report to the Chief Communications Office. I went in and sat down. He looked hard at me and said, "Did you get it out of your system?" "Yes." "Here's your next set of orders. You're going to Takhli, Thailand."

Itchy feet.

Takhli was supposed to be a two-year tour, but due to the fall of Vietnam, it was shortened to about a year. I liked Thailand a lot. Their beaches were fantastic, the food was cheap and good, and the girls were beautiful. What more could you want? I departed Thailand sometime in 1977 and headed back to D.C., where I received orders for Lusaka, Zambia. During this time, I took time to go home to Oregon to visit my family. When I got there, I was visiting with my Grandma when she sat me down and asked me why I seemed to have such a problem holding down a job. Keep in mind I could not tell very many people what my true occupation was. She, of course, didn't understand who I worked for and that all these assignments were just different *"covers"*. I *"worked for the State Department."* To her, it appeared that I was struggling to keep one job. I tried to explain and assure her that it was all government service with the same employer. I loved my Grandma.

I had about 3 months before I'd be leaving for Lusaka. In Virginia, I got reacquainted with an old girlfriend I had in D.C., and before you know it, we decided to get married. Wanda had two small boys, Ricky and David. We rented a Vienna, VA church, invited relatives, and got married. She and the boys were going with me to Zambia. After all the shots, getting new passports, and medical clearances, we were finally on our way to Africa for a two-year tour. We moved into a beautiful house with two large avocado trees and a nice garden. The kids entered the International School and Wanda got a job at the U.S. Embassy.

I had the privilege of working under two great Ambassadors while I was in Zambia, Ambassador Jean Wilkowski and Ambassador Stephen Low. Ambassador Wilkowski was the first female Ambassador assigned to an African country. She later served as the American Coordinator of Preparations for the United Nations Conference on Science and Technology. Ambassador Low played a key role in negotiations, seeking a solution to the conflict in Rhodesia (now Zimbabwe). After Zambia, Ambassador Low was appointed Ambassador Extraordinary and Plenipotentiary to Nigeria. He later became the State Department Director of the Foreign Service Institute.

Wanda and I got a message that our car had finally arrived in Blantyre, Malawi. We flew to Blantyre to pick up the car and drive it back to Lusaka. All went well until we were crossing the border into Zambia and a young Zambian military man refused to let us through. We carried Diplomatic Passports and when he stuck his rifle in the window at Wanda and tried to grab our keys, I grabbed his gun and yelled, "Diplomat! Diplomat!" while shoving our passports in his face. I think he got scared and let us go through. This incident had the potential of ending very badly.

As was the case in Asmara, I had to occasionally go TDY (temporary duty) to other embassies to help out. In this case, I had to go to Pretoria, South Africa, for a week or so. This was during a time of apartheid, and it was the first time I'd ever been someplace where segregation was the rule. The Consular Officer, with whom I became friends, was a black man who had to deal with these customs. As a Diplomat, he was issued a card declaring Honorary White Status so that he could go out in public and eat in restaurants. Yes, that was a thing. Even with the card, though, as you might imagine, he had to put up with a lot of hatred. One time he had sugar poured into the gas tank of his car. I asked him why he wanted this assignment and he smiled and said he liked it because any South African who wanted a Visa to the United States had to go through the Consular Office, which, of course, was run by a black man.

While in Africa, we took trips to Victoria Falls next to what was then Rhodesia. On our first trip to the Falls, we stayed in a small motel. Ricky was only 5 years old, young and inquisitive, and wandered off through a small field one day near the motel that had trees full of monkeys. The monkeys were very curious and started jumping out of the trees towards him. Ricky became very frightened and started screaming. I believe they would have attacked him if I hadn't run at them, screaming and yelling. A pretty scary moment. I took advantage of being in Africa and went on camping trips next to the Zambezi River. On one particular trip, I took my Avon inflatable boat that had a 10hp outboard engine. I took along Harley, a white African hunter, and one of our camp help, a Zambian National. We did a cruise down the Zambezi. The shoreline was riddled with crocs. So we were always on the lookout. We rounded a bend in the river, and, boom! It exploded with hippos! We spotted what we thought was a rock and headed to shore to tie up. That rock was, in fact, the back of a hippo! When we got close, he jumped, and we jumped! He headed to shore and we headed back across the river. We sat there trying to figure out what to do, as the water was full of hippos and, there were crocs all over the place, and it was too shallow to start the engine. To top this excitement off, Harley heard a large cat up on the hill stalking us. We had to get back across the river to get back to camp. Big dilemma. We sat there, smoked all our cigarettes, and decided we only had one option. We waded in the water, pulling the boat behind us, praying that the crocs would leave us alone until we got in deep enough water to start the engine and get the hell out of there. We made it back to camp; we were very lucky. The Zambian National that was with us got out of the boat, walked down the dirt road we came in on, and we never saw him again. Camping in Africa was definitely interesting.

During our time in Zambia, the Rhodesian War was going on. Rhodesia was one of the most beautiful countries ever. They had great farms and employed thousands of people, but mostly white farmers owned the farms. The country was under British protection.

They only gave limited power to the Rhodesian people, which really wasn't enough. There was much the British could have done to train the Rhodesians during their time of power. Not surprisingly, war broke out, they changed the name of the country to Zimbabwe, and all the white landowners were kicked out, and the Rhodesians attempted to take over the farms. Because they had no learned farming skills, they failed miserably, and the country went into an economic disaster. I must let you know that there are parts and places in this book that I cannot elaborate on because of my CIA cover, and this is one of them. Even though I'm far removed from this time and place, I cannot.

I talked to many Zambians about the time before independence from British rule. About what it was like under the Brits. One gentleman explained to me that during English rule they would drive up to the department store, which they were not allowed to enter, but instead could go to an appointed window and ask for the goods they wanted to purchase. The goods were then passed out to them. I thought that was terrible. But the gentleman I was talking to said, "Wait. After independence, I would ride my bike to the store, as I could no longer afford a car. I could go inside the store and shop. But, unfortunately, there was nothing on the shelves to buy. And even if there was, I didn't have the money to pay for it. You tell me, was I better off under the Brits or now, under independence."

I finished my tour in Zambia and Wanda, the kids, and I headed back to Washington, D.C. I'm sure it would not surprise you that the kids' first choice of a meal in the States was McDonalds. While in D.C. I received orders to an office in Sunnyvale, California. We moved to that South Bay Area of California, bought a house in Milpitas, and settled in, sort of. Not too long after settling into our new home, I was sent to Istanbul, Turkey, for three months to help out because of personnel shortages. I continued to travel overseas off and on. Wanda really liked it in Milpitas and mentioned she really didn't want to go overseas anymore and asked if I would get a contract job with one of the aerospace companies in the area. I admit I liked it in Milpitas, too, and was ready to stay put for a while. I met with some contacts at Lockheed Martin, resigned from the CIA on a Friday, and went to work for Lockheed on Monday.

Chapter 4

Lockheed Martin

A Continuation of Secrecy

As an ex-employee of the Agency, I was still required to maintain my various covers with the CIA pertaining to my employment record. Lockheed needed to use my employment resumé for contract bids as part of a team, showing expertise in a particular field in order to win the contracts. This process was tedious for me because I had been under numerous covers while working for the CIA. My employment history on my resumé had to list all the many jobs I had as cover rather than just saying I worked for the Central Intelligence Agency. In order to streamline the process, I contacted my old employer at the Agency and requested to be *"opened up"* (brought out from being under cover). A large amount of time had elapsed since my Agency employment, so it was agreed that I could now show my employer was the CIA continuously for all that time.

Lockheed always treated me great. I still traveled, but not as much. However, as life would have it, returning from one of my travels one day, Wanda announced she wanted a divorce.

She was heading to Hawaii with what turned out to be her *"new guy"*. Life isn't always easy.

Everything does have a silver lining, however. In this case, it was my youngest boy, Rick. When he turned 18, he wanted to become officially a Hasness, taking my name. We completed all the necessary paperwork and went to court to complete an adult adoption. He was now my legal son, Rick Hasness. Love that boy. I licked my wounds from the divorce and got heavily involved in the Masonic Lodge and the Shrine. I eventually became head of the San Francisco Shrine Drum and Bugle Corps. What a terrific time that was.

I also realized I wanted to start sailing again. When I was a young man, I read all the articles in **National Geographic Magazine** that were about sailing. One young sailor featured by the magazine, Robin Graham, set out to sail around the world alone as a teenager in the summer of 1965. National Geographic carried the story in installments, and he co-wrote a book titled **Dove**, detailing his journey. It piqued my interest. I'd taken lessons between tours with the CIA when I was back East on the Chesapeake Bay. Now in California, I joined a local sailing club in Alameda, CA called Club Nautique, which provided lessons and charter services. I completed all their lessons, got a charter license, and sailed as much as I could. I eventually wanted my own boat, so I met with a yacht broker in Alameda to see what we could find that would suit me. She suggested a few different brands of yachts, but we decided a Wauquiez would be well-suited for me. At the suggestion of my yacht broker, I flew up to Washington to look at two or three yachts. I found the perfect one on Lake Union in Seattle, Washington. She was a beautiful 33ft Wauquiez that I named *Moonglade*, which is the term for the long, magnificent glow on the ocean the full moon makes.

I immediately sailed *Moonglade* up to Canada and berthed her in a marina in Sydney Harbor 30 miles or so north of Victoria. This move saved me from having to pay Washington sales tax; a good idea on my part. I left her there for 3 months before bringing her down the coast to San Francisco. Two of my friends from Club Nautique agreed to crew for me on that trip down. We flew up and bought all the provisions we needed for the trip down on the boat. We went out to a celebratory dinner at The Stone Restaurant and Pub, came back to the boat, and immediately headed out the Strait of Juan de Fuca toward the Pacific Ocean. That ended up not being a great idea. The Strait of Juan de Fuca soon became the Strait of Juan de Puke-a. There went our nice dinner. It was cold, dark, and very rough with contrary currents. Finally, we were able to get *Moonglade* out into the relative comfort of the Pacific Ocean. Five wet days later, we sailed under the Golden Gate to the berth I had waiting in Alameda at Ballena Bay Yacht Club.

I decided to move aboard *Moonglade* at Ballena Bay Marina. It became my home for the next few years. It was a great place to live and commute to my work at Lockheed Martin in Sunnyvale. There's another book that could be written about life in a marina. The title would appropriately be **As The Marina Turns**.

Friday nights at the Yacht Club, after commuting home from working in the *'Blue Cube'* at Lockheed Martin, was the best way to end the workweek. So many great friends there, yummy dinners, and just plain good times sailing on our boats. On weekends, we would all take our boats on Cruise Outs to visit another yacht club in the area. As you can imagine, sailing the San Francisco Bay is second to none.

And that is when I met the love of my life in 1998. This is a good story because it ends with *"They lived happily ever after"*. A lot of us grew up with the notion of happily ever after because it was what we were read, or would read, in fairy tales of the time. Nothing wrong with being forever happy, that's for sure, but it takes more work than we imagined. We were introduced via a mutual friend who gave me her name and e-mail address. Ellen is a California girl, born and raised in Porterville, a graduate with a Bachelor of Science degree from Cal Poly, San Luis Obispo. Married to a dairyman she met in college, they lived in Gustine, CA, raising 3 amazing kids, Kevin, Lacey and Skip, and living the dairy and ranch life. The perfect place to raise a family. After struggling to keep her marriage of 20-plus years intact, Ellen and her husband got a divorce and she moved to Modesto. While there, now needing a full-time job, she was hired to take the place of a secretary at a private school who was on maternity leave. She loved it! Loved the kids. Having a substitute teacher credential in her hands, she was also asked to sub in the classrooms now and then. The Principal of the school saw her good connection with the students and suggested she teach Kindergarten the following year while working on a full teaching credential. Ellen was an excellent teacher and the kids loved her. The Principal asked her to oversee the school's summer program during her time there as well. Those were good years, but struggling years because of the divorce that resulted in her need for as much employment as she could get at the time.

Ellen had always been fond of sailing and had taken lessons in Santa Cruz with her ex-husband. Now she wanted to really go sailing. What the heck? When I got her email address from my friend, I emailed her… then we talked and talked on the phone; I invited her to come sailing, we dated, and we sailed, and then… she left Modesto after her 2nd year of teaching and moved up to Alameda where we lived together on *Moonglade!* The Fridays at the Yacht Club were now more fun than ever with Ellen on board.

Ellen secured a job before she left Modesto with a start-up charter school organization, University Public Schools, now called Aspire Public Schools. She became the Administrative Assistant to the COO of the organization and worked in their then small start-up office in San Carlos, CA. She was now commuting with me to work. Since we were both working, we had a lot of work clothes to deal with, and a 33ft boat doesn't have a lot of closet space. We decided to rent a small office at Ballena Bay Marina to house the extra work wardrobe. Two people living on a 33ft sailboat trying to get ready for work each morning provided an interesting struggle, but it worked and the memories that come from that time are amazing. Maybe even magical. Living on a boat was magical; just great.

Three or four years prior, I had purchased a small 800-square-foot condo in San Jose, CA, as an investment. An idea appeared. "Let's kick out the renters, clean and paint and move in there!" Well, we didn't 'kick them out', but you know what I mean. This proved to be a daunting task. Took a while to get the renters out. We had to go in and clean, clean, clean and then paint. It was worth it and an excellent move on our part; a bit more room for sure. Still a commute, but not as bad. Life was great. We'd spend the workdays at the condo and the weekends on the boat at the Yacht Club. I served a year as the Rear Commodore while at Ballena Bay Yacht Club and the cruise outs and, club dinners and dances and hilariously fun Jimmy Buffett Night events continued. The jukebox played, we danced and continued to enjoy our good times with friends. The *"Finally Friday"* song was our mantra. We could not wait for Fridays to get on the boat.

Itchy feet.

It was becoming more noticeable that the docks at Ballena Bay were worn, and the difficult approach to enter the marina from the Bay was starting to become tiresome. It's time to make a change. We decided to move over to the Oakland Alameda Estuary. We secured a berth at Marina Village on the Estuary and enjoyed our sails from that location. We continued to belong to the Ballena Bay Yacht Club, however.

And then…we married. May of 2000.

What a great marriage ceremony we had. The Commodore from BBYC, Robin Matt, married us. He managed to get an old admiral's uniform from a costume shop, I got him licensed to perform our marriage vows, and we made it final on the bow of *Moonglade*. Ellen and I sailed *Moonglade* back to BBYC on one of the most beautiful days on the Bay. It's more often than not pretty cold when sailing on the Bay but this day was warm and wonderful. That was a good sign for us. We secured a spot near the Ballena Bay Yacht Club for the big celebration that would take place the next day. I wrote our vows, my brother stood with me, and Ellen's daughter, Lacey, was her Maid of Honor. Our wonderful family and friends were crowded together surrounding the slip *Moonglade* was parked in, piling on adjacent boats, and standing on the dock ramp, a fabulous site for us.

Commodore Robin Matt began the vows by reflecting:

To paraphrase Jane Austin, who is big box office these days, "It is a truth universally acknowledged that a single man in possession of a yacht must be in want of a wife." This must be true, because – before Ellen arrived upon the scene – I heard Randy swear categorically that he would never be getting married again. Yet, here we are.

Samuel Johnson, perhaps somewhat cynically, referred to marriage, in this particular context, as "the triumph of hope over experience." But, at least in the case of Randy and Ellen, he may have been selling experience – and the wisdom of the heart that comes with experience – a little short. Friedrich Nietzsche, not usually thought of as a great cheerleader for the institution of marriage, nevertheless left

40

us some useful insights on the topic. He observed, "The best friend is likely to acquire the best wife (or husband), because a good marriage is based on the talent for friendship." I have only known Randy and Ellen for a couple of years, but in that short time, I have been the beneficiary of their talent for friendship. We have often whiled away a Saturday morning at Max's Deli solving the world's problems, and have agreed on almost nothing. But I can't imagine two other people it would be half as much fun to argue with. Randy and I go off on Election Day and merrily cancel each other's vote. But I can think of almost no other couple I would rather go sailing with. Their warmth and love of life create a special talent for friendship. So, if Nietzsche – or Jane Austen, for that matter – is right, this marriage is a sure winner. Most of the boilerplate marriage ceremonies I reviewed to get ready for this assignment seemed aimed at the inexperienced. They ran along the lines of, "As these two young people set off down the freeway of life together, etc., etc." Well, Randy and Ellen are almost as old as I am, chronologically speaking. But, where others might have let the passing years contract friendships and limit acquaintances, their talent for friendship seems perennial. Where others might lower expectations or limit horizons, their talent for enjoying life is carrying them on new adventures. Where others might give up on love, they have the courage of the young to pursue it. So please join me in witnessing the marriage of two very young people, Randy and Ellen.

The Vows:

Do you, Randy Hasness, take Ellen Brazil to be your lawfully wedded wife in both sickness and in health as co-captain on all vessels of land, sea and air, and in life itself? While navigating through life together, do you promise to steer a straight course, and never sleep during watch, always keeping a vigilant eye out for hazards? And when asked to descend to the galley, do you promise to gladly oblige?

Do you, Ellen Brazil, take Randy Hasness to be your lawfully wedded husband in both sickness and in health as co-captain on all vessels of land, sea and air, and in life itself? While navigating through life together, do you promise to steer a straight course, and

41

never sleep during watch, always keeping a vigilant eye out for hazards? And when asked to ascend to the mast top, do you promise to gladly oblige?

By virtue of the authority vested in me as a Deputy Commissioner of Civil Marriages of the State of California, in and for the County of Alameda, I now pronounce you husband and wife.

It is done!! The marriage bug captured the *itchy feet* and sealed the deal.

We had loads of family and friends, buckets of beer and champagne on ice at the yacht club, and even a steel drum band. The day was sunny and warm and perfect. What a great time. Ellen will prove to be the most intrepid woman I've ever known. She's not only my wife and co-captain. She's my partner, my rock, my fellow adventurer, and the best friend ever. There are not enough adjectives to describe her.

Chapter 5
9/11/2001

The World Changed/Our Lives Changed

Tuesday, September 11, 2001, our life was about to change. "Randy, wake up! Come see this on the news!" It looked like war. We watched, frozen in place as the plane flew into the second World Trade Center building. It was scary, eerie, and appalling. When we went to work that day, Lockheed was on high alert. They had already grounded all aircraft at the airports and the sky was eerily silent. The Lockheed campus is near the San Jose Airport, so the silence was very apparent. Shortly thereafter, and as a result of this devastating event, President George W. Bush issued a declaration to his administration to form the Department of Homeland Security. The plan would incorporate 22 federal government agencies under that new department.

My background comprised of knowledge of Physical and TEMPEST Security. TEMPEST Security is described as the certification of spying on information systems through leaking emanations, including unintentional radio or electrical signals, sounds and vibrations. As a result, I was asked by Lockheed

Martin to go to Washington, D.C., for 3 months to help get the DHS facilities infrastructure started. While in D.C. I was asked if I'd consider a permanent transfer with an offer of a substantial increase in pay if I took the transfer. I called Ellen, "Hi, Babes. Do you want to move to D.C.?" She immediately answered, "Wow! What???! What's going on?" I explained the offer I had from Lockheed over the phone and she was actually, really considering it. That kind of surprised me! But...she and I always lived by the notion that if opportunities arise, they need to be seriously considered and taken advantage of, as this is what living your life is all about. And opportunities arise for a reason. Ellen told me she wanted to call her daughter Lacey first to discuss it with her and get her thoughts on this big move. Of course, Lacey thought it was an amazing opportunity and told her to go for it!! Lacey, like her mom, is always ready to reach for opportunities, too. And Ellen has always been ready for the next adventure.

Ellen found her *itchy feet*.

Once the decision was made, with a bit of angst by Ellen because she loved her job with Aspire Public Schools and the people there, plus she did not want to be so far away from her kids and friends, Ellen flew out to D.C. so we could look for a house. After an extensive house scouting mission, we found a perfect house with acreage in Manassas, VA, about half an hour from the District, on the Occoquan River.

Our new house secured, Ellen flew back to San Jose to finish her days of work with Aspire, while I continued my duties with Homeland Security in D.C. There was a lot of pressure on Ellen in those days as she had to coordinate the sale of our condo, the packing and shipment of our effects, including two cars, get a one-way ticket to DC, and say goodbye to friends and family. When all was said and done, she landed at Reagan National Airport on November 3rd, 2003. When I saw her, she was a bit nervous, having taken a one-way ticket with no return, and wondered why I had not gone all the way to the gate to meet her. In her nervousness, she had forgotten that you were no longer allowed to go back to the gates to greet people. New rules set in place since 9/11. Not to mention that a ONE WAY ticket was pretty final and a new realization!

Usually, it was round-trip tickets we always purchased. Now it was a one-way. No return. At least not for a bit. New home. New state. New experiences to be had.

It was an evening of light snow when she arrived, which made it sort of magical. We stayed in a hotel in Crystal City, where I had been staying for my months there, until our effects arrived from California. That first night after her arrival, we walked down the street to Legal Seafood, sat at the bar and ordered Chardonnay and clam chowder with sourdough bread and butter. It was the perfect arrival dinner. We toasted our new life!

Itchy feet were in place.

We used our time after Ellen's arrival to do some painting at the new house and to do some fixing up of little things before we moved in. The house was so nice. It was in a cul-de-sac in a sweet neighborhood on 2 acres of wonderful woodsy land that led down to the Occoquan River. Meanwhile, at Homeland, I had a small office in Crystal City that was pretty skimpy. My desk consisted of a typewriter stand. My office stayed there for a month or two before moving to the General Services Administration building in downtown D.C. There was a lot of resistance trying to bring all these agencies together under Homeland Security. All those *"rice bowls"* no one wanted to give up. There were a few agencies, however, that were extremely helpful and the best, in my opinion, was the Secret Service. At the time, the Secret Service was about the most professional group of people I've ever dealt with.

45

Our furniture and cars arrived. Somehow, we ended up with an extra large fake potted plant, but everything else was there, much to Ellen's relief. The cars were delivered but not being taken off the truck. Wondering what the deal was, I went out to talk to the truck driver, who was looking kind of frustrated and I asked what the problem was. He apologized, and said he'd been driving trucks for 30 years and had never had this happen to him. He somehow lost the keys to our cars so he couldn't back them off the truck! Luckily, I had spare sets of keys and we soon got our cars delivered. Since the time of year was November, and being Californians, we weren't acclimated to snowy, cold weather. After arrival, Ellen took 3 months off before trying to look for work, so she could get us all settled in our home. One morning, we woke up to beautiful snow. While I was getting ready to trudge out in the snow to head to D.C., she commented, "Isn't this beautiful!" "Yeah, right", I said as I stepped into the slush that overflowed my shoes.

After searching and interviewing for several jobs, Ellen went to work for The Leadership Institute in Arlington, VA as Executive Assistant to the President of the organization, Morton Blackwell. Morton is a great man who worked in the Reagan administration as the Public Liaison. Since that time, Morton established the nonprofit Leadership Institute to recruit, train and place Conservatives in the Public Policy Process, a very interesting and successful organization. Ellen loved working for the Leadership Institute. Riding into the District on the commuter train and then the Metro, seeing the monuments as you go into D.C. gave you such a strong, proud, emotional, patriotic feeling. Ellen got to go to several bill signings and we both met President Bush at one of them. We also got to attend the second inauguration of President Bush, and sat across from the President's platform at the Inaugural Parade. We dressed up and went to the Inaugural Ball and watched the President and Mrs. Bush dance. We got tickets to see the Queen on the White House lawn. And the Christmas tree lighting was always an amazing treat to see.

Through Mr. Blackwell, Ellen was able to go to the Capitol Rotunda that displayed Reagan's body after he died, a very moving and memorable event. In fact, Ellen and I left work early on the day the caisson took Reagan's body down the avenue to the Capitol. The caisson is where the riderless horse with boots backwards in the stirrups passed by. We found a little knoll to stand on so we could see above the parade crowds. As we were walking back to the Metro to go home, the spectacular fighter jets flew over us in the Missing Man Formation, where one jet flies straight up in the air. Our hearts were fluttering and our eyes were wet. What a moment in time. The memories are incomparable.

I had the great experience of being invited by the Secret Service to walk through the White House and see all the Christmas decorations that first year. Unbelievably beautiful.

During my stint at Homeland, I was asked to be supervisor of the Physical Security Department, which was highly unusual, as civilians were normally never allowed to supervise government employees. I guess this impressed the folks at Lockheed Martin because they promoted me to Senior Engineer. This is one of my proudest accomplishments of my life. Having dropped out of high school to join the Navy, and later getting my GED while in the service, I would never have thought I would ever have Engineer Status.

In Apr 2007, Lockheed Martin won a contract with the DNI (Office of Director of National Intelligence) to work with the State Department to secure U.S. Embassies overseas, and I was reassigned from Homeland to the DNI office. I worked in that office on "K" Street until my retirement in April 2008. K Street in D.C. was THE place. Rarified air. It was the center for lobbying and the location of numerous advocacy groups, law firms, trade associations and some think tanks. Always a beehive of activity and very interesting.

Chapter 6
Kwanesum Enters the Picture

Island Packet 370 Sailing Yacht

Ellen and I decided to put our *Moonglade* up for sale while we were in Virginia, as she was all the way back in Oakland, CA, by herself. We were still paying for her berth there in Alameda at the Oakland Yacht Club and that seemed wasteful. We just cannot get back there enough to enjoy her anymore. Seemed like something we should do. We thought of possibly buying another boat on the East Coast. When getting *Moonglade* ready to be put on the market in California, we found she had a serious electrolysis problem from sitting so long in the water. Electrolysis had eaten away half the prop. Since we were so far away, a very good friend, Bob Martin, who was living in the Oakland Yacht Club Marina, arranged to have the prop replaced and we were able to list our boat with a broker. We sold *Moonglade* to a very nice guy from Seattle who was looking for that exact boat. She was such a great, classic boat, with a fin keel and hanked on sails and a tiller. Hanks are metal clips that attach to the luff of a sail to stay on the line. She had amazing wood bulkheads down below with dark navy velvet seating and a little furnace on the wall, blue square tile around the sink and a hand pump for water. She had an icebox for a refrigerator. Just a classic Wauquiez. We were so sad to let her go. So many great memories on *Moonglade*, not the least of which was our marriage aboard on the bow. There are many, many days we wish we still had her so we could run her about on the San Francisco Bay. But we were so relieved that the man who bought her loved her, too.

Believe me my young friend, there is nothing - absolutely nothing - half so much worth doing as simply messing about in boats.

- So says Ratty to Mole

The Wind in the Willows

Virginia is just adjacent to Maryland and we enjoyed taking day trips to Annapolis, with its Naval Academy and great restaurants. We loved walking the marinas and docks, dreaming again of our own boat and adventures yet to come. Because we still maintained our Oakland Yacht Club membership, we were able to visit the Annapolis Yacht Club. That was really very special. In the sailing arena you always heard talk of the prestigious Annapolis Yacht Club. And the Annapolis Boat Show.

We attended the huge Annapolis Sail Boat Show with our best friends Brian and Mary Cooley from Alameda who came to visit. We drank lots of Pussers Rum Painkillers, viewed lots and lots of yachts, and fell in love with the Island Packet 370, a full keel cutter rigged sailboat that is known to be a safe and competent blue water cruising boat. Perfect size. Island Packets had always been a favorite of mine whenever I saw them. We spent lots of time dreaming about how we'd fit her out to become our perfect boat. Looking through the internet for an Island Packet dealer, we stumbled upon a small town in southern Virginia on the Chesapeake Bay called Deltaville with an Island Packet brokerage run by a couple who had cruised extensively along the east coast of the U.S. There was a brand new Island Packet 370 sitting in the brokerage. We climbed aboard and checked every nook and cranny. We decided to go for it and make our cruising dreams come true. After an extensive list of options and upgrades was agreed upon, we signed on the dotted line and there began the long task of fitting her out to become cruise-ready. Our dream was coming to fruition.

Here are the specs of our new Island Packet.

IP 370-10

LOA	37'10	DISPLACEMENT
LWL	31'	BALLAST
BEAM	13'1	SAIL AREA
DRAFT	4'3	AUXILIARY POWER
MAST ABOVE DWL	54'3	HEADROOM
CABINS/BERTHS	3/7	STORAGE VOLUME
WATER CAPACITY	160 GAL	STIX
FUEL CAPACITY	75 GAL	SAIL AREA/DISP RATIO
HOLDING TANK	55 GAL	BALLAST/DISP RATIO
DISP/LENGTH RATIO	357	
DESIGNER		BOB JOHNSON, N.A.

Now, we had to think of the perfect name.

This was not an easy task. We came up with name after name, discarded them for one reason or another, and came up with more names. When you name a boat, it's as if you are naming one of your children. You want to make sure it is an appropriate name, as it will be with you forever. At the very least, it will be with you as long as you own the boat; and sometimes beyond that. When we purchased the boat, it was brand new...sort of. It was actually a 2004 model we purchased in 2006. Island Packet used this boat at boat shows, and now they were ready to sell it. As yet, it remained unnamed. We threw names back and forth at each other. Our last boat being *Moonglade*, the name for the bright reflection a full moon makes on the water; we thought perhaps something along those lines... *Moon Shine*, (umm...maybe not).... *Moon Glow*,.... *Moon Dancer*, *Moon Shadow*... Ellen immediately got online to be sure we didn't pick a name that had already been used a thousand times. We wanted to be unique.

A zillion "Moons" had been used.

OK...let's go in another direction. Perhaps something with Packet in it, since we're an Island Packet. *Packet Inn*! Been used...a few times. *Packet Up*! Used. Ugh. Let's try something else. How about *Intrepid*? That's what we are...intrepid. Intrepid... used many times. Darn. We get out the Thesaurus to find other words meaning intrepid. None sound good. Argh!

It's amazing how many boats have the same name: *Intrepid*, *Serenity*, *Indigo*, *Liberty*. When you're cruising, as we are going to do, you are remembered mostly by your boat name. So you don't want to be confused with another boat with the same name. The thinking process continued. "How about Popcorn!?" Ellen shouted. (I LOVE popcorn and our boat is a similar color.) "Then we can name the dinghy Kernel!" Ellen thought she was so clever. I actually really liked it! But we decided it was too cutesy. We aren't cutesy people. You also need to consider how it sounds when you use it on the VHF and SSB radios. "Ocean World Marina, Ocean World Marina, this is the sailing vessel Popcorn." "Yes, Popcorn, go ahead." Nah,...too cutesy.

Still thinking. Some people name their boats after a wife, girlfriend, or daughter. Always the woman, as boats are considered feminine. Maybe the daughter would be ok, but the wife or girlfriend might not stick around. The *Lacey Jane* (Ellen's daughter) sounds good, but you see mostly tugs or fishing boats with women's names like that. And we didn't want to slight our sons. Keep thinking.

We set our thinking beyond the obvious. I've always been a huge fan of Lewis and Clark and their Voyage of Discovery so we looked into something that might reflect some aspect of their trip. Lewis & Clark, the great explorers and cartographers that Thomas Jefferson commissioned to explore and map the new frontier, were intrepid. "How about a name associated with Lewis & Clark," I said. Great idea! OK...now...what name could we glean from that? Brainstorming begins.

We get serious. We want a name that is both unusual and representative of our feelings about sailing. By choosing the Lewis & Clark thought process, we've included our heritage, i.e., living and being raised in both California and the Pacific Northwest. With my interest in the Lewis & Clark expeditions, the Corps of Discovery, and specifically the winter they spent trading with the Chinook Indians, we decided to explore their language. The Chinooks created a trade language that was universally used by the native groups and European settlers. It ended up being used by nearly all who traveled and worked there, thus bringing together many different cultures in a common language. This is what we're doing in our own way...exploring and bringing together different cultures. Our common language...sailing.

Quote from **National Geographic**: *"The Chinook tribe had been trading with the British and American traders who came to the Oregon coast for decades. Their languages were mixed into 'Chinook* *jargon', which the expedition members picked up. It became the lingua franca from Washington State to California."*

MERIWETHER LEWIS 4 January 1806 *"These people, the Chinooks [sic]...have been very friendly to us; they appear to be a mild inoffensive people. ..."*

That would be us! Mild and inoffensive. Maybe...mild. Maybe ...inoffensive. Hmmm... Now to, explore their language for an appropriate word that might be used for a name.   Ellen jumped on the Internet. Skookum...we like skookum. We like how it sounds and it means strong and durable. But in researching further, there's already a line of boats called Skookum. Shoot. We keep looking. Ellen found old documents that have the Chinook Jargon in dictionary form. Interesting.

Ellen happened on a word. This might be it: Kwanesum, kwahnesum - always, forever.

Kwanesum: kwah'-neh-suhm. Ellen explores it further.

From one of the Chinook jargon books:

Kwah'-ne-sum, -or Kw'an-e-sum, adv. (C). (Chinook,- Kwanisum; Yakima,- Kwalisim.)   Always; forever; eternal; continual; everlasting; perpetual; unceasing.

Example:

Okoke steamer yaka kwanesum klatawa, that steamer is always going.

Kahkwa kwanesum, as usual.

Kwanesum mitlite, permanent; to keep.

We think it's fitting. We like it. Our boat will always keep us safe; we will always be together...forever. Taa daahh!

We shall call our boat *Kwanesum*.

We wanted to document *Kwanesum* and not register her in any one state. Documentation basically means that if the U.S. went to war, the government could take over our boat for use in the war effort. When documenting a vessel, you are required to provide a home port that can actually be anywhere in the U.S., it's not required that it be a seaport. We decided to be crazy and use Fresno, California as our homeport because that's where our daughter Lacey lived at that time. Now, by this time we had lived in Virginia for 5 or more years. For some reason, the Peoples State of California decided that we should pay them sales tax on this very expensive boat. That was a surprise letter to get in the mail! I wanted to tell them to go pound sand but Ellen said we shouldn't ignore this bill of over 10K but fight it legally, and that's what she did through letters and phone calls. The good news, no, GREAT news, was that the state of Virginia could only charge us sales tax on the first $3,000; this saved us *mucho denero*. So that's what we paid. After emails back and forth with the State Equalization Board of California, Ellen got the sales tax fiasco cleared up and sent the documentation that our boat is in Deltaville, VA and will not be in California for many years. That turned out to be everything needed to satisfy them. The gal was actually very nice. So, the next thing we did was change the home port stenciled on our boat to Seattle, Washington. Forget California. They seem to have tentacles everywhere.

We are going to be blue water sailing: definition - long-term open sea cruising, ocean crossing. This is the term used to define what we are about to set out to do. Ready or not! And we'd rather be ready than not! It is, of course, very important to have your boat prepared for the elements at sea and all the systems to stay safe. In order to get *Kwanesum* ready for this, we moved her from Deltaville to Rock Hall, MD, where the main Island Packet brokerage and service facility was located…Gratitude Yachting Center. In this location, *Kwanesum* spent her first winter up on stilts and shrink-wrapped while systems were being ordered. Shrink-wrapping was necessary to protect her from the cold Maryland winter. When Spring and Summer came, Ellen and I enjoyed going down to Rock Hall to check on *Kwanesum*'s fitting-out progress. There were lots of great places to eat and enjoy there. When we brought her down from the stilts and opened her up from the shrink-wrap, we moved her from Swan Creek Marina and were able to stay aboard in Osprey Point Marina in Rock Hall. That's where we had the boat commissioned. Commissioning a boat is the process of the broker's team going through all the systems, showing you how to use all the systems, and turning the boat over to you. Signed, sealed, delivered. A great feeling worthy of champagne!! We loved the people at Gratitude Yachts, Robin and Ed Kurowski. Their team did excellent work. As you read through our story, you will learn about all the systems that were added, as they will begin to unfold and be understood as we go. It was quite a process, lengthy and expensive, but one that was absolutely necessary for our safety.

We steered *Kwanesum* back down to Deltaville when the fitting-out process and commissioning were completed. We had a couple from Deltaville Marina help take her back down. And, yes, Ellen got seasick. We had to dodge a lot of crab pots along the way. We were NOT used to seeing crab pots on the water since we have always been sailing in the San Francisco Bay, so this was a new experience. Don't want those lines getting caught in our prop! You will hear more about crab pots a lot as the story goes.

The process continued. There was yet more to do to get *Kwanesum* shipshape. In Deltaville, we had the help and expertise of the local boat yard run by Matt Holloway. His wife, Jennifer, was the harbormaster at the Deltaville Marina. We sure loved that marina and the people there. It was very fulfilling watching *Kwanesum* come into her glory of being a tiptop blue-water sailing vessel. One of the reasons we chose an Island Packet Yacht was because of its integrity and intrepidness on the open seas. They are built for the challenge of blue-water sailing.

So there we were in Deltaville for a bit, waiting for all the parts and pieces we wanted to add to *Kwanesum* to get her ready for the blue water. We had become good friends with Jennifer and Matt and also with Speedy and his wife Nancy, whose boat *Marclicnez* was berthed across from *Kwanesum*. They had a condo there in D'ville and were awaiting their time to go South in November. Speedy was a retired Brigadier General with the Air Force and Nancy was an important part of the Community College system in the surrounding counties; such super nice people. And fun! Ellen and I enjoyed many evenings with them.

One evening, we were invited to dinner at Speedy and Nancy's and while chatting, they suggested setting a date to go to a new, neat place in the nearby, very tiny town of White Stone, VA. "It's a tapas bar called Seven that serves all kinds of great martinis!" Nancy said with excitement. "We need to try it out." Ellen's eyes lit up with curiosity and we, of course, said, "Sounds like fun! Let's plan it!" On the way home from Speedy and Nancy's, we discussed how modern and with it they were to want to go to a topless bar. But why not? We are game for anything. The next day, while in the marina office, we told Jennifer about Speedy and Nancy inviting us to go to the topless bar. We were very curious about their reason for wanting to go there, but we are willing to give it a try! I thought Jennifer was going to die of laughter. "Not a TOPLESS bar!! A TAPAS bar!" Well, I guess we were not up to date on the latest dining experiences and had never heard of a TAPAS bar. Holy cow, that story will live with us for the rest of our days. I'll have you know, that was the neatest bar. The walls and windows were covered in velvet curtains with a wonderful variety of antique, cushy chairs and couches and little tables spread around. And the tapas and martinis were wonderful. And that's an understatement. The whole atmosphere was perfect in this tiny town out in the middle of nowhere. And we love those kind of places. A memory that makes us laugh every time. A memory that's also quite special because Speedy and Nancy have both since passed away. Gone way too soon, for sure.

We only made a few sailing trips early on to get used to the boat and how she handled: to check out all the systems, to practice getting in and out of the marina, to practice anchoring this new boat. All in the positive effort of smooth sailing ahead! Different boats require different nuances in handling in and out of marinas and on the big water. We were so proud to learn everything about our *Kwanesum*.

One trip we took to get the feel of this vessel was north to Little Harbor off of Fleets Bay, where we had quite a storm, a warm storm though, and we were very thankful our anchor held. Good practice there. Another was a trip across the Chesapeake Bay with our good friends Brian and Mary when they were here visiting. It was fun having them come out and stay for a bit. We took them from our home in Manassas to stay on *Kwanesum*. We drank champagne and danced in the cockpit. The next day, we sailed across to the peninsula town of Cape Charles, VA. We had a great sail across and stayed at a very nice marina, walked about town, and had great dinners.

Virginia can be almost unbearably hot and humid. Of course, Ellen and I chose one of those days to sail, again, across the Chesapeake Bay to the little town of Onancock, VA on the peninsula. This particular trip sticks in our mind because the heat was terrible! Onancock is way up a little inlet off the Bay. There was barely a breath of wind going in there, winding our way, and carefully following our chart plotter. We finally got to our destination and secured the boat to the public wharf. We scooped water with our cloth bucket from off the side of the boat and poured it on our heads, and then laid down in the boat with cold washcloths on our face and took a nap. The heat had zapped our energy. After a bit, we spruced up and went in search of an air-conditioned restaurant. That iced cold beer and burger was the best.

But wait...there's more. On the way back to Deltaville, going across the Bay the next day, we encountered biting flies. A zillion biting flies. Maybe a trillion biting flies. Biting, biting flies. We could not get rid of the biting flies! We sprayed them, splashed water on them, everything and anything we could think of and there they were, sticking to us. It was a long trip back. Later, we learned that these flies actually live and breed on the water! No thanks.

During this time, we were preparing our retirement plans and sold our house in Manassas. We had a huge yard sale. We turned the keys over to the new owners and said goodbye to our wonderful neighbors. It was such a great neighborhood we were lucky to find. We moved into a hotel room in Vienna, VA, for the last two weeks of our work life. Every day as we got home from work, we put our perfectly good, but no longer needed, business wardrobe we wore that day in a neatly folded pile and left them for the gal that cleaned our room with a note to use herself, give away, or sell, whatever she wished. It was a weird feeling on that last day of work, to know you don't have to get up and go anymore! No more *"Finally Fridays"* to sing. We said goodbye to our friends at work and moved on the boat and then the final, final...we sold our car. That was big... a weird feeling. No wheels. No transportation. We now lived on a boat. Period. Ellen admits to having brought a few too many incidentals from the house that were piled in the rear berth, much to my dismay, but the process was to ease on in to see what we really needed and what "we" could live without. The process of what is now called tiny living. We were actually able to buy some super cool little Raleigh folding bikes from a person at the marina who no longer had use for them. So now we did have some wheels to ride to town.

This retirement adventure we were preparing for was going to be a once-in-a-lifetime experience, one we knew we needed to document. Ellen decided to create what was then, in 2008, a fairly new practice on the Internet called a BLOG. It will be the journal of this adventure for the next few years.

The story of *Itchy Feet* now takes the form of Ellen's BLOG posts and her voice from this point to play out the rest of this story; 7021.92 nautical miles, visiting 21 countries and the adventures along the way. The blog is written and narrated by Ellen. It is full of run-on sentences and ramblings from the heart as if you were sitting down with us, a nice glass of wine or cup of coffee in your hand, while the story is told. We hope you enjoy your visit here.

Mother, mother ocean, I have heard you call

Wanted to sail upon your waters since I was three feet tall

You've seen it all, you've seen it all

Watched the men who rode you, switch from sails to steam

And in your belly, you hold the treasures few have ever seen

Most of 'em dream, most of 'em dream

- Jimmy Buffett

**San Diego, CA 1964 Randy joins the Navy and becomes a
member of the Naval Drum and Bugle Corps.**

Iran 1972 Randy working undercover for the CIA.

1998 Randy meets Ellen and they dance to the juke box at
Ballena Bay Yacht Club in Alameda, CA.

May 21, 2000 Randy and Ellen get married aboard
Moonglade in Alameda.

April 2008 Randy and Ellen move aboard Kwanesum and celebrate their retirement.

Kwanesum – Island Packet 370 – cutter rig

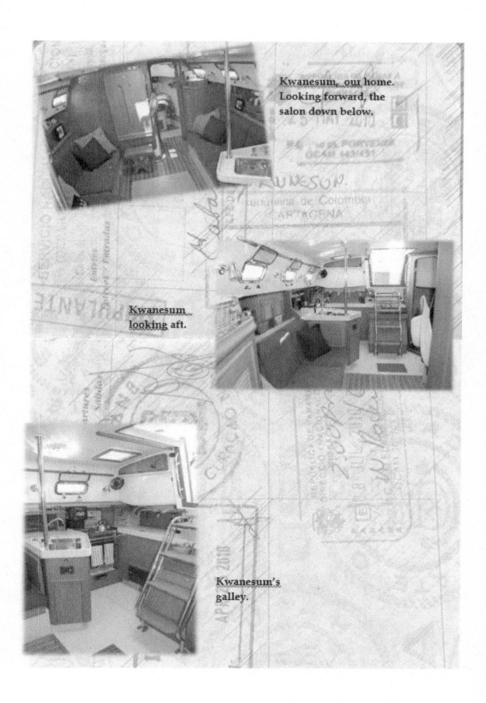

Kwanesum, our home. Looking forward, the salon down below.

Kwanesum looking aft.

Kwanesum's galley.

Early departure from Elizabeth City, NC.

The sailor, cigars and Sudoku while at sea.

The sailor setting sails.

Ellen at the helm leaving Charleston, SC. Freezing!!

Kwanesum at anchor in White Cay, Bahamas.

Meeting Foxy!

Cooper Island, Bahamas.

Corsairs with Terri and Lyman.

Jost Van Dyke - Kwanesum anchored between the palms.

Harleys in Bonaire.

Tall ships in Cartagena, Colombia.

San Blas Islands, Panama. Kuna Indians in their ulu selling wares to the sailor.

Roel, Isabelle, Tessa and Yoan Vrenken.

Panama Canal!

The Pirates of Kwanesum.

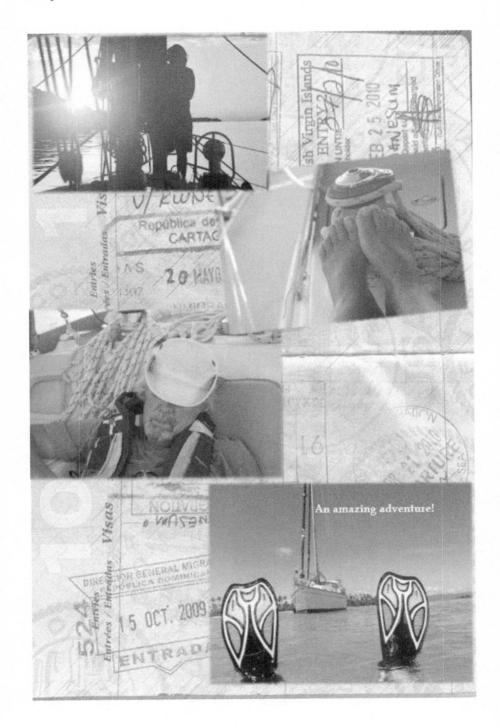

An amazing adventure!

Kwanesum Travels from Virginia to California.

70

Chapter 7
The Sailing Blog

Hit It Captain Ran!

A boat is sort of like a litmus test for relationships, the close quarters and solitude compelling people into either a warm bond or into mutiny and murder.

—from the novel **The Gold Coast**
—sent to us from our dear friend John Dobbs

"Welcome to our blog...our life...our retirement adventure!" That is the title of our blog. www.kwanesum.blogspot.com

A fitting title. As you read on in this, our story, you will experience this blog as it was written in real time, by me, Ellen...as it happened, or as soon as I could get it written down, usually with a glass of wine in hand or a great cup of coffee. You will see all the delights and, frustrations and crazy experiences that were new to us. Selling everything... the house, the furniture, the cars, then moving aboard and living on a boat, then releasing the dock lines to get going on the adventure we planned, is a bit scary, a bit daunting, a bit exciting, not for the faint of heart! But we are ready!

Let's hit it, Captain Ran!

Itchy feet.

The blog begins as we sit, waiting for good weather to depart Deltaville Marina. Posted the day after tropical storm Hanna passed through Deltaville, VA.

The Deltaville Marina and Boatyard was a beehive of activity in the days prior to the storm, pulling boats out of the marina and putting them *on the hard* (90% of the slip holders here) and moving the remaining boats to the safest locations within the marina docks. Putting boats *on the hard* means the boat is pulled out of the water and put on stilts on the boatyard grounds, in this case in a sort of protected spot on the grounds.

The storm was fast-moving with wind speeds up to 60 knots. The boats that remained in the marina docks had a really rough time, bouncing around and pulling at the boat docks...some pulling out cleats, others knocking over pilings and at least two roller furling jibs let loose. We're glad we decided to go *on the hard* and were well protected by the surrounding trees. And, as a bonus, one of the guys who was with us in the parking lot of boats on the hard, made chocolate chip cookies and brought them around to share! Hot out of the oven! Perfecto! Boy did they taste good. Staying up on stilts way up off the ground about 10 feet is not for the faint of heart. But chocolate chip cookies sure helped a lot! Plus, you learn to be intrepid living on a boat, ready to deal with whatever is thrown your way.

A lot has happened in the last year, and since we entered anything in our ship's log, not to mention on this blog. Every sailor keeps a ship's log of destinations and information concerning the boat. The blog is our story. We sold our house in Manassas, retired, took a road trip across the country to see our wonderful, much-missed family in California, up to Oregon, Washington and back, and sold our car. While we were living there on *Kwanesum* in the marina, we made a bunch of needed upgrades to the boat to get her fitted out for blue water sailing. The term *blue water sailing* is used to describe sailing on the open seas. It was important to us to be very prepared for open seas, which included a lot of equipment on the boat that gave us the ability to detect and deter any danger. These upgrades included 5 Group 27 batteries, which are large deep cycle, dual purpose batteries that can store large amounts of electricity and provide high levels of power. Much needed for our floating home. They were situated quite well under the seating in the salon down below on the port side. We also added 2 solar panels, a new 9.9 hp Yamaha outboard for the dinghy, dinghy davits to carry the dinghy on *Kwanesum* as we traveled, a motor lift for the Yamaha outboard to bring it up on the stern and sit securely there while we travel, a *"dripless"* packing gland for the propeller which keeps it lubricated with little maintenance, and... a new bottom job! A *bottom job* consists of painting the hull of the boat with an anti-fouling paint that will inhibit any growth that might want to attach itself as we sit in marinas, mooring bays, or as we go bobbing along. It's done every few years to keep the hull sailing smoothly.

The only sailing trips we made this year on our new boat was a trip north to Little Harbor off of Fleets Bay (we had quite a storm there, too) and across the Chesapeake to Onancock, VA, on a very hot, in-the-90s day, with only a whisper of wind. Man was that HOT!! We immediately found an air-conditioned bar with cold beer. With no A/C on *Kwanesum*, it was the best place to sit a spell.

What a feeling. Finally, *Kwanesum* broke away permanently from her D-31 slip at Deltaville Marina. It was beginning to feel as if there was a vortex holding us there. If not one more thing needed to be done to the boat…there was another. If you wait long enough, you'll own the whole boatyard with all those expenses! There was always something cool to add to the boat to make it better and better…or finding something that you might as well update now. So, as we figure it, the *Kwanesum* Room on the top level of the Deltaville Boatyard office should be open soon.

We popped out of that slip like a champagne cork at 0848hrs Thursday 18 September. It's bad luck to start your journey on a Friday, they say. We must be sure to keep up with the sailing superstitions for a safe journey…right?! Besides…it was time to get the heck going. "Put this puppy in reverse, Randy, wave bye to (our great friends) Jack and Marianne (berthed next to us for the last 4 months) and head out! Norfolk, here we come!" We are now truly on our way South…heading for Mile Marker Zero (which is actually red buoy 36…go figure) of the Intracoastal Waterway.

To make our departure perfect, dolphins swam by, and a little ladybug rode with us in the cockpit for a while. Now do tell…how do ladybugs get out there in the middle of the Chesapeake? We also saw several different kinds of butterflies fluttering by. Nature truly is a wonder and is apparently bidding us farewell. Except for the damn flies. Why are there flies on the water, anyway? Yucky, biting flies. Took us 2 days to get rid of them. Bad flies. Bad, bad flies. Go away!   But I digress….as they say.

Wait…back up a second. The night before we left, to make our departure even more perfect …our great D'ville friends came by to toast our journey on:

- **Matt and Jennifer** run the boatyard and the harbor. They are so fun and so helpful. We spent many late afternoons talking and drinking beer with them, dinghying out to the flats. (Is that a word…dinghying?)

- **Jack and Marianne** from *Gravyboat* next door came over. They are from Colorado and are going the same way we are, making their boat ship shape and perfect before carrying on. Again…many evenings talking, talking and enjoying each other's company. So fun.

- **Speedy and Nancy** from *Marcnicliz* berthed across from us, came by, too. Speedy is a retired Brigadier General and Nancy is an important part of the community college system in the surrounding counties. Randy and I enjoyed many evenings with them, too. You'll remember them from the *"tapas/topless"* story.

We will miss these people a lot, but we hope to catch up with them all on our travels to the Bahamas and the Caribbean. We told Jenn and Matt they have to join up with us somewhere. They are veteran cruisers but are back to working now. They're too fun to leave behind. We missed saying goodbye to Keith from the boatyard, but we are grateful for all he did for us. These are good people. We can't say enough about the Deltaville Boatyard and Marina. Bottles of ice-cold Yuengling beer and chardonnay were savored, and toasts were made by all in the cockpit of *Kwanesum* that night before we left. Isn't that what cockpits are for? I brought out my friend Penny's wonderful red wine she and her husband Al produce in the Alexander Valley of Sonoma County in CA. Perfect.

Still reminiscing…Deltaville was such a nice little town. So many interesting cruising people from all countries stop by the marina on their way to or from various places. They share their personalities and their information, showing good places to aim for on the charts…and bad places to avoid. Potlucks, swims in the pool, music outdoors… chats while on our computers in the marina lounge. But…now it's time. Time to get going.

Our sail away from Deltaville was actually a motor/sail away. The winds were directly behind us, so we went *wing on wing* and we kept the engine running, too. We were destined to arrive in Norfolk, VA, before dark. *Wing on wing*, for those who aren't sailors, means you put one sail to port and one to starboard. Like two wings on a bird. The wind from behind billows them out to float you along. You hold the jib sail out with your whisker pole and the mainsail needs a preventer to keep from jibing. We did it without our preventer, but all was well. It's one of our favorite points of sail and it made for a nice ride all day.

We arrived at Thimble Shoal Light around 1500hrs. This was the beginning of the Elizabeth River that took us into Norfolk, Portsmouth, and the ICW — the Intracoastal Waterway. Pretty good wind blowing at that time. As we took the long journey in, we were proud to see the presence of all the military bases and ships. We arrived at Tidewater Yacht Marina on the Portsmouth side at 1810hrs and slipped into a downwind berth between 2 powerboats. This is a lovely marina with floating docks, nice facilities and nice people. Immediately, we were invited over for a drink, but we passed...instead opting to open a bottle of champagne to toast the real beginning of our journey in the intimacy of our own boat.

We caught up with the invitation for drinks on a later day and enjoyed the company of fellow cruisers. Our immediate boat slip neighbors are from Ohio and are awaiting the weather to head up to Deltaville. Such nice people, boaters are. We are sticking here until the weather window opens for our trip down the ICW. Big winds have been hanging around...big, big winds. We want to enjoy it all and not have to fight inclement weather. After all...that's the point! We will head down the Dismal Swamp to Elizabeth City. A historic waterway. We are anxious to see this part of the East Coast going south. In the meantime, we are taking advantage of seeing what there is around Portsmouth and Norfolk.

Chapter 8
ICW

The Dismal Swamp

One of the gladdest moments of human life, me thinks, is the departure upon a distant journey into unknown lands. Shaking off with one mighty effort the fetters of habit, the leaden weight of routine, the cloak of many cares and the slavery of home, man feels once more happy.

- Sir Richard Burton

Greetings from the ICW, the Intercostal Waterway.

Position: heading to Camp Le Jeune from Beaufort, NC

Plan: to stop for the night.

We will anchor out there. We've come over 200 miles since I last reported in. Our daily rhythm is beginning to fall into place, but it is taking some adjusting. This is different than just being on the boat in the Deltaville Marina. We are constantly on the move and need to be heedful of where we are, where we're headed and if we're safe. Now that's a good idea, eh? It's a good kind of stress but it's stress none-the-less. Fellow travelers have said this all takes a while to get used to. And that's ok. We have time. And we love it!

Charting our course is like a game …I like it. Like the computer game *Myst*….trying to figure out how to get from one place to the next using all the clues….cool….ok, back to what I was talking about. We start with a Skipper's Meeting every evening at 5 pm. While sipping our favorite adult beverages and having snacks, we decide on our destination for the next day, how far we want to go and where we will anchor for the night or tie up to a free dock. We don't tend to go into marinas as they're more expensive and more trouble. Anchoring out is free! Free is good!

The waypoints are entered in the GPS on the chart plotter at our helm. The person not at the helm follows with the paper charts to make sure we're going along correctly, and watches for the red and green markers along the way to be sure the boat is in the ICW channel. It can be shallow along here so we need to be vigilant. Our *draft*, or *draught*, (the term for the vertical distance between the waterline and the bottom of the keel) is only 4 feet which is excellent for this kind of travel. Our fellow travelers we have joined on this leg have deeper *drafts*, so they must watch even more carefully. Through these ICW channels, we are motoring the whole time. We do put sails up to increase our speed and to balance the boat, but the engine stays on. Our boat carries 75 gallons of diesel fuel so we can go a long way before needing to refuel.

I'm sitting down below at the chart table as we travel today, working on this blog entry. I'm way past due. I've been waiting for the internet sources, but they have been infrequent through here. By the end of the day, I'm so pooped I don't feel like sitting at the computer. But, wait, Ellen….here's an idea…try typing some of this up while you're traveling and not at the helm! Taa daa! I may be slow…but I eventually come around to correct thinking. So now, when we get to an internet source, I can upload the blog entry. Brilliance doesn't always come easily. I intend to get an internet booster antenna but haven't decided which one I want to pay for yet. It's too bad I didn't make that decision already, as I could have used it through here.

Now…to the flashback sequence…. how we got to this point in our travel.

We left Portsmouth/Norfolk at 1145hrs Tuesday 30 September. We timed our departure to reach the first lock on the Dismal Swamp Canal by 1500hrs, which was the latter of the only two daily openings. The lock only opens twice daily now to conserve water. They had a peat fire here on the Dismal a month or so ago and a large amount of water had to be used for that. (Peat fires burn very slowly. They're hard to put out.) Our plan is to go through the lock and tie up at the dock just past for the night.

Several bridges had to be dealt with before we reached the sharp 90° turn into the Dismal Swamp. (Dismal Swamp does sound ominous, but that's what they named it!) This part of the Elizabeth River, leaving Norfolk, is very industrial and full of military ships. Tugs working all around us, pushing barges here and there. We like tugs. They are the worker bees. They have all sizes. While in Portsmouth, we got to watch 3 tugs maneuver a huge military warship, turning it completely 180° to get it onto a dry dock pad. Really interesting to see and listen as they tooted their horns to each other.

The first bridge we came to is *"always open"* they say. Nope. It was a railroad bridge and I'll be darned if a train didn't come just at the time we were ready to go through. Down came the bridge. OK…. we'll circle, circle until it opens again. Calling in to open a bridge and dealing with maneuvering through those bridges is stressful if you've never done it before. And we had never done it before. It's not easy to hold a sailboat still on the water while you wait for a bridge to open. There are always currents to deal with. "Hope this isn't a bad omen, Ran!". It wasn't. The rest of the way through here and dealing with bridges opening went perfectly. We called into the bridges ahead if we needed them to open or followed other boats and skedaddled through. Just past the Highway 64 Bridge, we made our right-angle turn into the Dismal Swamp. It's so beautiful! "Ran! We're finally going through the Swamp we've heard so much about."

The Dismal Swamp is the beginning of the Intracoastal Waterway, or ICW, at least as far as it's defined. There is a waterway that begins up the coast near Maine, but Mile Zero of the ICW is at Norfolk, VA. George Washington and Patrick Henry thought a canal was needed for the effective transportation of goods so that the country could grow and prosper. Construction began in 1793, dug by hand from both ends. This area turned out to be a haven for runaway slaves. HB Stowe and Longfellow both wrote of the Swamp. The completed canal finally opened in 1805. It is the oldest operating artificial waterway in the US. Edgar Allen Poe wrote The Raven during one of his stays at the Halfway House on the Swamp. James Adams' Floating Theatre was on the canal, which was the idea for Edna Ferber's "Showboat." Is this cool or what? I love it! So much history.

We got to Deep Creek Lock about an hour before the 1500hrs opening. There were 4 other boats waiting, too. Ok...so 4 boats makes it all a bit harder. Now 4 boats have to stay still in the current waiting for the bridge, or circle, circle with not much room. Stressful for us newbies! Just before 1500hrs, the lock master hailed us on Channel 16 on the radio to see if there were any boats behind us, and then turned on the green light. We all entered the lock, preparing to hold to the starboard side.

81

The lock tender, Robert, was unbelievably nice. This is the first time I had traversed a lock. Randy had done one up in Seattle. Lock Tender Robert walked down the dock and took our lines, hooking them to the side of the lock. In this lock, we prepared for 8 feet of water to raise us up. Robert had his dog UHaul or Uturn (I can't remember which) as his assistant. Dogs with Jobs. Dogs love to have jobs…and they're good at it! After transiting through, we tied up on the 100ft dock just south of the lock, with an offer of coffee in the morning from the lock tender. Can't beat that! One boat continued south, but 4 of us stayed. And this is where we met our new friends.

Theo and Marion, and their trusty dog Skye are on s/v *Double Dutch*. (s/v = sailing vessel) They are from Canada but originally from Holland. So, they have nifty accents. Skye is part husky and part border collie, so she's not Dutch, but she should have her pedigree known, too…and she loves us all. Always lots of kisses from Skye.

Lonnie is from *la la land*. Seriously a bit "out there". He's on s/v *Smoooth Move*. He hates that extra "o" in the name, but he bought the boat on e-Bay and he doesn't believe in renaming boats. Lonnie is originally from Iowa, but…he's been sailing for 30 years… and looks like the salty sailor: long ponytail, funky hat…. some teeth. He's great, with super stories! He's been there…and done that…in Key West, the Bahamas, at Le Select in St Barts with Jimmy Buffett…. He's writing a book about buying a boat on eBay. Well, there ya go!

Sue and Vick and Beauregard (dog, too) are from Washington, NC. They are on s/v *Sandpiper*, a cute little 27-foot Island Packet. They're just putzing around the ICW for a few weeks. We had great conversations in their tiny cockpit with Theo and Marion, drinking our beverages during a pouring rain. Great time.

Up early and over to the lock tender's hut the next morning for the promised coffee! UHaul, or UTurn, greeted us and the coffee was poured all around. Robert even microwaved us some little breakfast biscuits. How's that for service? A morning spent with nice people and listening to really great stories from the lock tender on some experiences he's had...quite the tales...started our next leg down the Dismal Swamp.

We left Sue and Vick at the dock to continue on their travels, which took them back through the lock, and we continued on with *Double Dutch* and *Smoooth Move* down the Dismal. After coffee and stories, Lock Tender Robert and UTurn/UHaul had to jump into the pickup and drive down to open up the Deep Creek Bridge for us as we departed. Lots of jobs for those two!

Our next stop was the Great Dismal Swamp Canal Visitor's Center, where we would tie up for the night. This Visitor's Center is right off Highway 17 and accommodates both boats and cars. I think it's the only one in the country that does that. We had a lot of people from their cars come down to talk to us. This area was also the site of a Civil War battle in which Confederate soldiers prevented the Yankees from blowing up the locks. So much history out here.

Later in the evening, we were approached by an Island Packet 445 coming down the Swamp. As there was no room left on the dock, they *"rafted up"* with us. This means they tie directly to our boat, side to side. This is done quite often in crowded areas. If they need to get off their boat, they must walk across our deck. The etiquette is not to walk through the cockpit but across the foredeck. And here we met Marthalou and R.T. How's that for some southern names? And their accent suited them perfectly. They were bringing their boat down from the Richmond, VA area to Oriental, NC, for the winter, traveling with their friends Chess and Karen. They use their boat as a floating condo. Nice, nice people. And that Island Packet was amazing. Huge, by our standards, but gorgeous. By the time we left them, I was talking just like Marthalou! Y'all!

The next morning, we were all up early and ready to go at daybreak, wiping the dew off the boat and enjoying the mist on the water. It's so pretty. I wish you could all experience this. We were headed for Elizabeth City. We're now in North Carolina! We had to traverse another lock, this time going down 8 feet. And this lock tender wasn't as nice or efficient. Oh well, I guess they can't all be Roberts. He wasn't even monitoring his VHF radio, so we had to figure out what he wanted us to do. The other boats filed in, preparing to tie up on the starboard side. We were prepared for that, too. Then suddenly, the lock tender motions with his arms to go to the other side! Like the guys do at the airport, but without the flashlights. "Ran! Does he want us to wait out here on that side or does he want us to go in on that side? What do you think?" "Hell, if I know!" Pretty soon we're so close we can hear him shouting. He wants us to tie port to. Good grief. Why don't you use your damn radio, mister? I pulled *Kwanesum* over and Randy frantically switched all the lines and fenders to the port side. A Chinese fire drill, for sure. (I probably can't use that term anymore, but it describes it perfectly.) As the water comes in, you need to tend the lines to keep them taut. Much harder for Lonnie, who's single handing. We were all on our way again in no time. Well, maybe not in no time, but we finally got underway.

As we arrived in Elizabeth City, all the boats decided to tie up at the same spot, the city docks. We fit in nicely except for s/v *Gift of the Magi*, which is Marthalou and R.T.'s boat. Too big! But there was room around the corner. We had lots of help tying up from gentlemen standing along the dock. Randy jumped off to thank them and low and behold, one is the mayor! Great service there in Elizabeth City. He invited us all to a wine and cheese reception at 1630hrs put on by the Rose Buddies, just for us. Apparently, it is a tradition in this town started by a gentleman in honor of his wife. He loved roses and had them growing everywhere in his yard. When he saw boats come in, he would pick the roses and come down to the dock to welcome the boats with a reception. After his death, the town continues the tradition in his honor. It was very special. It reminds us all to stop and smell the roses.

"As the gateway to the Outer Banks, Elizabeth City stirs memories of the time when Blackbeard sailed the waters, trains were still a way of life and Wilbur and Orville stopped for provisions on their way to Kitty Hawk," mentions a brochure we found. We did not experience these stirred memories, but perhaps they're there somewhere. We did, however, enjoy the little part of the town we were in at the water side in the short time we were there.

This was when we made the decision to travel on with *Double Dutch* and *Smoooth Move.* (you're right, Lonnie...putting that extra 'o' in there is a pain in the neck!) We had our first Skippers' meeting and decided to leave at o'dark-thirty in the morning, heading to mile 102.2, where we would anchor at Deep Point off the Alligator River. A power boat came into the docks and it was a couple Theo and Marion on *Double Dutch* had met in Norfolk. We invited them over and we met our second pair of Canadians, Monica and Al, on p/v *Painkiller!* Skippers' meeting is officially over. Let's just have fun! It is so damn fun just sitting and talking with these people.

We woke to a gorgeous morning and headed out, waving goodbye to Monica and Al. We decided to take a shortcut across the Albemarle Sound. In doing so, we played 'find the opening' amongst all the crab pots! We knew this would happen and it's not too bad, but they were everywhere. It seems as if they can put crab pots wherever they damn well please. And they can tag them with whatever kind of buoy they want...whatever color. Some of them look like recycled milk bottles. I don't think this would fly in California. They would have some kind of regulation on this. At times...regulation can be a good thing. We're zig-zagging our way through. I perched on the bow, keeping an eagle eye on all the weird, hard-to-distinguish, so-called buoys for their crab pots. Don't want to get caught in any of those lines, that's for damn sure. Our propeller would not take kindly to that.

Along the way, we saw the blimp hanger the mayor told us about. It is leftover from World War II and apparently, this is where they make 99% of the blimps today. Just not the Goodyear blimp. And by golly we did see Snoopy on the Met Life blimp as we sailed by.

As we were trucking down the river, who should drive up but *Painkiller*! They were going to stay in Elizabeth City for a couple of days, but the day was so beautiful, and they saw all they wanted to see there in 3 hours, so they decided to follow us. Good deal! Now, there were 4 of us buddy-boating.

We crossed the Albemarle, then the Neuse River and turned into the Alligator River. We turned into Little Alligator River and found our anchorage for the night. Ran and I have not anchored much...not a lot of anchoring to do in SF Bay, the area of most of our sailing experience... so we are still pretty new at the procedure, but we did well! We're still getting used to handling *Kwanesum* anyway, as she's a much heavier boat with a full keel, than our boat we had in the SF Bay. That makes her harder to maneuver and turn on a dime. Thus...the bow thrusters we had put on. Bow thrusters are our friend. Good, good bow thrusters.

Captains'/Skippers' meeting....1700hrs! All headed to the *Painkiller* tiki bar on her stern. It was such a beautiful night. A

86

zillion stars were everywhere. Because we are not used to anchoring, Ran and I were up several times during the night to check on everything. Every little noise would prompt us to check. At one time, around midnight, we heard a steady noise, and it was a tug pushing a barge…really pretty to see during the night. Kind of an odd thing to say about a tug pushing a barge, but it was neat. And again…the stars were amazing. Up at dawn to get going and another tug and barge passed by. Beautiful mornings and the tug and barge just added that extra touch. OK…you had to be there, but it was neat.

The next point of travel decided by the Skippers' meeting would be mile 157.3 on the ICW, the docks of the RE Mayo Shrimp Company in Hobocken, NC. We went through the Pungo River into Goose Creek. The docks here at our stop are….old. Very old. There are 3 old shrimp boats tied up to the docks but plenty of room for us, too. But be careful when you get off the boat. The docks are indeed precarious. Skippers' meeting on *Double Dutch* tonight. Bring the mosquito spray…they're on a roll. This is a narrow canal, mind you, and during the evening…the tugs come by with their barges. It is a sight to see. The next decided point of travel would be Beaufort, NC.

We woke up to fog. Well, there you go! I've done fog before…big, tule fog I was raised on in my hometown. No problem. We try to wipe off our dodger because of all the dew on it…so we can see. We're ready…everybody ready? Let's go. "Randy and Ellen…you lead today." "OK, no problem." I get behind the helm and off we go. I am watching the chart plotter, as you can't see much in front of you, and there's a little fishing boat right in the channel. Well, come on…why are you in the channel? Sheesh! And they're crab pots. Crap…we hate dodging the crab pots. Especially before we've had our coffee, pretty soon we hear Theo yelling…"Ellen! This way!" Turns out, I was so worried about the fisherman and the crab pots that

I was heading in the wrong direction even though we had the chart plotter telling us exactly where to go. Ugh. So much for being the leaders!! OK...now we are back on track. Then...after Ran wiped off the dodger window a zillion times he said, "Why don't we just unzip it and put it up out of the way?!" Duh... now there's a good idea! That way we can see! Yay! That would be a great idea! We are so new at this it's laughable!

Now, we're fumbling our way through the fog when Randy says, "I think I see a boat coming straight for us." Oh, jeez. OK. I'm really putting my Porterville fog eyes to work here, which is actually good training. Tule fog is a great training ground for future ship captains. I see the boat. It's *Painkiller*! They had left earlier, but because they didn't have radar and there was lots of fog, they thought they'd stop and let Randy and Ellen lead since they have radar. Only problem is...Randy and Ellen forgot they had radar and hadn't been using it! Hello?! Randy and Ellen?! Anybody home?!? We happen to have a super great radar that overlays onto our GPS. But if the brain doesn't remember that......it's useless. Ahem.... After turning on our expensive and wonderful radar...we trucked on down the waterway...headed to Beaufort, NC.

We arrived at Beaufort and tried to figure out where we're going to be for the night. Oops! It's getting shallow! We are at Town Creek Marina and wanted to anchor out there, but there are a lot of shoals in that area. We got on the wrong side. The dock master hailed us on the VHF radio, and we got back on track. We thought we might go into a berth, but the space was too tight. It's hard to maneuver *Kwanesum* in tight spaces. So, we decided to go back and anchor where everyone else was...but there's not a lot of room and a lot of depth. Crap. We aren't great at this anyway, and now we have to decide where to fit in amongst the boats so there's enough room to swing around. Our technique is still being polished. We found a spot.

Let's drop the anchor. "Ellen…move it back. Reverse. OK. I think we're good. Get me a beer." (Note from Ellen: we'll get better at this as we go. Practice makes perfect.) Phew. Wine for Ellen…beer for the Ran-man.

The weather's not great, but it's a nice anchorage. We can dinghy to the other side and go into their old town near the water. Very nice. Ran and I go in and walk to town, have some lunch…buy a couple of rugs for the boat and pick up some beer at a store. Back in the dinghy…back to the boat. Good day.

Skippers' meeting at the *Painkiller* tiki bar. Love that tiki bar on *Painkiller*. No…wait….I think we were at *Double Dutch*…oh well…doesn't matter. It's always good. Next point of travel: Camp LeJeune, NC. It's a marine base. You can't go ashore, but you're allowed to anchor in this one spot at Mile Hammock Bay. (Skye, however, was granted permission to go in and do her thing. Skye is special…and we know that.)

We're in…anchored…we're getting better at this…and the military are running some exercises. I love it. I just love our military. They have neato boats. They're running maneuvers around all around us…after dark, even…without lights. Cool. And the helicopters are flying right over our boats. It all makes my heart pound with pride. I applauded when they went by us. They appreciated it.

Skippers' meeting….I forget where….point of travel will be mile 295.1, Carolina Beach, NC.

This was quite a day. As we go down the ICW, it becomes more of a challenge. A lot of shoaling has taken place. We are following several cruising guides we purchased before we left Virginia that have details of what to expect and what to avoid along the way. We try our best to follow their suggestions and keep in the deeper part of the channels. It doesn't always work. The first to go aground was *Double Dutch*. They have a 7-foot draft on their keel, which is pretty deep. They got in trouble. *Painkiller,* being a power boat, was able to turn around, go back, and pull them off. Excellent. Otherwise, they would have to wait for the tide to rise. Really, really nice of them to turn around, come back, and do that.

We travel on and *Smoooth Move* gets in trouble. Lonnie turns the boat and, powers it forward and gets off. Excellent. Moving on down…being really vigilant of the buoys and the depth…Lonnie goes aground again. He, too, has a deep draft. We are just ahead of him and slow down…back up a bit…try to help. We've caught something in our prop. Crap, crap, crap! I hate when that happens. Lonnie turns his boat and gets off. Excellent.

We continue motoring on, feeling the boat shake knowing something must be caught somewhere on the prop or rudder. Not good…but it seems ok. We wait for the bridge to open. This is the second or third bridge we have dealt with this leg, and it gets old. These bridges only open on the hour! Some open on the half hour and the hour, but this one opens only on the hour! Ugh…. This means you have to putz around and wait and hope you don't get into some honking current that sends you where you don't want to be! *Double Dutch* got into trouble waiting for one bridge. The current caught them, and they had to put their anchor out to stop them before they started under the bridge before it opened! The mast would have been gone, for sure. But Theo got his anchor out pronto and held fast. Phew! They were ok.

The bridge is finally open and we all file through. We feel this thing caught on our prop. The boat is shaking. OK…just get through the bridge, *Kwanesum*! Randy powers up and whatever it was seemed to fall off and we smoothly powered through. All righty! Good girl, *Kwanesum.* All is ok and we're going on. Coming up on a spot, the guide said to be vigilant.

90

Stay to the red side, it said…more depth there. We do…we go aground. And we just have a 4-foot draft! Good grief. Randy turns the boat…turns on the bow thruster….we're off. No harm, no foul. We're on our way again. Love those thrusters!

We arrive at Mile 295.1 Carolina Beach. It was very beautiful along the way despite the stress of watching our depth the whole time. There are some beautiful houses. Some big boats! Mostly fishing boats. We're really glad to be here. Ran and I decided to go into a marina. We needed fuel, water, provisions and needed to do laundry. The others anchor out just around the corner. Randy also wanted to have someone dive on our boat to see if something is on our propeller or rudder. It's time to stop anyway. It's good to have electricity you don't have to worry about. When we're at anchor, we have electricity, but you have to be careful how much you use and it's all 12 volts. We have small inverters we can plug into but they don't like it when the power isn't up at a certain level. The solar panels we have really keep the power up. But it goes fast when you use it. So, it's nice not to worry about it for a couple of days.

The diver found the culprit today. A big, long ole piece of plastic. All twisted around. I'm so glad we stopped and checked this. *Kwanesum* is glad, too. There's a weather front here now. We traveled during a little rain yesterday, so it's good to stop for a few days. And there's internet here. Good deal. We slept in. Nice.

Skippers' meeting…where are we going next? (By now, I forget on which boat we had these meetings. We rotate boats. It's just too much fun.)

Well…the sailboats want to go outside to the Atlantic for this stint to Charleston, SC. The ICW gets even shallower from this point on. It's just too stressful and difficult for the sailboats…we want to go outside. It would be an overnight sail, but that's ok. We've actually wanted to do this anyway. Seems

91

like the best thing is to go out at Cape Fear Inlet and back in at Charleston. Because of the weather that's hanging around, it looks like we won't leave until Tuesday. Today is Friday. But we can rest here and prepare. It will be a different journey. So, we'll need to prepare the boat for that. We will need to travel straight through for 30 hours or so, so different shifts at the helm will be in order. Let's do it. I've been waiting for this.

Carolina Beach, NC, at Joyner Marina. Nice marina, but the weather was lousy. Really windy. We rocked back and forth like a cradle. Good for sleeping, 'cept the noise of the wind.

Our friends and buddy-boaters, *Double Dutch*, *Painkiller* and *Smoooth Move*, are anchored around the corner. They would dinghy on over to our dock and walk on the beach. Now, mind you…my idea of a walk on the beach is barefooted in my shorts with the beautiful sky showing a shining sun. Ahhhh. Not there…not during our stay. We did walk on the beach but wore our foul weather gear, hats pulled down over our ears, with rain pounding sideways and the wind pushing you back. "I realize this is exercise, but this is ridiculous!" Skye, the wonder dog, loved it…herding us all together.

Because of the wind and weather, we stayed a few days at Carolina Beach and then scooted up to Southport, NC to plan our route out the Cape Fear Inlet to the Atlantic… goal: Charleston, SC. I'm sure Carolina Beach is a nice area…certainly nice homes where we were, but the weather made it miserable, well, almost miserable. We were able to dinghy over to "town." Not much of a town. Sort of like Pismo Beach in the late 60s. Maybe not even that good. Pismo Beach was fun! We did find The Dive, where we had beer and good conversation. Those times are really fun.

While we were at Carolina Beach, we were able to catch up with one of my dear California friends I hadn't seen in years.

How odd that we were now on the East Coast! Mary Ann Miller and her beau Bryan live in Wilmington, NC now. They came over to the boat one evening bearing ingredients for Bombay Sapphire martinis …along with flowers and fresh basil for the boat. And…a wonderful bottle of Pinot Noir. Excellent! Though it was cold and windy, the martinis made for great fun and catching-up conversation before we jumped in their car and found a place down the road for dinner. What a great evening! We are actually hoping to catch up with them again out here on the coast before we get too far away.

Now, we had to plan our departure to Southport. Because of the wind and the big current where we were docked at the Joyner Marina, Randy and I had to plot our exit from our slip very carefully. We thought if we got up early….really, really early…the wind wouldn't be so bad and *Kwanesum* would slip out of this sideways-current/sideways-wind berth. We listened all night long to see if the wind would stop, and it kinda did…for a minute. "Well, let's get this over with."

We got up early, early…still dark and went out to survey the situation. Ugh…how are we going to manage this without damaging the boat somehow? We decided to physically pull her back a little, outside the pilings that defined our berth. At least that way, she would be in the fairway, somewhat, as a head start. She's heavy! Empty, she's 23,000lbs! But we got her where we wanted her. When in reverse, *Kwanesum* tends to pull to the port (left), which is not unusual for a heavy, full keel boat, with a regular prop. [Full keel: A keel that runs the length of the boat. Full keels have a shallower draft than fin keels.] It's called "prop walk." I do NOT like prop walk. Our other boat in CA had a fin keel and a folding prop and backed like a champ threading a needle.

Fin Keel: A keel that is narrow and deeper than a full keel. It looks like a fish's fin extending below the boat, and the boat usually has a rudder mounted some distance aft, often on an additional keel-like extension called a skeg.

Not so, on sweet *Kwanesum*.

It all worked well, though… our plan. Thank heaven. Her prop walk was in the direction the current and winds were pushing anyway. We eased her back, working the lines along the cleats of the dock and she went right back into the fairway. Yes! Now we just had to see where we were going and it was pitch dark. The plan was to go to the fuel dock and wait there until morning light and the rest of the crew were ready to go. We didn't have far to go so I stood on the bow and motioned to Randy which way to steer the boat in the dark. It worked. We could relax now and have our coffee and wait for daylight. Stress is gone.

The trip to Southport, NC, was short and fairly uneventful. We were there before noon, the point being that Southport was at the top of the Cape Fear Inlet we would be taking to get out to the Atlantic for our trip to Charleston the next morning. This would give us a head start. I am at the helm and it all went well…until we got to our docking spot. "We'll pull into the Provision Co. berths. They provide free docking for the night if you eat there." "Roger that, Ran, just show me where to go." "OK…pull in here…this looks wide enough. We'll tie up on the starboard(right) side so just pull over to drop me on the dock." "Roger that, Ran." "Good job, El; just a little closer and I can step off. Just a little closer…closer…uhhhh….why don't you back up and try again." "Roger that, Ran." Remember that prop walk we told you about? Well…I prop walked before I got past the port pilings. "Whoa….Nellie!! Dammit! I liked that BBQ! Why do we have that BBQ hanging on the side of the stern rail anyway, Ran? It's in the way! Ooooo….shoot." (…or a facsimile thereof). "No problem, El. We'll just tie up on the port side. I can work on that big dent in the BBQ later." I have the greatest husband in the world! There is still a big learning curve in getting to know how *Kwanesum* moves and handles in different situations. And at this point, I'm still a student learning, apparently! The BBQ was put back into shape and we don't think I damaged the stern rail. *"It looks ok, right Ran?"* I think we were good entertainment for those looking out the window while sitting at the bar at the Provision Co.

The rest of the crew took up the other docking spots by the restaurant. We all helped each other as it was kinda tricky, despite my stellar helmsmanship. HA! The tide change was huge and we had to account for that. Ours was not a floating dock. Placing lines and fenders for that large tide change required much planning and vigilance. All said and done...it's time for a beer...and a sandwich. Great spot. Reminded me of some of the fun spots in Cabo San Lucas, actually. Our kind of place.

The town of Southport was darling. The town is old and Southern. The very careful restoration was noticeable and very pleasing. A nice place to walk. Not all the towns we have visited have had their wonderful homes restored and well cared for. A lot of antique stores there, which drove me crazy. I love antique stores but we don't have a home for antiques anymore. Once in a while I'll look anyway in case there's something that would look fab on the boat.

Up at the crack of dawn and we're ready to go out to the Atlantic! Yay! Ran and I have been looking forward to sailing on the ocean instead of just motoring through the ICW. *Painkiller*, the power boat, was going outside for awhile and then back into the ICW to finish their trek to Charleston. *Double Dutch*, *Smoooth Move* and *Kwanesum* would do the Atlantic overnight. Hoping to sail. It was a beautiful day.

But no wind. Where is the wind when you want it!? Not at Carolina Beach when you're in the dock and you DON'T want it! But it was such a beautiful day it was ok. We motor-sailed doing about 51/2 knots to keep everyone at the same pace....at course 230° South to Charleston. Dolphins swam by...the ocean changed to a beautiful aqua color.

It was great—lots of shrimp boats about. Randy was in heaven and much more relaxed. Going down the ICW calls for a lot of focused diligence, which makes your shoulders tense when you're at the helm. This felt like freedom. *Kwanesum* could spread her wings.

Chapter 9
The Atlantic

Spreading Our Wings

The sun set as the full moon rose. What a site that was. We had *Double Dutch* in front of us and *Smoooth Move* behind. As it got dark, our radar was truly a gift. We could keep an *"eye"* on both boats as well as other traffic. Our running lights aglow, as we're still motor-sailing. We tried to sail a couple of times as we were making too good of time, but our heavy boat just flapped in the non-wind. Makes it very uncomfortable. We will need to get a lighter sail like a gennaker (a light sail for using downwind...a cross between a genoa and a spinnaker) for such times as these. We just didn't want to spend money on that one yet.

It was interesting traveling at night. It was still fairly warm which was very nice. The stars were out...though the moonlight kept them from showing their true colors. I was looking forward to seeing phosphorescence in the water at night, where things glow...like dolphins passing by. But, alas, it was not to be on this night — too much moonlight.

I had the helm a lot during the day. Unfortunately, our auto helm was giving us a bit of a problem so we had to actually steer ourselves quite a bit. For any length of time, this can be tiring, but we were so *"up"* and glad to be on the Atlantic that it was not bad at all. We looked at it as exercise. It's much harder when you're sailing with little wind…the boat is harder to keep on track, but when motor-sailing, it's not too bad. Toward the evening, Randy took over. I was ready to relieve him when 3 or 4 hours had passed, as that was our plan. But he was enjoying it. Therefore…I went below and went to sleep. We tried the auto helm switch one more time, and it turned on. Hooray!

Randy 'roused me at midnight and I took over the shift at the helm. Staying awake and alert is the tricky part at that time of night. But adrenaline kicks in. I had a Red Bull and some chocolate and that kept me going. But I decided I do NOT like Red Bull. So that won't happen again. I loved watching the radar and seeing if I could see the blips on the screen in the ocean around us with the binoculars. We had a lot more company out there at that time than we thought we'd see. Could see *Double Dutch* really well, but had a hard time finding Lonnie on *Smoooth Move*. Most boats have radar reflectors on their mast, which enables you to see them on your radar behind the helm. Lonnie's *Smoooth Move* did not have one.

I noticed *Double Dutch* turned off her running light and slowed almost to a stop. I hailed Theo on the radio to see if he was ok and he was. He just decided to sail for a while. You only turn on the running lights when you are moving under power. Their boat is much lighter than ours so it sails more smoothly in light winds. Not so, the *Kwan-ster*. I slowed the engine, which I didn't want to do, to stay even with *Double Dutch*. We need to keep the RPMs up to a certain level. Randy popped his head up. "What's going on?" Shoot…I didn't want to wake him but

I had a feeling he was sleeping with one ear open. You can definitely hear changes in the engine. Randy said he was awake, anyway (He had only slept 2 hours), so he told me to go down to sleep. I was glad to do that but didn't feel I was pulling my weight in the deal. But Randy was so stoked to be outside sailing that he was actually enjoying it all very much...no sleep and all.

As I lay down below and just sort of catnapped, I, too, was wired up, especially after the Red Bull and chocolate. I heard the engines go off. We are sailing! Woohoo! Finally enough wind to sail. Nice. It's so wonderfully quiet when you sail. It's so pure. We like that.

As we got closer to Charleston, Lonnie had to call Boat US to be towed. Boat US is for boats as AAA is for cars. He had been having trouble with his exhaust taking on a lot of water, and because he was single-handing, it was really hard on him. Boat US didn't respond, so he hailed the Coast Guard. Mind you, this is about 0300hrs or 0400hrs in the morning. Randy and I listened in on the calls. The Coast Guard was great and responded quickly and efficiently to him, even giving him suggestions of what to try. He had tried them all, however. They got a hold of Boat US, who then hailed Lonnie and lined him up to be towed into Charleston.

It's morning and we're almost there. You get to the mouth of the inlet and feel like you're there, but it takes a long time to get into the port. Lots of traffic coming out the channel from Charleston...including a couple of ships and a shrimp boat...with its nets...right in the channel! Sheesh! You have to watch them very carefully as they're dragging big ole honkin' nets off the stern. It would be ugly to get messed up with that. It was odd to us that they would be allowed to do that in the shipping channels.

I hailed the Charleston City Marina on the radio as we were getting nearer to our destination. We wanted to let them know of our arrival and find out where they wanted to put us. We decided to go into a marina and stay for a month here in Charleston. We can't go past Savannah River, GA, until the end of November due to our insurance restrictions during hurricane season. That's not too much farther down. We get a better price if we stay for a month, and we wanted to see a lot of Charleston anyway. It's a grand town. And Fort Sumter is here and the Citadel. And the CSS H.L. Hunley, the submarine of the Confederate States of America during the Civil War. We were guided into our berth past the MegaDock. And these were some MEGA yachts in here, I tell ya! Those yachts take more than a little fuel. Fascinating to me who these people are who can own such huge yachts. And I know these are just babies compared to what we'll see in the Bahamas and beyond. But there are some 150' yachts in here. Nice! We were greeted by two handsome young men who helped us tie up at our berth. They handed us a bag of information and made us feel right at home. Our neighboring boats came over and invited us for cocktails. How great is this life!

And, of course, Skipper Meetings on our boat and *Painkiller*! Love those Skipper Meetings! *Painkiller, Double Dutch* and *Smoooth Move* are all anchored out near us. Lots of current here, so they each had to put out 2 anchors. They were able to easily dinghy into the docks to do laundry and walk to town, etc. We even had Painkillers one evening on our boat in honor of Al's (*Painkiller*) birthday. Then Al, Monica, Randy and I walked the MegaDock after dark to check out the big fellas. It really was pretty as they all had their fancy special atmosphere-creating lights on, and we could peek in their ports to see what they looked like.

So...here we are in Charleston. Working on our second week. Our cohorts have since gone on farther south. We will catch up with *Double Dutch* and *Painkiller* in the Bahamas, we hope. Lonnie on *Smoooth Move,* stayed and sold his boat on eBay. He had had enough of that boat. Randy just took the dinghy over this morning to help him weigh his anchors (bringing them up after such a long time with lots of wind and current is not easy) and take his boat over to the marina, where the new owner will take possession. Lonnie is going on to Florida and back to school, where he's working on his master's in writing. He's glad to be rid of that boat.

There are two things I know for sure right now:

1. Charleston, SC, is a splendid, charming town.
2. We have the greatest boat.

Our stay in Charleston was enchanting. We immediately took to the town...you know that good feeling you get when you stop somewhere new? Like you've been there before in another life or something? Charleston definitely elicited a charismatic feeling. My kind of town...Charleston is.

We learned of pluff mud, saw dolphins play with their fish catch, mailed in our absentee ballots, shooed away the grackles, tasted gator tails, boiled peanuts, hush puppies, fried green tomatoes, rode our bikes to the Citadel and watched the dress parade, took a cupcake decorating class (well, Randy didn't), discovered our favorite pub after testing quite a few, found our favorite deli, had a perfect martini, had a great soup by a perfect bonfire by the water, walked, walked, walked and rode our bikes everywhere! What we didn't do? LEARN THE SHAG!

Pluff Mud: This dark, soft mud was all around the marina at low tide. It's a low-country term. Apparently, it's famous in this area for being great soil to grow rice in. Carolina Gold. But modern machinery can't manage this soft mud as it was earlier harvested only by human hands. It looks like chocolate whipped cream! But doesn't smell as nice. Great word, pluff.

Grackles: These are the big blackbirds that started visiting all the boats early every morning and at sunset. Unwanted visitors! Just like the movie The Birds! Lots of them!! They would come about 5:30 in the morning and 5:30 at night. Creating lots of noise above! They made a mess on all the boats, so we tried to shoo them off best we could. Ran would get up and bang the halyards against the mast to shoo them away.

Gator tails: Loved them! And, no, they don't taste like chicken. We had them as hors d'oeuvres. They tasted more like beef than chicken.

Boiled Peanuts: Quite the Southern delicacy. We liked them! Not everyone does. They're certainly different than the roasted peanuts we are used to, but they're served warm and they pop out of their shells like edamame. The shells being soft. Yummy!

Hush Puppies: Delicious. We tasted a lot of the foods I mention here at Hyman's Seafood Restaurant, which is renowned in Charleston since 1890. Always long lines at Hyman's. We were dining with new friends and one of the owners brought hush puppies out to taste. These are golden-brown puffs supposedly invented to stop the barking puppies at an outdoor feast. They're made by putting corn-bread batter into deep fat...'bout the shape of a donut hole. Hyman's also makes a great Bloody Mary, though I've never had one for dinner before. Of course, I had to try it. Delicious. But I like them better in the morning. Weird having one for dinner. But I guess it's what they do! Apparently, it's one of their specialties.

Fried Green Tomatoes: I loved the book and the movie and now I've tasted them. And, of course, they're delicious.

The Citadel: Randy and I were fortunate to have a wonderful tour of the Citadel at the invitation of our friend Speedy (you'll remember from the Deltaville, VA gang), a Citadel graduate and retired Brigadier General, and the existing General who replaced him, who was also a graduate of the Citadel. It was interesting watching the plebes all with brooms in their hands sweeping, sweeping at an already seemingly clean courtyard. A very special evening that we enjoyed with them over dinner later.

We wanted to see the Citadel dress parade so we rode our bikes a week later to the Friday afternoon ceremony. Terrific. Particularly the drum and pipes band. There's nothing like bagpipes. Thanks, Speedy!

Decorating cupcakes: A wonderful kitchen store, Charleston Cooks, held the class one Saturday morning. I signed up and, rode my bike in and had a blast! I can be the cruising cupcake maker.

The Blind Tiger: Voted by us as the best pub, best burger we found, tried Shock Top beer, and food was always good. Love finding the best burger and new beers.

Wentworth Station: Best deli, best BLT, according to the Hasness vote. This deli was suggested by the bike shop we frequented when we asked where to get a good sandwich. And they were right. Rode our bikes there many times.

Charleston Place: Best martini vote. Perfectly chilled, perfectly timed. I'm sure it was shaken, not stirred.

The Perfect Bonfire: Through our new friends Larry and Dona Jean on the p/v *Amilado* at City Marina, we met some very nice folks who lived on the outskirts of Charleston and invited us to their home. I am embarrassed that we failed to get their card and have forgotten their names! (On this cruising life, boaters have cards made up like business cards with all their information on them. It's a great way to stay in touch.) Their house is on a pretty waterway on which we took a cocktail cruise and came back to a warm bonfire, wonderful soup and freshly caught shrimp off the BBQ. Oh my.

The Shag: I have heard about this dance many times and want to experience this for sure! Another reason I have to get back to Charleston. Stay tuned for further news on this one. How fun to dance the Shag with the Ran-ster! I must learn this dance. And I think the Charleston dance was invented in Charleston. Is this place great or what?

We did not get to experience as many restaurants in Charleston as we thought we would. So many there… so little time. We need to watch our pennies, not to mention our waistlines. Waistline watching is NOT easy! I'm actually failing at that but hoping to snap out of it soon!

Second thing I know for sure…I love our boat! This will be evident as I explain our trip from Charleston to Florida.

Chapter 10
Florida

Submarines, Manatees, Alligators, Rockets

We arrived at Cape Canaveral, FL inlet, our destination, 21 September... in the morning ...0815hrs ...after 2 days at sea... two extremely tired sailors. It was a beautiful, crisp morning. We were unexpectedly and surprisingly greeted by the U.S. Coast Guard! Oh, oh! Oh great!...a CG inspection now??! ...when our boat is a mess and we are both dead tired?! But, no...thankfully, that was not their intent. They wanted to let us know that a nuclear submarine was leaving the area and they needed us to move 1000 yards south to get out of the way. Whoa! Cool! We can do that! That was exciting to see. That sub, barely above the top of the water with only the tower showing...just yards from us...was amazing. We waved to the sailors that came top side. I took pictures and Randy wasn't sure I was supposed to. But I did. No one said anything. Yay! Neat experience for sure.

Our trip from Charleston to this point in Cape Canaveral inlet was right out of Mr. Toad's Wild Ride. We left Charleston on a Wednesday morning about 0715hrs, and it was freezing.

Freezing, freezing! Plus, there were some big winds! But we were ready to go. I was at the helm all bundled up with a t-shirt, a turtle neck, another long-sleeved shirt, a hooded sweatshirt, and a foul weather jacket, as well as pajama bottoms, khakis, and I had on Randy's sweats over that. And a woolen ski hat with the hoodie of my sweatshirt pulled over my hat. Oh...and gloves. My sailing gloves. This is NOT the kind of weather we want to sail in. We are used to cold sailing, being from the California Bay Area, but not C O L D sailing! It had to be in the low 30s. The wind made the sea coming out of Charleston really choppy. But *Kwanesum* was amazing.

I loved how *Kwanesum* responded to the seas. Hence, repeating the number 2 thing I know for sure...I love our boat. She works the waves really well and smoothly. Like a surfer choosing his path. No pounding. And the auto helm was amazing. Held us right on course with not a falter. Love it! One of the great things about sailing is the response of the boat to natural elements.

We turned south from Charleston out of the channel down the Atlantic and the seas calmed down. Our goal was to head to about 20 miles offshore. Our friends from Deltaville, Jack and Marianne on *Gravyboat*, who spent that last week in Charleston, were going to head out that morning as well. We hailed them on the radio in the morning but they missed our call. They told us later, they had decided to leave later and let the winds calm down. Their destination was St Augustine, where Marianne's brother has a home. We do hope to catch up with them again in the Caribbean or sooner. They have sailed many years in the Caribbean and were anxious to get where it's warm! And that's what we want, too! Warm sun and water we can swim in.

It's still really cold and it's hard to warm up once you get that cold. We decided to motor-sail the rest of the way. Running the engine with the main sail up. Randy tested the wind at this point, with just sails, but it was not enough for us to make good time; *Kwanesum* being a heavy boat. We just wanted to get there. Plus, our auto helm takes power. Running the engine keeps it powered up. We were doing 6-7 knots while motorsailing. The engine just purred like a kitten. We were so proud of our boat. We do have an advantage in this kind of weather over others in that we are used to being miserable while sailing. We've sailed those rough, cold seas like this a zillion times out in Northern CA, as I said before, so this was just par for the course for us. We knew it wouldn't last forever.

We did 3-hour shifts, which worked well. As the sun started setting the seas started getting larger. The weather was perfect...clear skies, but the winds picked up to 20+ knots and the seas responded to that. The course we were on had the seas hitting us sideways, which isn't the most comfortable way to go! But again, *Kwanesum* rode them like a surfing champ.

I, however, didn't ride them as well. After a while, I went below to try to sleep and the creepy, crawly, roly stomach stuff got a hold of me. Darn it! I hate when that happens. I did take Bonine and it worked really well for me, but when the seas are big and I'm down below...the 2 don't always add up correctly for me. But it passes.

By now, things were shifting off the starboard shelves down below, too. Books that we had secured, but obviously not well enough. Kind of a mess down below. I did end up puking over the not-so-porcelain bowl in the head and tried to sleep a little more, telling Randy I needed a little more time before my shift at the helm. He's amazing...just kept going out there even though he was freezing, too.

Thank heaven for our dodger and bimini setup: the canvas covering the opening of the companionway (stairs down into the boat) and over the cockpit. It was perfect in that we'd check the helm and the seas and the instruments, making sure all was well, then tuck in under the dodger to stay warm and out of the wind and seas, and let the auto helm do its remarkable thing. We had a kitchen timer we put on 15-minute intervals, then do our checking again at the helm. It was a good system for us. And we were able to stay warmer and dry in these conditions with this routine of getting under the dodger and bimini at intervals. God Bless our auto helm.

The seas calmed down and we moved along. It started getting warmer, too, which was a great relief. Still, we had all our gear on, but it was a more comfortable temperature. During the day, the seas remained calmer. We found we had a hard time getting our sleep in. It's hard to relax long enough to really sleep. We catnapped often when we could.

That evening, I had the 1800hrs – 2100hrs shift and it was magical. The seas weren't bad at all. The weather was warm enough that I could enjoy sitting at the helm. I leaned back while at the helm and watched the stars for a long time. Do you know how bright the stars are when there is no light around from any source? It's wonderful. When Randy came on at 2100hrs, I just sat out there with him and dozed until my next shift. Of course the seas picked up again, so we were riding the wild ride once more. This time, my stomach handled it well. YAY! *Kwanesum* was a crusty old sea salt by the time she got into the marina. It's amazing to see all the salt that accumulates on the boat after a bout at sea.

We are tucked in now very comfortably at the Harbortown Canaveral Marina at Merritt Island, FL. Near Cape Canaveral. If we had gotten here a little earlier, we could have witnessed the shuttle launch! We're hoping to catch the landing. Not much around here, but just a bike ride to many stores. And the price is really reasonable. Considerably more reasonable than City Marina in Charleston. It gets chilly at night but much warmer than Charleston. We've had some beautiful warm, sunny days.

When we got here, we checked in at the marina office and then had a yummy hamburger at the restaurant here. It was perfect! Neither one of us ate much on the way, though we had plenty to keep us going. We came back to the boat and went to sleep for 4 hours. Ahhhhhh.

We got our bikes out and found lots to explore. We have also, of course, found a sports bar that serves my Shock Top beer and great bar food. What waistline? The burger here at the restaurant is a top runner for the best burger in the area. For Thanksgiving, we were missing our family so we decided to put together food for a picnic and ride to the beach. We rode our little fold-up bikes all the way to Cocoa Beach. I made fried chicken and macaroni salad and off we went about an hour bike ride to get there. It was a beautiful day and a nice beach. A little trivia here...Cocoa Beach was the place where astronaut Larry Hagman lived in My Dream of Jeannie! (I didn't remember that. Randy gets the credit. Why would he remember that?)

It feels so good to be in Florida! We're getting closer to the warm, sunny beaches of the Bahamas. It's definitely warmer here. We saw one little gator and the tails of some manatees since we've been here. We're hoping to see more of them before we leave.

We are going to rent a car and go see the sites… and tour the Island Packet factory in Largo. Maybe even venture to Disney World! We also want to get to Cape Canaveral and do a tour there. We took a couple of weeks and headed to California for Christmas. When we returned, we thought we'd be on our way. Apparently not. We're still here in Florida! We're stuck in another vortex! Didn't I think by now we'd probably be basking in the warm sun diving for lobster to put on the barby when we got to Florida? Yes. Didn't I think I'd be swimming every morning around the boat after I had my coffee? Yes. Then why am I freezing here in Florida? It was so beautiful and warm when we first got here in late November. But...the weather wasn't great for moving on, which we thought we'd be doing by now. Big winds... and then it got terribly cold for Florida, in the low 30s, and since we don't have heating when we're *'on the road'*, only when we're in a marina, we decided we didn't want to freeze each night. So we'd wait that out. They said it's the coldest it's been in 7 years. Great.

Then...Randy got a chest cold, down for the count.

So, what do they say about the best-laid plans?....'tis true. They often go awry.

The plan right now, this second, is to head out on Sunday, 25 January. The weather is getting warmer by the day and next week looks good. Our escape is imminent! I started getting concerned about the length of time of our stay here in Florida. Florida has a 90 day rule, I believe it is, in that if you stay more than 90 days you get to pay them money! I guess they figure you're homesteading or something so they're going to tax you. Like the omnipresent Tax Man from the old film Popeye...always knocking on your door.

The Tax Man: You just docked?

Popeye: I has.

The Tax Man: Ah ha, let's see here, that'll be 25¢ docking tax.

Popeye: What for?

The Tax Man: Where's your sea craft?

Popeye: It ain't no sea craft, it's me dinghy and it's under the wharf.

The Tax Man: Ah ha. ahh-ha. This your goods?

Popeye: They is.

The Tax Man: Yeah. You're new in town, right?

Popeye: If you call this a town, yes.

The Tax Man: Well, first of all, there's 17¢ new-in-town tax, and there's 45¢ rowboat-under-the-wharf tax, and one dollar leaving-your-junk-lying-around-thewharf tax, so all together, you owe the Commodore $1.87.

Popeye: Uh, who's this Commodore?

The Tax Man: Is that the nature of a question? There's a nickel question tax.

No escape if you stay too long. Good grief. We'll be gone in plenty of time, but seriously…this tax stuff is ridiculous, even WITH representation.

In the meantime, we've enjoyed our stay here at Harbortown Marina. Haven't done too much but we did rent a car before we left for California and toured the Kennedy Space Center; unbelievably neat. Saw the gantries that hold the space shuttle (I love that word…gantry), and saw the HUGE engines from the Apollo flight. Unbelievable. They have a wonderful complex there. I learned something I never thought about: Cape Canaveral and the Kennedy Space Center are 2 different things. Cape Canaveral had the Apollo launches and some of the earlier launches. Kennedy has the shuttle launches. Just last week, we witnessed an NRO (National Reconnaissance Organization) spy satellite launch from Cape Canaveral. Really cool. It was delayed so I got on their website, where they had a webcam with live action from command control. As we waited on the deck of our boat to see the launch, we could watch what was going on prior to that on the computer. Really interesting and spectacular to see in the middle of the night.

We drove out to Port Canaveral one Sunday for a late afternoon lunch. And as we were sitting enjoying our wine, we got to watch the big cruise ships leave. First, Carnival Cruise Line, nice. Royal Caribbean Cruise Line, very nice, then the Disney Cruise Line, super duper nice! That was fun. I never realized Canaveral was a big port of call for cruise ships.

We drove across Florida to Largo to see the Island Packet plant…where they made our boat. We had a great tour. It's so interesting and reassuring to see how well-made these boats are.

We didn't get to Disney World or Epcot Center, etc. We weren't sure we wanted to spend the money or deal with the crowds; perhaps another day. What we DID try to do before we left was an airboat tour around the swamps with our friends Jack and Marianne. You know…see some alligators and manatees. (Jack and Marianne, you'll remember, were berthed next to us in Deltaville, VA. We have run into them along the way here and there.) But it ended up being way too cold and windy to be out on the water in an airboat. We wanted to be in our shorts and flip flops and would have had to wear our ski hats, gloves and heavy coats! NOT what we had in mind.

We did have a great late lunch with Jack and Marianne before they took off for points south. Dixie Crossroads. Apparently a very famous fish restaurant in Titusville. You could tell they served a lot of patrons as their waiting area was huge! Because of our timing, we got right in, and out come hushpuppies; those wonderful warm hushpuppies. But get this! This time they're covered in powdered sugar! Oh, good grief. Warm with powdered sugar. And they keep bringing you more. It's so not fair that this stuff puts on pounds. We all ordered their rock shrimp with drawn butter and the best coleslaw ever. I'm telling you people… you gotta experience this great stuff out here! Unbelievably good.

112

Did I tell you how much we're enjoying our bikes? We've particularly ridden them here in Florida as well as in Charleston. They are so fun. Really makes you feel like a kid again. I could ride forever, except my rear-end starts getting really sore. Now, operator error can be a problem. Remember the old man on Rowan and Martin's Laugh-In? He would ride his bike, I think it was actually a trike, and then just stop and fall over... that would be me. Twice. "Mommy, why is that lady lying on the sidewalk laughing with her bike beside her?" Can you just picture it? Lord. Randy's no help. He just laughed at me. But twice should be enough. You'd think. Each time I've done it... only twice, remember... we stopped at a corner, I put my foot out,

to brace myself ...and the ground was on a slant...unfortunately, a downward slant. So there I go, in slow motion. Awwww yeah,...not an attractive site. We're going to ride our bikes one more time before we put them away for this leg of the trip. We'll go visit our favorite pub for yummy wings and nachos and then hit the store for some essentials. Never know what kind of stores will be available for a while.

We're anxious to get going. We'll anchor at night as we head again down the Intracoastal Waterway to Lake Worth, our next destination and point at which we will leave to head across to the Grand Bahamas. Anchoring out is a bit more rugged in that we can't use our lights or run our water as we would if we were in a marina. We have some LED lights that we'll use at anchor, so we don't need to use the energy normal lights take. There will be no heater, but we can turn a clay flower pot upside down on the stove, which actually gives out quite a bit of heat. We'll take navy showers and quickly wash any dishes. Our solar panels and our big battery bank keep us in good shape. We'll be running our engine a lot along the way, which will keep the batteries purring. The ICW isn't conducive to good sailing. We purchased an internet booster antenna, which should help us pick up internet sources along the way, but we won't have TV for a long while! Back to the basics. We're ready!

We left Merritt Island just as we had planned. What a concept! Sunday 25 January. It was a beautiful morning. Very calm. Backed easily out of the berth we seemed to be 'stuck' in and headed to the fuel dock. Added fuel and pumped out the head...always a charming event, but necessary. Paid our bill and we're off! Down the Barge Canal... headed to the ICW south. Seagulls followed behind our boat...must have been stirring up fish. And dolphins. I love it when the dolphins are out there. We had them appearing a lot on this leg of the trip. They just make you feel GOOD!

First day, we anchored out behind a spoil island on the Indian River, which is this leg of the ICW. That put us around mile 925. The spoil islands are created from dredged material, and sediments removed from rivers, oceans and estuaries to enhance navigation. Dredged sediments are deposited in the water to create new islands or to add to existing natural islands. Spoil islands can be less than an acre to more than 50 acres. The island we anchored near had a little sandy beach that several power boats pulled up to on the sunny Sunday, where they were having a great time partying. Considering we started at Mile1, it's pretty fun to know we've almost gone 1,000 miles.

We are getting so much better at anchoring and knowing our boat; much more patient now. We just drop the anchor and get a beer! Works for me. Or...I'll have white wine... depending on the mood. We let the anchor just sit on the bottom and do its thing, then let out more chain...the rule we go by is 5 to 1: five feet of chain per foot of depth, depending on how we feel the holding is or how strong the winds are. We let that sit through at least one beer, then back down 'til we know we're not going anywhere. We open another beer and just smile! That's the *Kwanesum* way of telling the length of time... by beer. We do mark our anchor spot on our chart plotter. That way, we can check if we have moved during the night.

We started again the next morning, heading down the river to Ft. Pierce, FL, at Mile 965. We plotted out a nice anchorage in front of another Harbortown Marina just past the North Bridge. We've become more patient about dealing with opening all the bridges, too. 98% of the bridge tenders are really nice and efficient. There's always a couple that you wonder why they pursued this type of job. There were about 10 of us anchored there. A nice, quiet anchorage.

Up again and off to Lake Worth, FL, our final spot on the ICW until we head over to the Bahamas. We've had great weather on this leg of our trip. Not as warm as we'd like but nice. Always the dolphins poking up to make us feel good. We're starting to get into more fabulous real estate on this leg heading into the Jupiter/Palm Beach area. We leisurely motored down the river admiring the homes along the banks. Some of these places have totally screened-in backyards. I mean the WHOLE backyard! I guess they must have some honkin' bugs out here! Just before Jupiter, we passed Mile 1,000! High five, on the side, under the leg, bump the behind...!! Here we are drifting along in our home, down the eastern seaboard, experiencing this part of the country from the water. It's very surreal.

This leg of the trek along the ICW is open-bridge-city. But remember...we are now very patient people. Uh huh.

MILE 981.4: Jensen Beach Bridge – no problem, 65ft.

MILE 984.9: Indian River Bridge – no problem, now it's a high rise.

MILE 995.9: Hobe Sound Bridge – opens on the hour and every 20 minutes, no problem.

MILE 1004.1: 707 Bridge – opens on request, no problem.

MILE 1004.8: Jupiter Federal Bridge – opens on request, no problem.

MILE 1006.0: Indiantown Road Bridge – on the hour and half hour…problem!

"Indiantown Road Bridge, Indiantown Road Bridge, this is Kwanesum, Kwanesum over." "This is Indiantown Road Bridge, go ahead." "Yes, this is southbound sailing vessel Kwanesum requesting your 3:00 opening over." "Can you please spell the name of your vessel over?" "Uh, roger, that's K-W-A-N-E-S-U-M, Kwanesum, over." "Sorry folks, there's a delay while we do some repair. We'll open in 15 minutes." "Roger. Kwanesum standing by on channel 9, over." Arrghh! That's going to put us at awkward times for the next 3 bridges that open on the hour and a half hour. We slow down, circle around, circle around…circle around…

"Southbound sailing vessel, the bridge will be opening in 5 minutes. What was the name of your vessel again?" "Uh, yes, that's Kwanesum, over." "Can you please spell that over?" "Uh, Roger, that's K-W-A…."

The alarm sounds, the arms go down on the road, the bridge opens… "Put the pedal to the metal, El!" We get under that one and race to make the next bridge, so we don't have to wait around.

MILE 1009.2: Donald Ross Bridge – on the hour and half hour.

"Donald Ross Bridge, Donald Ross Bridge, this is Kwanesum, Kwanesum, over." No answer. Again, we hail. No answer. There is another sailboat hailing the bridge so we're not worried. Not sure why she couldn't hear us. The other bridges heard us fine. As we head under the open bridge, we hear the

116

bridge tender hail the Indiantown Bridge tender, the one we last passed. "Indiantown Bridge, what was the name of the southbound sailing vessel that just cleared your bridge over?" "That would be Kwanesum, over." "Can you please spell that, over?" "Are you ready for this? K-U-A-....."

We laughed as we went along the way.

MILE 1012.0: PGA Bridge – on the hour and half hour, no problem.

MILE 1013.5: Parker Bridge – quarter after and quarter to the hour. Ok, so the last bridge we have to encounter has to be different. But we're patient, remember?

No more bridges! We have arrived at Lake Worth at Palm Beach. We travel past Peanut Island to an anchorage next to the inlet out to the Atlantic. There are about 25 other boats anchored there but plenty of room. We find a nice spot and settle down for the night. It's beautiful. The water is the most beautiful aqua color and clear enough to see the bottom. We now wait for a weather window. What we need are south winds; south, southwest or southeast. We need to travel over the Gulf Stream that flows north and you want a south wind to do that in the most comfortable fashion. We're not sure how long we'll have to wait here. Some of the other anchored boats are heading south to Miami and crossing over to Bimini. We want to cross here to Freeport/Lucaya, Grand Bahama Island. Then we'll work our way down to the Berry Islands and then to Nassau. From there, we'll go on to the Exumas. We'll stay in Georgetown there for a while. The plan is to leave our boat there while we travel back to California in April for our son's wedding! It's a place where cruisers love to stay for a while. It should be tons of fun and a good place to fly out of and leave our boat safely behind until we return.

Chapter 11
Gulf Stream Bahamas Bound

We Have Arrived!

As luck would have it, the south winds were available right away. So we decided to leave Lake Worth at 2100hrs the next night. We're ready to go.

As Randy and I try to get a little sleep before we leave on Wednesday night, we both look at each other and decide…let's just go! Up comes the anchor and we feel our way out of the anchorage in the dark at about 8:15 pm. I'm at the helm…Randy is standing on the bow, letting me know if I'm going to run into anything. I plotted my course out before we departed and had it on the chart plotter, too, just the way we wanted to go. It's not easy to see in the dark! But we did fine. "See that red marker, El?" "Yeah, that's the one I want to turn around…whoa! There it is! A little closer than I thought!"

We made our way out just fine, despite the little drama part I put in above. It makes for good reading to have a little drama, especially when the drama really happens. (We weren't really that close. Well, not too close, anyway.) It is always a challenge to exit an area in the dark. Thank heaven for the green/red lighted channel markers. The saying is Red Right Return to remember on which side to go. When you return to a harbor, red markers are on the right/starboard. When you exit the red markers are on the port side, green on the starboard. Just stay in between. We can do that.

The seas weren't too bad. Winds, of course, were right on our nose as we were traveling south. We did our usual 6 knots or so motor sailing since the wind was on our nose. We did 3 hours on/3 hours off watches. After a bit, we were slowing to about 3 knots! Which is crawling! We had hit the Gulf Stream. The Gulf Stream goes about 2.5 knots in the opposite direction. Like watching paint dry. Did I mention patience? Yes…patience. We need patience as we're on this adventure. Longer/faster boats can power across the GS at a quicker pace. We aimed our departure at 160°, which put us more south than we needed but then we'd ride the Gulf Stream up a bit to aim across for Freeport/Lucaya.

The seas got a bit steeper, and yours truly did pretty well most of the way. I put a patch behind my ear this time to be ready... just in case. As you know from the previous posts, I don't always do well on rough seas. Randy powers through better than I do. On my 0200hrs-0500hrs shift, I started getting a little queasy. Crap. I wasn't too bad but wasn't very comfortable. Randy came on at 0500hrs, and I stayed in the cockpit and slept on the port side. After a bit, I heard Randy rustling around putting up the sails, and whoa, I almost fell out of my spot! Randy had turned the boat up, and it was a great point of sail with strong winds. Woohoo, we're sailing now! 8 knots, which is really fast for our boat. But it's rough... I didn't do so well on that leg of the trip. Doggone it! But it didn't dampen my enthusiasm one bit for what we're doing. Not sure why, but it didn't. When later analyzing my sailing tummy situation, I discovered that the patch behind my ear had disappeared! Somewhere along the line, it fell off. Well, no wonder! Right?! Next time, I'll put super glue on that thing.

The sun is up, I am green, and the sea is the most beautiful sapphire blue color. Just beautiful! I can't move. I tried to get up to relieve Randy, but I couldn't. I had to stay perfectly still, or things wouldn't go well. I have a little bucket by my side. Don't want to lean over the rail... might fall off! Attractive, right? I'm going to do better. I just know it!

With winds a-blowin' at a pretty good pace, we enter Port Lucaya, Bahamas, at the Bell Channel. I can't believe we're here! We're in the Bahamas, mon! I immediately start feeling better as the water is calmer in the channel, the air is fresh and bright, and the excitement has got ahold of me. Taking my mind off things. The water turns a wonderful turquoise blue. And clear, clear, sparkling clear. We weave our way around to the Grand Bahama Yacht Club where we'll stay and check into the country.

We were tucked into our berth here by the nicest of people. Randy was dead tired from having to man the helm by himself all night, but he cleaned himself up, and, after we filled out all the paperwork, went with the

harbor tender over to the Immigration office to check into the country. A procedure we will do over and over many times on this adventure. I stayed behind and cleaned up two very messy areas down below. One of my plants I optimistically brought with us for what I thought would be nice ambience, jumped off its perch, despite my thinking it would be ok. So we had a lovely pile of broken pot and potting soil. I also had some coffee ready to be made on the stove, safely tucked into the fiddles on the stove so it wouldn't fall...it did. So I had coffee grounds in the galley to deal with, too. What a mess! It smelled good, though! Like yummy French roast! Coffee grounds are the WORST to clean up. I know from experience.

All went well with immigration and checking-in. I did have to count the ammunition we had aboard ...every bullet, which is in our safe...and get that info over to Randy, but no other problems. Except...when Randy returned and we checked over the cruising permit for the Bahamas, it only had 8 days down! Eight days?! I had filled out part of one of the many forms, thinking it was only for the length of our stay here in Lucaya, which we anticipated to be for only about a week at the most. Oh dammit. Well we'll deal with that tomorrow. Right now we're hungry and tired and need to have a beer!

Taken from Skipper Bob's **Bahama Bound** publication and **History of the Bahamas**, by Jerry Wilkinson.

The Bahamas were discovered in 1492 by none other than Christopher Columbus. He landed at San Salvador, located at the southeast edge of the Great Bahama Bank. Of course, while Columbus may have "discovered" the Bahamas, it was already inhabited by a race of people called the Lucayans. Apparently, the Lucayans are descendants of the Arawak tribe of Indians from Hispaniola. Lucaya means *"island people."* The Spanish forced or lured the Lucayans into slave labor on Hispaniola, destroying the entire indigenous race. The Spanish brought to Florida a West Indies native word, "*Cacique,*" pronounced "Ka-SEEK-ee" by some, but "Ka-SEE-eh" by the Spanish, meaning Chief. The fierce Caribe tribe, Spanish for "cannibal," gave rise to the name Caribbean. The slaves were mostly taken to Cuba, where they were worked to death. By 1600, there were no Lucayans left.

Over the next 150 years, the Bahamian Islands were mostly uninhabited and largely ignored. Water routes to the Bahamas were dangerous. With the Gulf Stream and tidal current to

121

contend with, at a time when navigation equipment was at a minimum or non-existent, getting a large ship near an island was not easy. Many vessels met their end against a Bahamian reef. Once there, there was little to keep anyone. No mineral deposits, no farmland, little if any fresh water, and a rugged terrain. The Bahamas eventually became British property and were granted to Sir Robert Heath in 1629.

Captain William Sayle led the first organized group to try to settle the Bahamas. Seeking religious and personal freedom, his band of about 70 tried to land in 1648 on the northeast coast of Eleuthera and were shipwrecked. Most of their provisions were lost and over the coming years, the group struggled to survive in a very hostile environment. Little local fruit, almost no game and soil that begrudgingly grew meager crops meant life was hard. They survived, but never flourished. Even today, a living can be earned in Eleuthera from the land and the sea, but it requires a lot of effort.

Over the coming years, numerous groups would try to settle the Bahamas with great ideas of success and riches. All would fail. The land would provide a place to live and a refuge from the sea. But only fishing and tourism would keep the Bahamians alive. Pirates chose the Bahamas for refuge and a place for a base of operations. After 100 years, they were hunted down and eradicated. Wrecking would become a profession as more and more ships plied the oceans and came to an unexpected death on an uncharted reef. The locals would collect all the material of the wrecked ship and sell it or use it to buy goods to augment their life.

The American Revolutionary War caused a large influx of settlers in the Bahamas. Those American Colonists who chose to remain loyal to England during the war were treated harshly after the war. (They were called Loyalists.) Many fled persecution in the new country of the United States of America and went elsewhere. Some went to Bermuda, others back to England, but almost 4,000 settled in the Bahamas. They started cotton plantations (eventually killed off by a worm), salt ponds (could not remain competitive to modern mining methods), farming (land would not support long-term crop growth), etc. This English ancestry is clearly visible today in the many small towns and villages throughout the Bahamas. Even more obvious are the many failed ventures. There are visible remains of plantations, resorts and other ventures that have been tried throughout the years.

During the period of 1780 to 1805, the last group of Bahamians to enter the stage emerged. They were slaves. Before the Loyalists fled to the Bahamas, there were probably not more than 1,000 slaves in the Bahamas. The Loyalists brought an estimated 4,000 slaves with them. Over the coming years, thousands of additional slaves were imported to the Bahamas. However, slavery was abolished in 1833, and the slaves became citizens of the Bahamas. Years of hard work followed, but the black population in the Bahamas has been largely absorbed into the mainstream. With interracial marriage a common occurrence, racism has been virtually eliminated in the Bahamas.

Today, the black population outnumbers the white by three to one. As you might expect, blacks hold most government positions. Over the years, the Bahamas was to endure pirates, liquor smuggling, and drug smuggling. Each flourished until the authorities could bring them under control. Because of its history, the Bahamas often gets a bad rap as a "dangerous" place to visit on a boat. The truth is that there is very little danger from pirates or other criminals in the Bahamas.

By 1973, when the Bahamas was granted independence from Britain, the Bahamas had transformed itself from a deserted group of islands to a functioning nation with industry, a government, and very valuable assets: its geography and climate. Today, this independent nation plays host to thousands of cruisers each year.

So…we had an 8-day cruising permit to stay in the Bahamas in our possession. That is for the whole enchilada! The whole nine yards! The complete set of dishes!   All …of… the…Bahamas. Well, THAT'S not going to work. Randy and I looked at each other and decided we needed to check on this as soon as possible. But…we have 8 days, so we'll do it tomorrow. We need to finish cleaning up the boat, check email and take a nap.

Up early the next day…well, not EARLY…early is different when you're retired. At least it is for us. That won't surprise a lot of people who know me. Our morning routine, when we're in a marina or have internet coverage, is that Randy makes the coffee and we sit and read email and the news online. We have breakfast and then start the day. All comfy and cozy in the salon of our boat.

On this day, we catch the ferry across to Port Lucaya and climb the stairs to the immigration office. It's not far away. We could easily dinghy there, but our dinghy was still on the davits at this point. We hadn't put it in the water yet. The ferry is free and the guys are so nice. Everyone here is so friendly and nice. I love that.

Because I didn't go with Randy when he checked us into the country, I hadn't seen the office. When you come into a new country, the routine is that you haul up a yellow quarantine flag on your mast and the courtesy flag of the country you're visiting. Only the captain of the boat goes to the immigration office with all crew passports and paperwork to check everyone in. We decided to stay here at the Bahamian Yacht Club as we were advised that they are very helpful in checking into the country. This was true. If you are not in a marina, the authorities see your yellow flag and either come out to your boat to check you in or advise the captain to go into the immigration office. The yellow flag shows that you are new in the country. Once you are checked in, you remove the yellow flag but still fly the country's courtesy flag.

Ran and I are in the immigration office, which is very small. Apparently, this is only a satellite office…and out comes this very tall, buffed Bahamian with his dark green uniform on. Looks like a bouncer! And sunglasses. He's wearing sunglasses.

Sunglasses always make you think…." *he's bad*". Holy moly. But he's very nice…but he's very somber. To our relief, he says this happens to others, but unfortunately, he has entered everything into the computer and we have to go to the main office to remedy the situation. He said a couple of days before we leave Lucaya, go to the main office downtown and get an extension. OK. We can do that, sir. Whatever you say, sir. Now…clearly, again, I wax dramatically. He wasn't wearing sunglasses, but tinted regular glasses. And he's probably not as tall as we imagined since Randy is 5'11". But it felt like he was enormous and ominous! "Well, Ran, at least we have 8 days here!" I mark on my computer calendar the exact day we need to get our extension, so I don't forget. I tell you, if I don't write it down or put it on the calendar, I get lost in the ambiance of cruising and forget! Don't want to forget this one!

In the meantime, in true *Kwanesum* spirit… we go have a beer. Right away, we discover what will turn out to be our Port Lucaya hangout: Rum Runners. Appropriately named, I would say, as during the Prohibition period, I do believe the rum runners kept this place in the pink! Servicing everyone in the states with their booze/hooch/spirits. Of course, I step right up and have a piña colada… although the beers are 2 for $5.00. That is a darned good price considering that a case of beer here is

$45.00 or more!!! The beer at the marina where we're staying, and those at the hotels down by the beach, are $5.00 apiece. Even the local beer. The local beers are Kalik and Sands. I think you can get a case of those for a mere $35.00. The liquor, in the liquor store, seems to be about the same price as you can get in the states. And of course, there's rum (called ron here) to be had by the dozens at a good price. All shapes, sizes, and flavors.

We hang out where it's cheap. At the Port Lucaya Marketplace. I want the fancy drinks. Because... my name is Ellen and I'm fancy. So here, I'm the expensive date in a cheap place. Which is not as expensive as an expensive date in an expensive place, right? The guys behind the bar are so fun. It's an outside bar so it's perfect. My fancy drinks are $5.00 each, which I didn't think was too bad considering the beer at the beach was that price.

Our days in Lucaya are spent mainly waiting for weather. We had hoped to just be here 2 or 3 days; we've been here 2 weeks. We walk, we explore, we drink beer, or Bahama Mamas and Pina Coladas. The expensive date. We dinghy around a bit, though it's still very chilly for the Bahamas so we wear our jackets. Not what we thought we'd be doing here.

We met new friends who were docked near to us. Robyn and Peter on s/v *Sequel II*. They are from New Zealand. They just sailed their beautiful 60ft boat over from Fort Lauderdale. We had tea (read coffee for Randy and Ellen) with them aboard *Sequel*. As you can imagine, it's a magnificent boat. We roamed around the Marketplace with them and had cracked conch and fries. Yummo! Cracked conch reminds me of Calamari, which I so love.

Robyn and Peter went on ahead to Nassau after a few days. We spent a fun night prior to their departure drinking wine and the ever popular beer on *Kwanesum*. With their boat having a longer waterline, they were able to ride the rocky seas better than *Kwanesum* so they took off during the still unsure weather. We have a weather service guy by the name of Chris Parker that we listen to each morning on the Single Side Band radio. We subscribed to his service, so we are able to receive emails from him with weather updates as well as talk to him on the SSB to ask him when the best time of departure would be for our particular upcoming trip. It gives us peace of mind as we are still learning about the weather.

So now…it's the 6th day of our 8 allowable days in the Bahamas. I don't want to get thrown out of the country so we make our departure for the main immigration office downtown. First, we need a cab. No problem, mon, cabs are everywhere in the marketplace. We ask the price…$14.00. Ok. What do we know? We don't know how far it is and we need to be taken to just the right spot. Sounds like an ok price. He ends up being a super nice man. He told us his son is a professor at a university in New York. Randy chats away with him while we ride into town. I guess the town is Lucaya. I don't think it was Freeport. I forgot to ask him. But it's not very far away. Oh well. It's good to have been driven to the right spot. I asked if he would take me to a grocery store, too. As it turns out, the store is right next door to the immigration office so that's not a problem. He waited for us. All the buildings and surrounding areas look very run down and unkempt. Even the grocery store area. I'm not sure why they don't fix things up or clean around. It reminded me of areas I've been to in Mexico.

Our visit to the immigration office to extend our stay in the Bahamas was pretty uneventful. I know…you're probably disappointed that there wasn't more drama, which is more typical of us. But it went very smoothly. We just had to wait here, get that form there, go back over there, and wait here. We finally got in to see the main officer and we thought great…they're going to charge us more money. It cost us $300 cash for the original filing of our forms. But that didn't happen! We sat in his office for quite some time while he chatted away about the Bahamas and asked about us and where we were going, etc. I'm telling ya, these people are nice here! Most of them, anyway. We extended our stay until May. He did inform us that when we leave for our son's wedding in April, leaving our boat in the Bahamas, we will have to alert the immigration folks there and then check in again when we return. I never thought about that! More of our learning process.

We went to the City Market, which is their supermarket after we visited immigration. Our cab driver is still waiting for us. (I feel like I'm on the Amazing Race... having the cab waiting for us, except I'm not arguing with my husband and running from place to place with my backpack flopping all around.) Food is expensive here and not too abundant on the shelves. A gallon of milk is $6.29. A bag of Fritos, which I grabbed on the way to the checkout stand, was $5.49. No more Fritos for me! Apples are $.99 each. We passed on the apples. I bought a head of romaine lettuce that was $2.79. Bread wasn't bad, $2.72, but there wasn't much choice. The racks are pretty bare. I didn't check meat prices. There wasn't much available, it appeared. Fortunately, we stocked up really well before we left Port Canaveral. The dollar and their money are even-steven here, so there's no problem with currency. We previously went to an ATM for cash, and it handed out $50 bills instead of the usual $20s, and it didn't charge us any fees! We were surprised about that. Our driver delivered us safely back to Port Lucaya, and we were good to go. Why we didn't have him deliver us right to the marina is beyond me, but... we took the ferry back across. A good day, and now we can legally stay in the Bahamas for more than 8 days.

This has been a good place for us to get our feet wet on traveling in the Bahamas. It's been easy to get around, and our facilities here at the marina are A-One. The marina price is fairly reasonable, $1.20/foot. So, for *Kwanesum*, at 37+ feet, that's about $45/day. Then we pay $5.00/day for water. (Therefore, we're taking long showers to get our money's worth.) Marinas in the Bahamas, as a rule, are not cheap, so we felt this wasn't too bad. And it's been a nice safe place for our boat considering the weather and winds we have had. There is a small place where we could have anchored just adjacent to the marina, but the good positions were already staked out. So, staying in the marina, it is.

We had a great Super Bowl day, beginning at Rum Runners. Lots of people milling about and they were setting up big-screened TVs all around. We ate conch and chatted with people at the bar. One young man was off a cruise ship he worked on. He was from Malta. We chatted for quite a while with a young couple that comes here often to fish. Spent the day exchanging stories all around. So fun. We then decided to go back to the marina to watch the super bowl at the bar there since it's on so damned late on the east coast! We met up with Robyn and Peter (obviously, this was before they left) and had great fun eating bar food. By then, I was drinking water. However, we did smoke 2 Cuban cigars we purchased. Nice...

We decided we're off on the next leg of our adventure on the Thursday coming up. Our weather guru said it's a good time to go. We will leave about 2100hrs again with me at the helm feeling my way out of the marina in the dark and into the ocean. I think there will still be a big moon that will help light the way. We will head to White Cay, which is in the Berry Islands. We have used our ever-reliable cruising guides all along the way so far to help us decide our destinations. Also, sites on the internet were helpful. Written by people who have gone before, their knowledge of the area and the waterways are invaluable. We're hoping to stay there one or two nights and then head on to Nassau, where we'll meet up with our friends

Jack and Marianne aboard *Gravyboat*. My cousin Deb and her husband Tom, from Nebraska, are meeting us in Nassau for a couple of days. That will be really fun. They will experience life on *Kwanesum*, *"on the hook"*, as they say, when you are on your anchor.

So, hey, now! We are anchored in White Cay and there's Randy…naked as a jaybird prancing around the cockpit of the boat. Does that mean we've arrived? I guess so!

What fun we had in White Cay. Our trip from Lucaya on Grand Bahama Island to the anchorage at White Cay in the Berry Islands went really well. We had previously scouted out the destination on our charts and as I said, I had researched it online via other cruisers' blogs and articles from different cruising forums. It sounded like a perfect place to stop on our way to Nassau, which was our final destination on this leg.

We left Lucaya at night... again, we leave at night!! One of these days, Randy, I want to be able to see well when we leave a spot. But we had good moonlight, so that helped... a lot. And if we left at 2100hrs, we would get to our waypoint at White Cay at a perfect time in the morning. Because we had been at Lucaya so long, I knew the way out, so it was easier. It was a nice calm night. I easily backed *Kwanesum* out of her spot and slowly made way out of the port with Randy standing on the bow to make sure we didn't hit anything, a.k.a. Proactive Boat Protection Management. Got out, no problem, and off we go. The seas weren't bad at all, and we motor-sailed the whole way. Randy and I both put seasick patches behind our ears this time to be sure we did well. We put them on and then covered them with bandage tape to make sure they stayed on. This shall be named **Proactive Puking Management**, or **PPM**.

We did our 3 hours on/ 3 hours off, traveling all night routine. There was plenty of company out there at night. Lots

130

of cruise ships all lit up. But nothing that came near. It keeps you entertained. We arrived at White Cay in the morning. It was a beautiful day. We found our plotted waypoint and worked our way into the anchorage, lining ourselves up with the various islands per the guidebooks. This shall be known as Shoal Avoidance Management. We anchored just as the guidebook suggested and started our day. We relaxed a bit, napping a little. I did not like how the patch made me feel. Though it did keep me from getting sick, it made me feel lousy otherwise: dry mouth kept having to clear my throat... just a funny feeling. I think next time if I use them at all I will cut it in half and see how I do.

Randy jumped in the water with snorkel and fins and checked our anchor. Ahhh... to be able to see your anchor. This shall be known as Clear Water Excellence! We put the dinghy down and went exploring on the island. We are by ourselves except for one boat anchored far, far away. We did, later, have a few boats come in and out, and one catamaran anchored that first night in our little area but far away from us. It was a Saturday and people were out and about. Even way out there.

The next day was a beautiful morning and we put on our bathing suits. "Today, Ran, we are going to take champagne to the island and do some snorkeling. We need to toast our arrival!" What a great day we had! We toasted ourselves and prepared to snorkel.

We just love to snorkel. We could do it for hours. The water was so clear. There was plenty to see, too. Randy found a huge conch. Unfortunately, we didn't know how to get it out of the shell or prepare it so we put it back. This shall be known as Conch Survival Management! It was so big and beautiful with lots of yellow on its shell edge. I found what I thought was a jackpot underwater. There was a pile of shells just waiting for me. But Randy signaled to me underwater, no, no, no! I surfaced and he said, "That hole that's next to the pile of shells might be an eel's hole." You do NOT want to put your hand anywhere near there...just in case. That eel might pop out and bite your hand. All...righty...then! I don't need to do that. This shall be known as Ellen Survival Management! But it killed me to leave all those neat shells behind. It was still so wonderful to swim and snorkel and to see everything so clearly. More! More! We want more!

We went back to the boat and continued to celebrate. The sun felt so good. We put on music and, drank wine and danced on deck. What a fun day! This is what I've been waiting for! I could have stayed there for a week.

But...we were headed to Nassau so off we went the next morning. At least we're leaving in the daylight! Woohoo! Having had so much fun the day before, with all that sun and adult beverages, I wasn't sure how I would do the next day. I didn't want to wear the patch so I took a Bonine and put on my Sharper Image wrist electrifier doo dad band I purchased just for this purpose. It gives you a little electric shock every so often that you feel up your fingers. I guess it helps. The day was nice and sunny, and the seas were calm so it's not a good test of whether it worked or not, but I felt just fine on this trip. I manned the helm the whole way until we docked for diesel.

Chapter 12

Nassau

Active Attitude Adjustment

Before you come into Nassau harbor, you have to hail the harbor patrol and ask permission to enter the harbor. We had never had to do this before. They get your information and ask where you will be and that's it. Apparently, before you leave, you also have to let them know.

Once we were in the harbor, Randy pulled *Kwanesum* into the diesel dock like frosting a cake. That's sort of a lame analogy but it was so smooth! We are definitely getting better at handling our boat. Our friends Jack and Marianne, who had been in Nassau a few weeks, recommended the Texaco dock. Best price. It's good to have friends in the right places. We filled with diesel and water and were on our way to the anchorage near Jack and Marianne on *Gravyboat*.

Drop the anchor...have a beer. Wait, and wait, and have another beer. Back her up at 1200 rpms, hold that and wait. Finish that beer and stop. Holding good. By golly, Tonto, we're getting this anchoring thing! Take a reading with the handheld compass. Mark our anchorage on the chart plotter. Get SPOT out and send off our location to the kids. Get that dinghy down, we're going for sundowners on *Gravyboat*!

We're in Nassau! Cheers! This shall be known as Active Attitude Adjustment.

It's Wednesday. We're currently in Nassau at Nassau Harbor Club. And we're waiting for Global Warming. It's cold, been raining and it's very cloudy. Maybe not cold per Virginia standards right now, but cold for the Bahamas. We're rocking away in our berth, reading books and uploading pictures on the computer. A good time to work on the blog. I tend to go on and on when I'm writing these blog posts, so I need to set aside a lot of time anyway.

We have had some awakenings about what we expected in the way of weather on this trip to the Bahamas. But I guess everywhere has sort of had a lot of cold weather...or different weather. My friend Linda, who lives in Texas, said on Facebook they were having 80-degree weather today! Guess we should take our boat there. I'm holding out hope for the Bahamas.

We've had a great time in Nassau so far. But, as you've heard me say before, we didn't expect to be here quite so long. The weather is truly our schedule maker. We were at anchor in the harbor for the first 2 weeks. I like anchoring because it's free! I've said that before, too. And it's kind of a neat way of life...on the hook. The dinghy is your car. So when you need to go to shore...you drive the dinghy...*Bob*. Our dinghy is *Bob*. Now, mind you...getting in and out of the dinghy is not attractive. It sits in the water behind the boat just waiting for you to take a drive, just like your pet dog. You pull it up close to the boat and pray that a big power boat doesn't go by and start the wave action just as you're attempting to climb aboard. The first attempts at this was more of a plop action. You turn your back to the dinghy, stick one foot in and plop down, hoping the boat doesn't flip over. (Not really, it won't flip ...but you might flip out!). As we get more agile… we just step down in the dinghy and ...be seated. Makes you feel like you've really accomplished something…going from the plop action to the be seated action. You learn to balance your legs standing in the dinghy. I figure it will keep us young and agile and use up a few calories. Stomach in…one arm out, the other holding on to something for dear life, er…I mean to guide you down….step down…balance, balance…be seated.

Being on the hook in our Nassau harbor location was not always pleasant. Love the mornings, as I do anyway on the boat. I get my cup of coffee and go up to the cockpit and watch the goings on, as long as the weather is nice and the wind is not making it too rocky. Usually, mornings were calmer. Then the action starts. The wind comes up. A zillion boats go by…right through the anchorage and NOT at no-wake speed! Even the big ole Mail Boat would saunter by on occasion making you pause with held breath. A little too close there, pardner! But they never hit anyone. That wouldn't be good. Apparently, the anchorage we were in was also a path to the docks. In the states, boaters are usually very cautious and drive slowly AROUND anchorages. But I guess this is not the case here in this particular spot. Even though there were a lot of boats anchored here.

Next…you have to be concerned about where the newcomer anchors. "Uh, excuse me! We have 130 feet of chain out. You may want to move away a little!" This anchorage is squirrelly in that the wind turns you one way and the current turns you another. Usually sail boats all turn the same direction which helps insure you're not going to bang into each other. Interestingly, at this anchorage, if the wind was pretty strong, the boats end up facing all sorts of directions.

We had warned one particular boat, who was flying a country flag that does NOT have a good anchoring reputation (other cruisers will know the country I'm referring to, but it will remain nameless on here) that he was too close. No response. None. Mind you, this particular boat had been seen anchored around this area in two or three different places. He would take his boat out somewhere, then the next day or two come back and try to anchor. He was getting a bad reputation. He attempted to anchor too close to our friends Jack and Marianne on *Gravyboat* and also tried a spot too near our new friend marc on *Opal*. Both of them had to ask him to move. In this particular instance, Randy told him we had a lot of chain out and that he should move away more. He stood there staring…saying nothing…and did nothing. OK…maybe he's ok.

Later, that afternoon…I'm down below cooking some potatoes for dinner on the stove, when I glance up out the port above the stove and see him about 2 feet away from our boat! "Holy s#$t, Randy! Here…take the horn and get up there!" We both climb up the companionway to the cockpit hollering and sounding our horn. NO RESPONSE!!! He didn't even come up from down below. Marc heard us and came up from his boat…the other 2 boats around us heard us and came up…but NOOO…not this particular imbécile. We honked and hollered again! By this time we're both swearing up a blue streak. (Marc said our people skills were not exactly in line.) His boat eventually drifted away from our boat, but he needed to move. We were NOT going to stay awake all night worried that he was going to hit us.

OK…that does it…Randy jumps in the dinghy and blasts over to his boat and bangs on it…and bangs on it. Now the water is not docile…it is rocking around pretty good. So the dinghy is flinging all over the place with Randy screaming at this guy. HE STILL DOESN'T COME UP!! I was ready to tell Randy to steal his dinghy. Finally, he saunters up from down below as if nothing was happening. Looking as if he was wondering what all the fuss was about; these 2 maniacal people are screaming their heads off. I wish I had had the presence of mind to grab my camera. Marc said the same thing. But we were too mesmerized by this ding dong who wasn't even courteous enough to find out what's going on when he almost hit our boat. Finally, after Randy was grabbing the guy's lines to keep from tipping over,(now that would have been a picture...Randy hanging on that guy's boat in the water asking him to help him get back to our boat...or back in the dinghy after screaming at him for 15 minutes.) (Fortunately that didn't happen.), ...finally, Randy got a response from him and he said he would move. I was still in a high anxiety/ madness state. This guy...saunters around his boat...looks at his anchor...slowly checks things....driving me CRAZY!...and finally makes motions as if he's going to move. Randy is now safely back on *Kwanesum* and we are both just staring at the guy. Unbelievable how slow he was. Like the lights were on and no one was home! Hello! Move your damn boat! He finally did. He only had to move back about 100 yards. There were tons of areas where he could go that weren't next to our boat or any other. He finally found one. OK...I'll have some wine now please.

This instance was actually the 2nd of a close encounter of the remain-nameless country-flag kind. The other was a couple of days after we anchored and also by a gentleman in his little boat Gilligan. It was a particularly stormy windy night and Randy slept little all night. You worry that your anchor will drag on windy nights. But at least this gentleman was also monitoring the situation. He had the courtesy to be up watching the boats to be sure they didn't hit. And he left first thing in the morning. His 3 hour tour was over! He did anchor near us again but far enough away. That's all we're asking...far enough.

In the meantime…we had some fun. We of course were so glad to see our friends Jack and Marianne on *Gravyboat*. And they introduced us to Marc who was anchored near us. Single hander. Fun, fun, funny guy. And knows all the locals and the local hang outs. My kinda guy. We shared cocktail hours and dinners back and forth with Jack and Marianne and Marc… fresh conch, giant hot dogs and potato salad, Marc brought the Cheez Wiz…we had rum punch, beer, wine (not all in one night…whew!)…margarita cocktails…lots of fun.

A ray of sunshine on *Kwanesum* was a visit from my cousin Deb and her husband Tom from Nebraska, coming to stay for 4 days. OK…guests are coming…boat is ready. Now we need to figure out how to get them out to the boat without scaring them to death. Neither one of them had been on a boat before, let alone at anchor. We decide our usual dinghy dock won't suffice. It's at the Texaco station…not a really attractive place… and you have to climb up from the dinghy 3 or 4 feet, depending on the tide. Sometimes rolling on the dock before you can get up! (Can you picture that? It truly is NOT attractive.) We figured that might not be a good first impression. So we told them to meet us at the Green Parrot at 1400hrs. There's a better dinghy dock there. At least you don't have to roll on a dock to get up or down.

Now… there are 2 Green Parrots here in Nassau. One is on the Paradise Island side near Atlantis and one is on the New Providence side, which is where we are. (The other side of the 'tracks.') "Deb, be sure to tell your taxi driver it's the Green Parrot on the New Providence side, not the Paradise Island side."

Randy and I are ready…we have the boat all ship shape for our guests, so we jump in the dinghy and head for the Green Parrot. It's quite a ways from where we are anchored. We have to go through the boat traffic and under both bridges, and the water gets some pretty good waves started now and then. We get there and order a beer, and some nachos and wait. It's a fun place and the view is very nice. There are a few boats anchored in front there and they seem so calm and serene in this beautiful aqua water. "Randy...why didn't we anchor here?!" That was answered when we ran into some people we knew from Deltaville, VA. Roy and Doon are originally from Scotland. They are anchored out there but had to re-anchor 2 or 3 times. The anchorage doesn't hold well. Ahhh,...glad we didn't choose this spot. Despite all the wind and currents we haven't moved an inch in our anchorage.

Tom and Deb finally arrive. It's so fun to see them. They spent some time in Miami before flying over to Nassau. They have 1 suitcase and its pretty good size but it's doable. They said their taxi tried to take them to the Green Parrot on Paradise Island, but Deb in her wisdom remembered that I told her the New Providence side. But the taxi driver didn't know where that was! So, they asked other drivers and with Tom and Deb's help, the taxi found the place. It's not very well marked from the road. That doesn't seem to be important to Bahamians I've noticed. A lot of things aren't marked prominently when you're looking for them.

We had a drink and are now ready to load on the dinghy. I told Deb that if they didn't enjoy staying on the boat at anchor there was a little hotel nearby that could be used. I actually went over to check it out and see if they had rooms just in case. Being the troopers they were...they wanted to give it a try. So we load Tom, Deb, their suitcase and carry-ons, Ellen and Randy in *Bob*. And off we go. Thank goodness the weather was cooperative. We made it just fine with no one getting wet. Miracle! We looked like the Clampetts coming in to Beverly Hills...Gilligan style!

We had such fun with Tom and Deb. And the weather pretty much cooperated while they were here. We had a fireworks display for them on their 1st night. Well…ok…it was Atlantis doing the fireworks but what perfect timing! We had been sitting below drinking wine and talking in candlelight when we heard the commotion of the fireworks. What a display! Very impressive. Tom and Deb were the ultimate guests. They fit right in. They were troopers, learning the nuances of living on a 37-foot sailboat at anchor. They slept through the rocky nights, had great conversations under candlelight as we tried to conserve power, they took navy showers, and learned how to use the head. Our mornings were leisurely with coffee and breakfast in the cockpit. They climbed in and out of the dinghy as we trooped to and from the shore and even got sopping wet one ride back to the boat. Fortunately, it was warm enough, but Tom and I sitting in front were soaked to the bone. And…yes…we made them do the Texaco dock once or twice. Never a complaint!

We all walked down to the Greek Festival downtown that weekend with Jack and, Marianne and Marc. We met Michael, a friend of Marc's and a local here, along the way. Fun time. Who knew they had so many Greeks in the Bahamas? The next day we walked over the bridge to Atlantis. Beautiful day, beautiful place. We ate pizza and had too much Ben and Jerry's ice cream. Fun time. It was sad to put them in the taxi when they had to leave.

After rocking and rolling at anchor …Randy and I were not liking it. "Let's get off the boat for awhile. Go get a burger and a beer." Sound familiar? "Good idea." PAUSE FOR A DISCLAIMER: the amount of alcohol portrayed in this story is not quite as bad as it sounds. Not quite. It makes for good copy and enhances storylines. And it was always fun. (Randy made me write this.) We hop in the dinghy and see Marc outside in his cockpit. "Hey Marc! We're going to the Green Parrot for a burger and a beer." "Outstanding! I'll meet you there." Ran and I decide to dock the dinghy at the Texaco station and walk down. It's about a mile walk and it would feel good after sitting on the boat for a couple of days. We stop by Jack and Marianne's boat but Jack isn't feeling well so they aren't joining us. We reach the Green Parrot and Marc has already arrived via dinghy and is on the phone with his insurance guy. Michael is there, too. Eureka! Marc has finally gotten insurance for his boat, not easy for a single hander, so he can go further south. Time for celebration. We have beer...Kalik or Sands, the local beer, and Ran and I share a burger. We talk for hours. After a while we discover the beer is costing us $4.50 a pop. (It used to be cheaper...they JUST changed the price. Now you tell us!) So ...in the interest of continuing our world-problem-solving/relationship-savin conversations...we decide to go across the street to Hammer Heads...for, you guessed it...more beer! Cheaper there. Hammer Heads is a local hangout. Odd location, odd looking...and fun! Of course, there are people there Michael and Marc know so we end up staying for a long time. So fun. Finally we oldsters have had enough and leave the young guys carrying on for the remainder of the evening. Super people...super fun.

After 2 weeks at anchor Randy and I decided to move into the marina. We thought we'd leave our boat here in Nassau when we travel home to CA for our son's wedding. Originally, we were going to sail farther south along the Exumas and leave the boat down there. But the weather wasn't cooperating like we anticipated and we have remained longer in Nassau. We figured we'd get flights from here, which are less expensive anyway, and leave the boat in a marina for the month of April. Now, we decided to move in for the month of March, too. We're glad we did. It costs money, but it's nice. We have budgeted for marinas and there won't be many more once we go south.

Therefore, in the interest of comfort and pleasure, we decide not to go any further until after April and treat ourselves to marina life. And it's nice. But I feel like I'm cheating! We have electricity. We have water ($6/day). We aren't rolling as much. They have a laundry facility and a nice pool. We're right across the street from a shopping area that includes Starbucks, City Market, Radio Shack, a video store, a clothing store, etc, etc. We've frequented most of them and now we don't have to climb out of a dinghy to get there! Or lug jugs of water back to the boat. Much more relaxing. Sorry Tom and Deb! We put you through boot camp! But that was so fun.

The day we moved into the marina, we had plans to dinghy over to Atlantis with our friends Jack and Marianne. It was her birthday celebration. We parked the boat and gussied up a bit, climbed in the dinghy with J and M and off we went. It was a beautiful day. We dinghy'd right into the Atlantis marina where the *'Big Boys'* are parked. (*Big Boys* meaning… HUGE yachts!) So pretty seeing Atlantis from the water. You can park your boat there if you're at least 40' and no longer than 220'. It costs you a mere $4 - $7/foot, depending on where they put you. On top of that, you have water and electric fees. We decided not to put our boat there. HA! As if we would be able to. But there is a little dinghy dock and that's where we parked our 'car' and walked to the casino. It's a great casino. So fancy, and they have fun machines for a nickel so Marianne and I worked on those while Jack and Randy drank beer and solved the world's problems. That sounds like Hammer Heads redux but in a glamorous location. After M and I made our millions…not… we walked across the street for a late lunch and dinghy'd home….getting sopped again! Always a treat. At least it's on the way back.

So here I leave you as I started. Sitting down below on this gloomy day but nevertheless in a great spot with my favorite guy. Randy is reading **Caribbean** by James Michener. And I plan to read it when he's done. We figure it's a good way to learn the history of where we're headed! Tonight…dinner at the Poop Deck with Rob, our next-door neighbor here. He's a captain on a fishing boat my 2 boys would love. We will be off to CA in April and when we return will head south. Stay tuned!

Wake up early one morning.

Kiss my momma goodbye.

Goin' back to da island

Don't worry momma, don't cry.

Dwang d' dwang d' dwang dwang dwang

Dwanggg, dwanggg, dwanggg…..

Everybody now….

Dwang d' dwang d' dwang dwang dwang

Dwanggg, dwanggg, dwanggg…..

…as taught to me by Mike Thompson, our island tour guide and Bahama native. (I asked him to teach me a native song while we were driving around the island.)

Before I get into Nassau, Part Deux, I must digress to the wonderful trip we had to CA for 3 weeks. Then back to *da island*.

As I've said before, Randy and I purposely stayed in Nassau longer than we intended so that we could fly easily back to CA and enjoy our family and the wonderful wedding of our youngest son Skip. It was the best place to leave *Kwanesum*. And it was easy… other than the flight out…which was fraught with delays. FRAUGHT! But …we had a good price on our tickets and we allowed plenty of time, so we can overlook that one. The trip back, other than being a redeye, was a snap.

Actually almost felt like home, coming back to Nassau. Does that mean we've been in Nassau too long?! HA! Of course, our boat feels like home…but we get to take her everywhere we go anyway. Nice. I like that part a lot. LOVE our bed. Ahhhh…..Everyone took good care of *Kwanesum* while we were gone: Peter, the Greek and Dudley, the Bahamian…our main men. She was just as we left her, making us glad; again, we decided to remain in Nassau.

Now to Nassau, Part *Deux*. When I last left you in Nassau, we had just moved into the Harbor Club Marina to park *Kwanesum* for our trip to California. We had gone in to the marina earlier than we had planned due to weather and tiring of being at anchor. It would be our last marina for a long time, so we took advantage. The weather continued to be so-so, and we continued to rock, even in the marina. But at least we could rest well knowing no one would park too close and drag into us. Ahhh…peace. Our friends Jack and Marianne found a weather window and went on south. Marc remained at anchor in Nassau preparing his boat for his trip south. In the meantime…we had some fun. We wanted to explore more of Nassau, so we decided to walk to see Fort Charlotte.

We asked Marc if he'd like to go, and one of the greatest days ever was begun. Fort Charlotte was quite a walk from where we were, so Marc called his friend Mike Thompson who lives in Nassau to see if he wanted to go along and be our chauffeur and guide. We'll buy the gas and the beer! We met him down at the Texaco station and piled into his funky old Suzuki jeep vehicle. Perfect way to sightsee! He dropped us off at the Fort, and we made plans to meet him for lunch at the Cricket Club, which was just down the hill. Yes…they play cricket in the Bahamas, though I never saw them playing. The Club was great, casual, and not too expensive. (The Fort was amazing, by the way.) We immediately ordered gin and tonics and toasted. It was so hot this day that the drinks were seriously quenching. Had a really good lunch, Mike joined us, and then we were off on our tour of the island. First...a stop for beer/water/ice for the cooler. Pop open a beer and we drive off. Can't do that in good ole USof A! Mike drove us all over the place. Down the other end of New Providence from where we're staying, to the area that is a little more ritzy. Big hotels down there, too. Compass Point Resort was gorgeous. Saw a wonderful little out of the way place that was very romantic, *A Stone's Throw Away*. Fun name for a hotel. Highly recommend it. Drove out to Lyford Cay where some definite ritzy places are. Did I mention what a gorgeous day it was?! Couldn't have been more perfect. Drove on to I-can't-think-of-the-name point where Mike decided to jump in...30 feet down. OK... go ahead. Now the other 2 guys had to decide if that's what THEY wanted to do. It's actually a beautiful spot. Crystal clear water...but it's a long way down. Mike had obviously done this before. The 2 amigos, Randy and Marc, prepared themselves to jump. Mike swims around, climbs up, and gets ready to jump again. The 2 amigos are still deciding. "Had a lot of beer, you know...not quite as young as I once was, you know....it's a long way down there, you know...and then you have to swim around to get out, you know...not sure how far that is since we can't see where Mike climbs out, you know...I'm a strong swimmer, but...you know...maybe next time." "More beer please" and off to the next destination. (I would have done it, but...you know.)

From there we drove around to a cool place where they kept horses and had a neat nursery with lots of fresh veggies and a little funky store that reminded me of places in Oregon or Napa. We fed some carrots to the horse. Love those kinds of places.

Then on to a bar on Sand Dollar Beach, I think it was... for, you guessed it...more beer and some hors d'oeuvres. There we met another friend of Marc's who was just delightful. He lives over on that side of the island. A British fellow that had done a LOT of sailing...even on tall ships, which is very cool. He's a contractor and very busy here and there. Nice conversation. He mentioned Quiz Nite at the Green Parrot and we decided to do that. It was getting on to evening so why the heck not! Got to the Green Parrot and we needed more people on our Quiz team. Wasn't long until our 2 handsome single guys found some good-looking girls to fill in our team. What a hoot! We did pretty well I think, but we didn't win. But we thought we were very smart. Fun time. After all is said and done, Ran and I were tired and Mike took us back to the boat. It was a long day. Mike and Marc? On to Hammer Heads to continue the night. We can't keep up with that bunch. What a fun, fun day. We had a fun, surprise encounter in Nassau with our boating buddies Al and Monica from our trip down the ICW! They stopped their boat Painkiller in Nassau on their way home to Canada and surprised us in the grocery store. What a fun, fun thing to see them there! Well, this calls for some do-stuff-days so we started with a bite to eat at the Poop Deck...next day walked downtown.

I wore my pedometer to see how far the walk was, so we thought a good thing to do would be to stop for a beer every mile we walked. Worked out really well! It was a 5-mile trek total. Ha! Then back to the boat where Al cooked up some lobster that he had caught on his southern trip. Soooo good. Sooo fun to see them. Way too short a visit. We're hoping to catch up with these 2 again. Even if we have to fly to find them somewhere! Our kind of people.

Our dear friends Speedy and Nancy from Deltaville, VA also came back through Nassau on their way back home. They had been further south, and they, too, had great luck getting lobster and conch. We so enjoy being with them. We had a wonderful dinner across the bay at the Columbus Tavern. What a great place. Before Nancy flew home and Speedy took the boat back up to Deltaville, VA they decided to stay 2 nights in the marina at Atlantis. They asked if we would help crew the boat in and then we could have passes to see the backside of Atlantis. Speedy had a crew coming in to help him take the boat north, so before they arrived we indulged in their offer and helped Speedy slip the boat neatly in their berth at Atlantis.

While they relaxed by the pool we explored the rest of Atlantis. What a great place! Of course we stopped to have an adult beverage…Kalik for Randy and a Pina Colada for me! Why not?

There is so much to see in Atlantis: a wonderful aquarium, a zillion pools for kids and adults, water slides, an area where you can swim with the dolphins, wonderful beach spots, bars everywhere. And it was a perfect day. We should have brought our swimsuits! We said goodbye to Nance, and Speedy 'speeded' us back to our boat in his dinghy. We will miss these good, good people and hope to catch up with them again one day.

Chapter 13
South Bound

Are We Having Fun Yet?

The answer is: It's an adventure. We're testing our mettle. It's been our dream. It's so fun, so beautiful, so many great people. We're exploring a part of the planet from the sea point of view.

What is: I'm doing this … why?

There are days…

- When you want to take a bath and there's no bath…and you have to save water so you can barely rinse off.
- When you've worn the same clothes so many times you have to 'hose' off with Febreeze!
- When you haul your laundry to the little laundry shack (when you can find one), there are 2 washers and only one dryer works…and it costs you $30.
- When you're trying to sleep and the boat is rocking and rolling so badly that you move into the aft berth where it doesn't rock quite so much and you can't hear the anchor shifting around.

- When you want TV...or something on the radio besides Cuban music, which really isn't too bad but doesn't come in very well.
- When you want a piece of toast so, you do it in the oven and hope you're not using too much propane.
- When you want a tortilla and there are none to be found.
- When you just want to be on the internet...for awhile...and you don't want to use the inverter and use power...and you can't find a good signal anyway.
- When you're sure you won a million dollars and you can't get your voice messages. OK...maybe not this one.
- When you want to phone home...and there's no coverage and the internet is too low for Skype.

Trade-offs... for a pretty darned fun, adventurous, interesting, back-to-basics, great people-meeting life. It's a hoot! Living *la vida loca*, baybee!

So on we go...South.

Itchy feet.

We left Nassau...finally! After saying farewells to all who helped us there...Peter, Dudley...all the guys at the dock who were so kind...we pulled out of the marina and made a right turn. Excellent. Now we'll work our way down the Exuma islands heading toward the Dominican Republic. We had a great weather window. It feels so good to be moving again!

To Highborne Cay: We motor-sailed on. A 7-hour tour. It was beautiful...a beautiful day. I love it! The seas are gorgeous, the day is bright and sunny ...the wind is in my hair... I'm on the bowsprit singing with my arms spread wide.....NOooo! Bad analogy! But you get the picture. The direction we're going is the wrong way. That's what Randy says. "Ellen, we're going the wrong way." We're always heading into the wind. And it's usually directly on our nose! Hence the reason we leave the engine on > > to make progress. We put up the sails, again, as it does speed us up and help balance the boat. But if we turned off the engine we'd have to tack off course to pick up enough wind to make speed, and then it would be a longer distance. We toodle along as is. So... we're actually going the right way... but the wrong direction in this wind.

We reach Highborne Cay. Let's anchor. I am the one that takes us in to the anchorage, finding the best place to 'park.' OK...I've spotted where we're headed. I slow the boat down and make my way there. We're about to have a Safeway-Parking-Lot experience. I've almost got us to my scoped-out spot when I hear on the radio, "*Love Affair*, can you slow it down a bit in the anchorage." I look around and to my right, a large power yacht is making its way too quickly through the anchorage and, yep, headed right to the spot I had picked out. Hmmmm....not sure if he's going on through or going to anchor there. I continue on course, and Randy says, "El...you might want to stop. It doesn't look like he's going to!" I put the boat in reverse and wait for him to pass. But sure enough...he speeds in, slams on his breaks, (that's putting it in reverse in boat talk) and starts lowering his anchor. "Ummm *Love Affair*, *Love Affair*, this is the sailing vessel *Kwanesum* just to your port. Just letting you know we had been heading this direction for quite some time and I find it rather discourteous that you sped in to anchor with no awareness of other boats approaching this spot." No response. Another boater gets on, "I guess there's no love for *Love Affair*!" "Roger that, roger that," I say. Then, "This is *Love Affair*, was someone trying to hail us?" "Roger, *Love Affair*, let's go to 18." We dial up on the VHF from the main channel 16, which you constantly monitor. Now Randy's on the horn... "Uh, *Love Affair*, this is the sailing vessel *Kwanesum* just to your port. Not sure how long you've been sailing but you usually don't speed through an anchorage and stop right in front of someone making way to an anchor. Over." "Uh, this is

Love Affair. I've been boating since 1940! I'm 83 years old and have been doin' this for years!" Silence. Whoa...83...OK. He probably didn't even see us! I think we'll turn around and anchor a little farther away. Bless his heart...83 and still handling a big boat, but goodness! No love for *Love Affair*.

We found another great spot in the anchorage. Back ...and away from *Love Affair*. It was just plain weird having a Safeway-Parking-Lot encounter on the water. Not to deter us, by golly! Randy put on his swim trunks and snorkel gear and dove on the anchor to be sure it was set. I jumped in and just swam...around the boat. Felt so good! Lots of big boats here. Highborne is a stopping point for cruisers going north or going south. Just to the north of our anchorage was Allans Cay. Allans is famous for the iguanas. This area is the primary home of the remaining iguanas that live only here and on some of the remote Out Islands.

We're up early the next morning and jump in our dinghy to go see the iguanas. It's a beautiful area...Allans Cay. Very peaceful. There are a few boats anchored there but it's not a large anchorage area. At first, we were not sure where to find them. As we look around the beaches, I spot Indigo, a Hinckley 49, at anchor. We had met Gary and Mike off *Indigo*, 2 nights before, at the Poop Deck bar in Nassau. They were headed the same way, and by golly there they were! We pulled up to their boat and knocked. They welcomed us aboard and showed us around their boat. We told them we were looking for the iguanas and they pointed to the beach where we'd find them. We head out for the beach with an invitation to come back for Bloody Marys when we're done! All righty! We shall do that.

Off we go, and the iguanas are fascinating. I, however, do NOT get out of the dinghy. Those puppies scurry pretty quickly and they head right for you... expecting food I suppose. They are NOT attractive. They have very long claws. Randy being the macho, hero type immediately got out and started taking pictures with his new little camera. Thank you...I'll stay right where I am. I can get my own pictures from the safety of the dinghy. There are a bunch of them. We finish our pictures and off we go back to *Indigo* for one of the best Bloody Marys I've ever had. Always interesting conversations with other cruisers. As we're sipping on our drinks we see a big commercial cigarette-type speed boat piled with people headed for the iguanas. I'm so glad we got to see them in the peaceful quiet morning. Back to the boat, another swim around...some gin and tonics...life is good. The sun sets and we hear a sound. Someone is blowing through their conch shell. Then another boat responds. Then another. How cool! Apparently, in these Out Islands, that is a tradition signaling sunset. A perfect ending to the day. Now off the next morning to Norman's Cay.

To Norman's Cay: Hang on to your hats, folks, we are sailing! The winds are at the right angle. We're doing 5.5 knots, which is not bad. This is great! A beautiful day and just the peaceful quiet of the sails. By the way, I must tell you that my **Proactive Puking Management** (hereafter known as **PPM**) has been working well. Either that or I'm getting used to the motion. I have NOT been sick since our trip across to Lucaya..: knock on wood:: Loving that, sports fans! This is the kind of travel we have dreamed of. Sailing... sails without the engine... with bright sunshine and crystal blue seas and doing a respectable speed to our destination. We pull in; I find a spot; no speeding power yachts coming out of nowhere... nice. It was a sweet 3-hour tour, or so. It's only 1000hrs and here we are!

Norman's Cay is a small Bahamian island that served as the headquarters for a drug smuggling operation from 1978 until around 1982. Part of the Medellin Cartel action. Hope we don't see any Cartel action.

You will remember in my earlier posts I mentioned a captain on a sport fishing boat, Rob, who was next to us in Harbor Club Marina in Nassau for a brief time. He works his boss's boat, *American Beauty*, out of Wax Cay. Wax Cay is a small private island next to Norman's Cay. Rob told us to give him a holler when we got to Norman's and he'd give us a tour. So that's what we did. We hailed Rob on 16 and we arranged to meet him over there via dinghy about noon. We were expecting some good ole boys' area and maybe a couple of buildings for the fishing fanatics. Not so! It was quite a place.

Wax Cay is owned by 2 guys that I think live in Nassau. Rob's American Beauty is owned by a gentleman from New York. Rob's boss somehow negotiated with the 2 owners to use Wax Cay during the season for fishing. Nice move on his part. As we turned the corner to Wax Cay, I thought we had the wrong spot... there were so many buildings! We saw Rob waiting for us and he guided us into the little harbor that had been made. What a magnificent place! We went up to the main building that had a restaurant style bar and kitchen and a lovely eating area. We popped open three Kalik beers right away and toasted. What a view! Rob explained that all the main buildings on the island were purchased in Vietnam, parts numbered, disassembled, shipped to Wax Cay, reassembled, and finished off. Very chic... shabby/beach chic. Done very tastefully. We toured the game room and one of the cottages and then jumped in a golf cart and toured the whole island.

The spa... they have a building they call the spa. Apparently, the wife of one of the owners wanted to have an open building where she could get massages. Of course, it has a magnificent view... all open sides. There are maybe 6 or 8 cottages on the island, some little, some bigger, and are all fitted out for visitors. Most have their own beach. There may be a time, Rob said, when the owners will lease out this side of the island and they will put their own private buildings on the other side. How fun to be able to see this!

After our tour, Rob poured me some wine and, got more Kaliks for Randy and him and made us an early dinner of mahi mahi. How can you beat that? I felt like I was on The Rich and Famous program. It included a perfect weather day. Rob found a conch shell on the property and gave it to us for our sunset calling. We're going to try it!

We said our goodbyes to Rob and scooted back to *Kwanesum* in the dinghy. The tide was in …good… we can cut a corner to get back to the boat. Whoops! A little too close there! Poor *Bob*! Ran into a little reef! Boom! We climb out and push *Bob* off the reef, hoping we didn't put a hole in him. One of the dumb decisions we made when fitting out our boat was to get an inflatable bottom dinghy. These are good dinghies, and they fold up for stowing on long passages, but are not very practical for where we are. Going over coral reefs? Not so good. And the hard bottom dinghies ride better, too, it seems. And I think our outboard engine doesn't like *Bob*. It's always cavitating when we want to go fast. And most of the time, you want to go fast. We tried to remedy the problem, but so far, it really hasn't worked well. Yahama 9.9 + Avon inflatable bottom = not a good combo. However, our *Bob* did handle the little reef like a perfect dinghy. No holes. A few dents in the propeller, but that adds character. Off we go back to the boat. Our next dinghy will be a hard bottom. And in my opinion… the sooner, the better. No offense, *Bob*. Anyone want to buy a 10ft inflatable bottom dinghy? Meet us in the DR.

Back on the boat… put on some Gordon Lightfoot… again, a couple of gin and tonics… nice. Again, a conch shell announces sunset as we watch from our waterfront property… life is good. Randy gets our conch shell out. Blows… sounds like one of the cows from the dairy. Don't think that's the one, Ran! We'll keep looking.

To Staniel Cay: Up and off to Staniel Cay the next morning. Still cruising the Exumas... headin' south. A 6-hour trip. Another beautiful island with water different shades of blue and so crystal clear! It is one of Earth's great splendors. Two days at Staniel. We swam around the boat... Randy checked on the anchor, and a barracuda was following him. Hmmm... I swam a little and was going to go in later in the afternoon when I thought I saw a ray! And another fish.

The ray turned out to be a nurse shark. I think not... on the swimming. Nurse sharks, they say, don't harm you. But I don't think I'll test that one. And I think the other fish was a barracuda, too. He was shading himself under our boat.

We need to go check out the Staniel Cay Yacht Club we've heard about. Plus... we're hungry. It's another great funky place. Good conch burger, good cheeseburger, got online briefly, and toasted to Cinco de Mayo! Happy Birthday, Nancy and Deb! Happy Hour munchies and specials on Coronas. Can't beat that. They were having a big to-do, but we passed on that. It was starting later, and it would have been dark when over. I didn't want to dinghy in this new area after dark. But, too, sometimes we can just be wimps. So back to the boat.

The next day, we dinghy'd to Thunderball Cave. Thunderball Cave was made famous by the James Bond movie. You can dive there, but there are strong currents, so you need to be there at slack tide. Supposed to be wonderful diving, which would have been great. Our timing wasn't at slack tide, and we still haven't made a good method to help get back in the dinghy from the water. Not an easy task... unless you're buffed or under 40. Although if you get a good kick with your fins... you should be able to get in. Should is the key word. And one of us would have needed to stay with the dinghy. I want

Randy with me when I snorkel something like that. Sounds like a bunch of excuses to me! So, we just dinghy'd out to look and then back to SCYC for a beer. Nothing wrong with that!

They were cleaning fish in front of the SCYC, and the wild animals... sharks... appeared! Cool.

Ahhh... and the pigs. We were actually anchored off the island of Big Major Cay, which is next to Staniel Cay. And Big Major has pigs. Not sure why, but there are pigs on that island. Actually, I found out Big Major is an uninhabited island, and the pigs are not native to the island. Some say they were left by a group of sailors, who planned to come back and cook them. Others say the pigs swam over from a shipwreck nearby. So, I needed to find the pigs. We dinghy'd over to the beach and walked around and did see little pig footprints. But no pigs. I called them... but no pigs. Back to the boat we go.

Sitting outside, I noticed a boat from one of the big yachts going over to the beach. "Randy... they found the pigs! We must go see the pigs!" Back we went. I guess we're too cheap to feed these wild critters, so they didn't put on a show for us. This boat brought food. Should'a known. They didn't impress me anyway. No food for you! It was funny to see, though.

To George Town: Up early and off at 0600hrs. George Town is on the Great Exuma Island, a destination we'd been trying to get to for quite some time. We read a lot about what a great spot GTown is during our phase of gleaning all the information we could from cruising books before we weighed anchor on our adventure! I was originally going to have my cousin Deb meet us there. But one thing I've learned about what we're doing is to have patience. And be ready to wait. And sometimes that's not easy. But I think we're getting closer to accepting it. We arrive in George Town at 1630hrs. Not a bad trip. We anchor off of Monument Beach on Stocking Island, which is just across Elizabeth Harbour. Plenty of room.

We have missed the party. During the cruising season, which is November through June (Hurricane Season is June through November), there can be up to 300 – 400 boats anchored around George Town. It's a favorite destination of cruisers going south, like we are, and for those who just want to get there and stay for the season. Tons of things going on. Like Spring Break for the cruising crowd. Boats start leaving in May, and now there may be 50 anchored there. Part of me is glad we missed the crowd... and part of me is sad. But there's still fun stuff to do. There's a fish fry Friday night on Stocking Island right where we're anchored. We dinghy in and have conch and ribs. No fresh fish, I guess. And Bahamian music. Very nice... but only about 20 people. We have good visits with all and enjoy the music.

The next day, we dinghy into town to get an internet card so we can pick it up from the boat. The dinghy is giving us trouble again. "Come on, *Bob*! Knock it off." The motor starts fine, but then it just quits. Well, that's not good! We've had this problem before, but not so frequently. The float sticks in the carburetor, and that's as much as I know. Randy takes off the cowling (can you believe I even know these words?) and bleeds it a little, taps on it, and all is well. But it's a pain in the neck. So, the day didn't start the best.

We find our way into George Town proper and start the hike to the Car Wash/Pet Store, where we will buy our internet card. It's quite the place, and it was a bit of a hike to get there. We get there and realize we only have a $100 bill with us. Duh, they're not going to have change for that! So, back we trek to the bank we spotted near the dinghy dock, or back Randy treks while I wait for him in the shade. Not enough pets to keep me interested in the Car Wash/Pet Store, and not any car wash customers. Kind of a useless endeavor with all the dusty, sandy roads, but whatever works! Randy comes back, and we pay our $15. Now we're hot and thirsty, and I'll be damned if we can't find a bar with a beer! Hold on, I thought this was the happening town! Just because we missed the party, they must have beer someplace.

We settle on water from the store and dinghy back. We find THE place: The Chat 'N Chill on Stocking Island. I knew there had to be some rockin' joint on this island. Loved it. Again, a funky bar with volleyball courts off to the side, quite a few people anchored in here, and dinghies pulled up on the beach. A great bartender, Kendell. I feel better. It's the simple things that please me, like finding the nearest funky beach bar.

The next day, it's Mother's Day and my birthday! We head to the Chat 'N Chill, where they're having a pig BBQ and my favorite, Bahamian Macaroni and Cheese. And I always love the coleslaw in the Bahamas and their peas and rice. Great food. My birthday, so I'm going to have fun drinks. Started with a blue something, which was ok, and I went to a piña colada, which was great, and then a Goombay Smash. Excellent. Again, good conversations with people. We wrote our boat name on the bar. Good day, this birthday. Now back to the boat to call our favorite kids and our favorite mom up in Oregon. Yay! Miss them so much!

In the meantime, during the days we're anchored there in GTown, Randy goes back and forth in the dinghy, into town, to get fuel and water, two or three times, to make sure we're topped off. Again and again, going through the steps to unstick the float in the carburetor. "Come on, *Bob*! Knock it off." Anyone want an outboard engine to go with that dinghy that's for sale? What a pain in the inflatable.

To Rum Cay...make that, **Conception Island**: Gotta keep going, so we're up and at 'em and on the way to our next stop. The weather is starting to turn. The seas are bigger, a lot bigger, and the winds, of course, are on our noses. The day is beautiful, but the ride is not. But the **PPM** is keeping me puke-less. To make me happy, because the seas are *trying*, Randy stops at Conception. A beautiful anchorage, this island is an uninhabited National Park. Lots of nesting birds and hatching green turtles are the only inhabitants. Nice to have these little islands where you can stop. This tiny island is known for its wonderful coral reefs to snorkel. Unfortunately, we had the dinghy put away and we were worn out from the ride over. And we wanted to get on to Rum Cay before the weather turned worse. I hate missing stuff, but it just wasn't practical. Always gorgeous sunsets to enjoy. "Randy! We need to find our own conch shell and make it into a horn." The one Rob had given us on Wax Cay had not worked out.

Now, **to Rum Cay**: Not far, about a 5-hour trip. The weather is starting to become a factor. The skies are still beautiful, but the waves are big, and the winds are strong – from the wrong direction. We have a bouncing trip into Rum Cay. **PPM** still on full attack mode.

Found the anchorage… one boat there. Hmmm… not sure that's a good sign. We anchor and set a bridle on our anchor. The purpose of the bridle is to keep you in the swell so you're rocking like a rocking hobby horse instead of rolling side to side – a much better motion. Otherwise, your boat is just at the whim of the wind.

Now to relax.

Chapter 14

Rum Cay

You Can Check Out Anytime You Want

We last left Randy and Ellen at anchor in Rum Cay...a bit breezy. Rum Cay was to be just a brief stopover on our way south. It ended up being quite a bit more. More weather...more excitement....more new friends...more socializing...more learning... more patience.

As we motor-sailed into Rum Cay, the weather was changing; bigger seas, bigger winds...still beautiful sunshine, but big everywhere else. We had huge waves coming in, breaking over the bow and onto the dodger; aqua blue, clear water but big waves over the bow. Waves don't often make it all the way to the dodger. We carefully picked our way into the anchorage. There are a lot of coral reefs around this island. Our technique in coral areas is to enter with the sun high and behind us and Randy standing on the bow of the boat, watching for the reefs, signaling which way to go to avoid them. There was only one other sailboat anchored at the time.

We dropped and checked our anchor, and we added an anchor bridle. It was suggested by the cruising guide authors for this area to add a bridle in the Rum Cay anchorage to keep from rocking/rolling so much. Add the bigger winds to rocking/rolling and it becomes even more uncomfortable. The bridle should help. We were moving around pretty good out there...adjusting our bridle to find the most comfortable position. As I said before, the see-saw motion offered by the bridle is more comfortable at anchor than the cradle, sideways motion.

In the meantime, we are joined in the anchorage ...throughout the day...by 5 or 6 other boats. From listening to their conversations on the radio, some are going north and some are going south, like us. One boat, *sans clés* (yes, spelled all lower case), a Passport 43, anchored in the late afternoon near us. I heard them on the radio asking the marina about coming in for dinner as they had a birthday to celebrate. I got on the radio and wished them a happy birthday and welcomed them to the *'neighborhood'*. The day continued to be very windy and a little choppy. We decided not to put the dinghy down and go in to see the island. Perhaps it will be calmer tomorrow. All is well with the anchor, so we relax and enjoy the evening.

Wind continues. Days are pretty; the water is sparkling and clear, but it's still windy and very choppy. We decide the next day to still not go in to explore the island ...yet. We are now on day two. We notice *sans clés* pulling up anchor. Shoot! I was looking forward to getting to know them. Ahhhh...it looks like they're headed for the marina. Guess they decided to go in there for the duration. In checking with our weather guru (remember we contracted with Chris Parker, our weather guy; we check via the ham radio)...there's no weather window opening to leave, so we're still stuck here. Our trip from Rum Cay will get us eventually to the Dominican Republic, which is our destination for hurricane season. The plan is to stop at Mayaguana, then the Turks & Caicos on our way down.

Relaxing, reading our books in the cockpit on a lazy afternoon...rocking and rolling... boom! Hmmm....? Boom, again! OK...what was that? "!#$%^*! ...we're on a reef!"

"Quick, El, start the engine. I'm going forward to the anchor." I look down and sure as shootin', we drug onto a coral reef. Holy moly. This is precisely what you do NOT want to happen! OK. I started the engine and manned the helm. Randy cut the bridle loose and went forward, trying to see if the anchor would pull itself off. Try, try, try.... not to be. It's pretty damn stuck on the coral. Crap. I decide to hail the other boats on the VHF radio to let them know our situation. My fear was if we kept banging against the coral, we would eventually put a hole in the boat. Now THAT wouldn't be good. Not to mention hurt the coral reefs.

Within minutes, I had other boats and the folks in the marina responding on the radio with concern. Zoom... over come 2 dinghies from nearby boats. It was amazing the help we got so quickly. The dinghies were pushing against *Kwanesum* to try to keep her off the reef while Randy struggled with the anchor. I'm trying to turn the boat to clear the reef, but the anchor held too tightly. Randy had to cut the anchor, and 250 feet of chain loose. Heck sake...that's an expensive bunch of equipment!!! Mind you, all this time, the seas that got us on there in the 1st place were still wreaking havoc. The dinghies were dancing around in the choppy water, trying to hold us clear. With the anchor gone, I was able to back away from the reef to clear water, away from the reefs. With my heart pounding, I hailed the marina and told them we were coming in. We needed to assess the damage. Going into this marina is not an easy task in itself. Lots of coral around that you need to avoid and the entrance is shallow in many places. A boat was sent out to help guide me in and the marina was on the VHF telling me what to avoid and where to go. And the water is still its old, choppy self. Beautiful water, always beautiful... but big and choppy.

I follow the advice, and the buoys, head around to the marina entrance and slink my way in. There are still big winds that push us as I try to dock. I got her in at the first immediate spot. We decided we needed to stay in, so they directed us to a berth farther inside the marina. The problem is...the wind and current are strong against us. I make Randy take it from here. I have a lot of confidence steering our boat, but thought he could better maneuver her in the tight spots under these conditions. I need to trust my skills more. I could have done it.

With lots of help, and some missteps, we are in our spot. Actually, we are in an adjacent spot, but it will do. We had that experience already, and you will remember from my Southport docking, jockeying foray ending with a banged-up BBQ. Missed the first spot and was blown into the second spot.

This will do, thank you very much. Soon-to-be new friends were all there with their hands out, ready to take a line and help us get in our berth. It's so hard doing this with winds and fussy seas. We are glad to be here. Randy takes the box of wine (yes... box) up to the dock and offers one and all free happy hour for their help. The cruising way.

Now we worry. Worry about damage to the hull and worry about retrieving our anchor. But we are damn glad to be in the marina, safe and, what we hope is, sound. One of the dinghies, off the *Wanderlust* that came to our aid out in the anchorage motored in to check on us and let us know they dove on our anchor after we left to make sure where it was. Fortunately, the water wasn't too deep out there. They put out a buoy to mark it. They attempted to pull it up, but it was planted in pretty tight. One thing that is a given in the cruising community is that all are there to help. This is a perfect example of going above and beyond to help fellow cruisers. *Wanderlust* certainly did not have to spot our anchor or try to pull it up, but that's the mettle that runs through the cruising backbone... always there to help. We were grateful to Bruce and Nick off *Wanderlust* for marking our anchor so we could try to recover it. Grateful, too, are we, for their quick response, along with s/v *Indigo*, to fend us off the reef. We'll figure the anchor retrieval out in a day or two. Right now, we want to make sure the bottom of our boat is okay. There doesn't seem to be any leaks so far, but what does it look like?

Here's the dilemma we'll face... sharks. Normally, Randy would put on his snorkel, mask, and fins and dive the boat to check it out. But we've been warned. Sharks swim in *'them thar'* waters in the marina: lemon sharks, nurse sharks, and bull sharks. Bull sharks are the 3rd most aggressive of the species. Oh yay! This marina sees a lot of big fishing boats... hence fish that are cleaned... hence sharks. And they're smart, too. They make a little drive-by once or twice daily to see if any new fishing boats are in. Niiiiccee. Some big barracuda in there, too. Makes getting on and off the boat a little more deliberate.

So, again, as this exciting day ended and the evening progressed, we popped that beer, brought up that boxed wine to share with all who helped, and joined others up at the *'Nut House'* on the dock for conversation, analyzing the day, and how we should proceed. Nice to be in the marina.

A new day. Wind still blows, so being tucked in the marina is comforting. As luck would have it, there was a boat at Rum Cay we knew from Nassau. Not a sailboat, but a funky, power, work boat that is based off of an old converted coast guard ship permanently anchored in Rum Cay. Their purpose... to keep Rum Cay full of fuel at the marina. The converted coast guard ship was originally here to house employees working on major construction on the island. It has been converted to a fuel storage vessel. The work boat had been in Nassau a few days at

164

the marina where we stayed, and in usual Randy fashion, he got to know the guys.

The next morning in Rum Cay, as we are trying to decide how we can retrieve our anchor and check the bottom of *Kwanesum*, the work boat pulls into the marina. Randy took his coffee up to the '*Nut House*' again for good conversation. Before I know it, a very tall young man is standing at the dock near our boat, in his swim trunks with diving gear on. He's going in. He's going to check the bottom of *Kwanesum*. You're kidding me?! Nope... he's not afraid. He had his sidekick there... watching for sharks. It's still early in the morning, and the sharks don't usually make their rounds 'til late. O...K... This should be interesting. In he went and very quickly made the rounds around the boat. And out he came with his sidekick pointing to the marina entrance... "Shark headed this way." Those damn sharks must hear every time there's a splash in the water! Looked like a nurse shark, which isn't known to be dangerous, but who wants to test that one!?! Out just in time. "*Kwanesum* looks okay," he said. "Just some surface, cosmetic scratches." Whew! Dodged that bullet! High Fives all around. Such relief... as the shark swam slowly by.

One of the worries down. Now... will we get our anchor back? We actually thought it was a goner. However, there were two very ambitious young men on a sailboat in the marina who thought they might be able to get it. Again, the cruising community rises to the occasion. Neil and Nick off of s/v *Conch Pearl* said they'd try to dive on the anchor and retrieve it. Fantas-tic! Off they go in their dinghy. Back they come. They found it but couldn't get it up. "But we'll keep trying!" Fortunately, it's not too deep, but the water is still pretty choppy, and the anchor is stuck in there really tight... not to mention the 250 feet of heavy chain attached to it. At least we know where it is, and we have help. Excellent.

We see Neil and Nick go out again in their dinghy. We gave them our 'look bucket' to help spot the anchor and it was well marked by the guys on *Wanderlust*, so finding it again won't be a problem. Bringing it up off the bottom, however, remains the problem. I notice the workboat parked next to us go out. Noisy, old workboat. RastaMan and his sidekick, Billy. Yes…he looks the part. A perfect specimen example of the Rastafarian style. Out they go…back they come… with smiles on their faces and our anchor in the back of their boat!! Holy Cow! You've gotta be kidding me?!! They got our anchor! Chain and all. Oh my gosh! They didn't even tell us they were going to try. With Rasta-man at the helm, the always-smiling Billy dove in and got it. Somehow, they were able to dislodge it and pull it all up. Not sure if Neil and Nick were there to help but Randy and I are beside ourselves with glee! How unbelievably lucky are we!?! We are now whole. There will be no glitches in going forward as we now have an anchor with all the chain rode again. This is so excellent. Randy gives the R-Man and Billy a large token of our appreciation. Later, Neil told us he and Nick renamed Rasta-man and Billy the Sneaky-Rastas. Neil and Nick were trying to find a way to carefully take the anchor and chain off the reef so as not to harm it. Rasta-man and Billy just manhandled it off when the *Conch Pearl* duo weren't looking. Well…not to harm the environment is on all cruisers' agenda, but apparently not the locals'. Either way…we were ecstatic to have the anchor and chain back on the boat in working condition.

Now we can enjoy Rum Cay. And wait for the weather window. During this hullabaloo we got to know some great new friends. Terri and Lyman off *sans clés*. They were the boat originally anchored next to us. Mike, Karen and Samantha off s/v *Mschiana,* who have been in the marina waiting for weather for a couple of weeks. Neil and Nick from s/v *Conch Pearl,* ditto. All great people. Not to mention the people that live on the island.

Not much to do on Rum Cay. Not much at all. It's a sleepy, peaceful island. A small island, about 10 miles by 6 miles. Buildings were mostly sparse and plain. Beautiful beach with interesting shells. Evidence of the Lucayan-Arawak Indians that once lived there can be found in the island caves. I loved walking on this beach. I found some wonderful shells.

A great cast of characters occupies the island. The marina area is great. Covered shelters off the docks where we sit to chat often (the *'Nut House'*)... at sunset usually with a cocktail. We play the cruising game, consisting of a ring... on a string... which you swing... up to a hook. If you're really good... you can even do it backward. I'm not good. Lyman was the expert, followed by Randy, Mike, and Terri. Samantha got pretty good at it, too! There's a nice restaurant and bar here that is not often open except for happy hour and dinner... if you let them know you're going to be there. If you're not there... they're not open. Still... a great place to gather when we do all show up.

Terri and Lyman rounded us up to take a taxi tour of the island. And why not, since we had so much time on our hands. George's Taxi... the taxi on the island is George's Taxi. Not sure why they need a taxi on this island, but we were glad to acquire his van and his knowledge for a tour. $40/hour... but if we share it, it's manageable. I'm going to digress right here a moment to say we learned a lesson. Cash on hand. Cash... not credit cards. Establishments on islands like these take only cash. The marina, however, will take the credit cards from the big fishing boat coming in to fuel up. We have a coffer of cash we keep on the boat. We should have beefed it up before leaving Nassau. You never know when you're going to get stuck on a remote island for 2 weeks. An island that doesn't have a bank... and can't give you a cash advance on your credit card because there's no expendable cash on the island... and the mail boat comes in only once a week, if it can get in... and the cash it brings is for payroll. Dammit. Ok... we need to watch our cash. This lesson will creep up several times on our stay at Rum Cay. But... back to the tour. We're all now in *"Us Against the Weather"* mode, as Mike would say, so having a tour of the island is a great way to pass the time.

The land in the Bahamas is rugged and rough. These islands are made from atolls, which don't offer a lot to foster flora and fauna. However, parts of this island found a way. What does grow is interesting and beautiful and often useful! Many of the plants are used for medicinal purposes. Terri and I had many questions about the plants we saw, and George was very forthcoming in informing us all about their attributes and if they were useful... or dangerous.

We learned of the island's past... locals are descendants of slaves. Of yesteryear... plantations... cotton. Still a few remnants of cotton plants here and there. More recently... several attempts to make tourism prosper on the island, to no avail for various reasons. The latest attempt left big scars on the island where a huge marina was to be developed. Very sad when you look at the large, dredged areas just left there. Expensive equipment sitting, rusting. An airport that doesn't see much action. But the locals prevail with their wonderful attitudes.

George took us by the local grocery store... The Last Chance... so we could provision before returning home. Again, the money coffer rears its head. We buy just what is necessary.

"Welcome to the Hotel Rum Cay.... You can check-out any time you like, but you can never leave!"

We wait. We form the Breakfast Club... or Coffee Club. Every morning at 0630hrs, we gather on *Kwanesum* for coffee and to listen to our weather guru, Chris Parker, on the single side band radio. (Glad I brought lots of Starbucks French roast.) We need to find a weather window to carry on. For reasons of location in the marina, our boat is able to pick up the broadcast on the single side band radio better than the other boats. We all need to get moving, but we want to have good weather, and the tropical wave that went through is still hanging on with big winds and chop. As a matter of fact, 4 other boats that have been waiting at anchor decide to come into the marina to wait. The anchorage is getting uncomfortable. Now there's a full house at the Hotel Rum Cay.

We learn a lot while we're here... waiting. We learn more about weather. Karen on *Mschiana* is very skilled in the weather department. We learn more about our single side band radio and getting new weather reports using that medium. Lyman is skilled and experienced with that. He's very tech-savvy. Nice. Mike and Karen have many years of experience cruising beneath their belts. They share their knowledge. Terri shows me websites that are useful for my needs on the blog. We all become fast friends and it's fun. We celebrate birthdays and anniversaries. We watch the big sport fisher boats come in, clean their fish, and 'play' with the sharks. Then fill their tanks with fuel and leave again, $7,000 added to their credit card. (We were hoping they paid in cash.)

Randy carves his conch horn. There are many, many, many conch shells on the beach at Rum Cay. Randy chooses one, George (the taxi man of many talents) carves a hole in the end, Randy taps it out, and the conch horn is born. Quickly, the conch blowing talents go from sick cow to... it's 5 o'clock somewhere! Hooray! We have our official sunset/happy hour horn.

Still waiting....things happen:

1. A cruiser falls in the water, missing his steps as he tries to get off his boat onto the dock. It's not an easy task, that...getting off onto the dock. Not a young man, and sharks are about. He quickly scurries out of the water. Whew!

2. A boat slams into the pier. And it wasn't one of us! The fuel boat...reverse didn't engage...wham! Another exciting moment.

3. Nick catches a mahi mahi and fries it up as hors d'oeuvres for the evening happy hour...excellent.

4. The South Africans, both boats of which were the dinghies that helped us when we were caught on the reef, come by to check on us. To see if we're ok. Such delightful people.

5. The guys off the S African catamaran *Indigo* come aboard for drinks and tell us great stories while enjoying wine.

The delightfulness of times like these is hard to explain. What a rich life we lead. Even while stuck on a remote island...waiting for weather.

Hang on to your hat, folks; I think we have a window of opportunity. The Morning Coffee Group...or whatever we decided we were...has spotted a weather window...of more than one day. And it's been consistently forecasted for a couple of days, which is a good sign. If the weather states the same forecast for at least two or three days, it's a good indication that it might be stable.

So, we set the date to leave... finally. Since we've been here so long, Randy and I decide to forego the Turks and Caicos and head straight for the Dominican Republic where we will stay for hurricane season. *sans clés* is going to do the same, but they will then go on to Puerto Rico and the Virgin Islands after stopping in the DR. *Mschiana* and *Conch Pearl* will head to the Turks. *Mschiana* will leave their boat there for the season. *Conch*

Pearl will continue on but wants to see the Turks first. But we'll all leave Rum Cay together. The other boats are leaving, too, but are heading North. Their weather window hasn't been any better in that direction either. They leave before we do. We wave goodbye to our fellow cruisers and wish them fair winds.

The plan is to leave first thing in the morning. The plan fails. We wait another day. The plan works. We're all up early, getting ready to go... to peel off the docks one by one. We are being eaten alive by mosquitoes and no-see-ums... ugh. But we're excited. The morning is calm, the water very still. Too still... the bugs were eating us alive! The calm water, however, will make it easier to get out of the not-so-easy-to-get-into marina. For that, I am grateful. For the zillion bugs, I am not grateful.

Conch Pearl in the lead, then *Kwanesum, Mschiana,* and *sans clés.* Our next journey has begun.

The *Hotel Rum Cay* has let us go.

Itchy feet.

Chapter 15

At Sea

Mother, Mother Ocean

We are on our way south again. Good. We're headed to the Dominican Republic. Straight to the DR....not stopping in Mayaguana...not stopping in Turks and Caicos, as originally planned. Maybe we're moving too fast? We do think of that, but the long wait in Rum Cay sort of tired us out. We want to see new country. Mayaguana and T&C are more of the Bahamas. As a matter of fact, T&C used to be part of the Bahamas years ago. We decided instead to go on to the Dominican Republic with *sans clés*.

We are anticipating a good trip. We've searched the weather window and it called for 4-6 foot seas, winds starting at 12-15 knots, going down to zero at times, for 3 days or so. The winds we did have are out of the east which is not a good direction but it's okay. Specially if they aren't big. They are on our nose, or at best '*close hauled*,' a sailing term for when sails are trimmed flat for sailing as close to the wind as possible. 'Close hauled' is doable but not great. On the nose is stupid bad. Works against you. We put up the main sail as it makes for better riding and

172

any wind that might be to our advantage will pick up in the sail and help us move along. Would be nice at some point if we could strictly sail, but we shall see. We stacked up extra fuel. The direction we're going doesn't really play into a good sail. But we're excited. Excited to leave Rum Cay and get on with our adventure.

We settle in for the duration. The 4 boats with our sails up... looking good. We chat back and forth on the radio to see how we're all doing. It should take us about 3 days to get to the DR. I have made sandwiches and hard-boiled eggs and other stuff to have on hand... particularly during the night shifts. You don't want to spend much time below (**PPM**... remember?) (**Proactive Puking Management**). We will again do our routine of 3 hours on/ 3 hours off at the helm.

Our destination in the Dominican Republic is Luperón, on the north side of the island. It's considered a *"hurricane hole"*. We had several options of where to spend Hurricane Season, which our insurance company defines as 1 July – 1 November. It's defined by some as 30 June - 30 November. We are abiding by our insurance company information since that's who calls the shots for us. The insurance companies give parameters for the zone you should be inside during this time in order to remain covered. Our insurance company defines the *'zone'* as between the Savannah River (between South Carolina and Georgia) to the southern coast of Grenada. So a decision needed to be made. At the time, when making this decision, we were in Nassau, with the beginning of May being our departure date south, depending as always on the weather. Do we go back to, say, Charleston, SC, which we loved, and then redo the miles we had already traveled? Do we head quickly down to Grenada? This would hurry our trip and determine it to be a little less relaxing. Should we head through the Gulf and straight for Panama? We would miss the Caribbean entirely but get to the west coast sooner. Should we keep on course, head down the Exumas and over to the *"hurricane hole"* in the Dominican Republic? The *"hurricane hole"* or Luperón, would not be sanctioned by our insurance company. We could, if we spent more money, get a rider, but it had a huge deductible.

So what do we do? This is our home. We must make a good decision. We decide to email our weather guru, Chris Parker, and give him our options and see what he thinks. Chris immediately emailed us back and gave his opinion on our options:

1. **Going back to Charleston?** – That would be backtracking, which doesn't really suit us. Chris said: *You're also more likely to get a Hurricane there. With an April or May departure, there's no reason you couldn't be somewhere secure by July 1 (Luperón, the ABCs, Trinidad, Venezuela, Colombia, Panama, the RioDulce).*

2. **Heading quickly to southern Grenada?** - Would this even be feasible from Nassau? Chris said: *Yes, but not until late May or June do cold fronts stop, making it tougher to get to the E Caribbean.* We asked additionally…what route should we take if we did that? Chris said: *It depends on the weather pattern in place when you're ready to go. If you want to enjoy the Bahamas, hop down the chain…but there, you'll be more pressed for time in the Caribbean. If you want more time in the Caribbean and don't mind a longer offshore passage, go E or ENE from Nassau (or anywhere in the Bahamas), then make a gradual turn SE-S as you get far enough East to lay the E Caribbean in the Trades.*

3. **Heading straight to the Gulf and the Panama Canal?** - But we would miss the Caribbean, the Dominican Republic and Puerto Rico included, which would be a shame. And Chris agreed: *Yes, a shame. No need to miss areas to the East.*

4. **Heading to the Hurricane Hole in the DR?** - Our insurance would not cover that decision if we get damage from a named storm, but they say there are good "hurricane holes"

there. It might be nerve-wracking. Chris's response: *Given the orientation of the Dominican Republic, the only way you could get a significant Hurricane in the Luperón area is from a SW-moving Hurricane (approaching from the NE) or from a hurricane paralleling the DR's N Coast. While neither is impossible, both are highly unlikely. Plus, I believe there are reasonable "hurricane holes", though there's no such thing as a perfect "hurricane hole."*

We made the decision. And it didn't take us long. Let's keep going. Let's go to the DR and wait. And we're on our way...pounding against the wind and the seas but happy as clams to be heading in the right direction. We're betting on the 'Come Line.' Kinda.

On we plod, pounding on the seas. We thought we'd have smoother sailing. We actually did have one great morning along the way. Woke up to nice, calm seas...coffee in the cockpit. I loved it. Wish it could be like that all the way...wind at our back...sailing. Oh well...once we get down into the Virgins, we can get the wind in a more favorable direction. Can't wait.

We pass into the Tropics.

The Tropic of Cancer, according to Wikipedia: *"one of five major degree measures or major circles of latitude that mark maps of the Earth. It is the northernmost latitude at which the Sun can appear directly overhead at noon. This event occurs at the June solstice when the northern hemisphere is tilted towards the sun to its maximum extent. The Tropic of Cancer currently lies 23° 26' 22" north of the equator. North of this latitude are the subtropics and Northern Temperate Zone. The equivalent line of latitude south of the equator is called the Tropic of Capricorn, and the region between the two, centered on the equator, is known as the tropics."*

Kind of thrilling, passing into the tropics. Randy is down below sleeping, so I take a picture of the chart plotter passing the latitude mark. I notice something out of the corner of my eye. Something was jumping in the water. Shoot, I missed it! Wait…there it goes again!

I have my camera in my hand so I get ready, in case it jumps again. Holy cow! It's big! It looks kinda like a dolphin, but it's not graceful like a dolphin. It's very clumsy. Like a whale, but smaller like a dolphin. I get some good pictures. I still have no clue what this odd thing is that's jumping in the water, but I'm so glad I had my camera in my hand. Later, when I have time, I'll zoom in on it and try to figure out what it is. In the meantime, we continue…into the Tropics. (Turns out, it was a Bottle Nose Whale.)

Gets kinda hairy at night. Lots of lightning going on…in the distance, but at night, it looks very menacing. Some people don't like to sail at night. It doesn't bother Randy and me. As long as we stay vigilant, watch for ships.

As a matter of fact, one night along the way, I was concerned about a ship I saw heading across our path. Even though I had it on the AIS (Automatic Information System), and it told me we were plenty far away, it looked like it was going to cross right in front of us! "Uhhh, Randy… can you come up here for a minute?" I wanted him to validate that we were far enough away. And as the ship got closer, it looked like it was right in front of *sans clés*! That's the weird part about nighttime. Things look closer than they actually are! We were fine; we were plenty far away, as the AIS said. And *sans* clés was, too. But better safe than sorry, I say!

To divert here a minute, I'll explain the AIS. Not sure that I've done that before. It's part of our chart plotter system, and it's very cool. It picks up any ships that are in the area and puts them on the chart plotter. They show up as a little triangle. By clicking on the little triangle, you will get all the information about that particular ship. How big it is, what the name of the ship is, where it's coming from, where it's going, what it's carrying, the closest point of approach... all the information you need to avoid it. Very cool and it wasn't that expensive. It's almost better than radar sometimes. We are very glad to have it onboard. And it's interesting to use.

As we carry on the first night, we actually all changed course to try to avoid an oncoming squall. It seemed to work. As we stand now, *sans clés* is leading us... by far the fastest boat. We are next, and *Mschiana* and *Conch Pearl* are behind us. We want to stay with *sans clés* as we're heading to the same destination. The fin keel on *sans clés* is hard to keep up with, so we really push *Kwanesum* hard. We are motor-sailing and averaging about 5 knots, sometimes faster, sometimes slower. We want to make sure we arrive at our destination in daylight. Timing is important. Our rule, and one that is advised and used by most cruisers, is never to go into a new anchorage or marina at night. This is a general rule of sorts that cruisers follow, but there are some that dare to do it. If you are familiar with the anchorage or entrance to a harbor, it is not as disconcerting. But we are not familiar with any of this, so we must reach our destination before dark or stay outside until morning.

The next morning is the calm and wonderful morning I mentioned before. We are near Mayaguana, and this is when we will part from *Mschiana* and *Conch Pearl*. Kinda sad! But we will catch up with them on down the road in the Dominican Republic, Puerto Rico, or the Virgin Islands. We bid each other fair winds and promise to meet up later and stay in touch via email. When you're stuck on an island together for two weeks, you get to be darned good friends. Part of the blessing of this opportunity of cruising the seas in your yacht.

We have now changed our exact destination to enter the Dominican Republic. Instead of going into Luperón first and checking into the country there, *sans clés* and *Kwanesum* will go into Ocean World Marina at Puerto Plata and check in there. We both researched it and decided this would be the easiest. It's easy to get into the marina, we can check into the country, refuel, re-provision, do laundry, fill with water... and relax after our long trip. Sounds good. That's what we'll do. Then *Kwanesum* will go on to Luperón for the season, and *sans clés* will head to Puerto Rico. The destination for *sans clés* will be St. John in the US Virgin Islands, where they will celebrate their anniversary.

So... on we go. Day three. Are we there yet? We're getting anxious to get to our destination. Sandwiches are about gone. Boiled eggs are gone. 3rd day of wearing the same clothes and no shower (it's just easier that way.) It's kind of hazy today... the seas are still big. Give us a break! Ugh. I think I spot some hills but I'm not sure. Hard to see through the haze. But I'm pretty sure I see hills. There are NO hills throughout the Bahamas and T & C. They say you can smell the DR when you get close. Smell the earth. My smeller's not that good. But I'm testing it nonetheless. We're now starting to worry about our fuel. We calculated we had plenty, but didn't expect the seas to hold us back so much. We figure we use a little more than a gallon an hour. Our tank holds 75 gallons. And we carried an extra 10 gallons. We've already poured the extra in. Let's see how we do.

Now we can see the hills. Hooray! Beautiful, green hills. It's still pretty hazy, but we can see them nonetheless. We aren't far off now. But sometimes that last bit, when you know you're almost there, takes forever! We radio sans clés and they informed us they alerted Ocean World that we're on our way in. Cool. As we're plodding along, a fancy, schmancy power yacht zooms by, bouncing wildly on the water. "Oh yeah??!! What else did you get for Christmas??!!" We had boat envy at that time. Speed envy. "Show offs!!!" We watch *sans clés* make their turn to approach the entrance. We hail *sans clés* again. "Lyman, we're coming in on fumes. Just want to let you know we may need assistance." Our gauge registers... very... low. OK, *Kwanesum*... get us there. "She'll get us there, Ran. She always does." I'm at the helm, and we make the turn at the yellow marker to head our way inside. Tired, excited, kinda smelly, and ready to stop, we bounce our way in. It's a straight shot in once you turn, but the seas are still very, very bouncy. Makes it a bit of a challenge to keep the boat straight. I'm on the helm and on the radio with the harbor master finding out where to go.

"Make a port turn just after you enter and head to the back F docks." "Roger that."

I make that left turn, and it's nice... so nice... and calm... hooray!!! What a nice marina! Cement docks... lots of room. We decide to get fuel later as we're exhausted, and it's already getting close to 1800hrs.

I find the spot they want us...F Dock...I pull *Kwanesum* right in. F12...our spot is F12. We tie up...there are many hands helping...we are so excited! So glad to be here. We have our DR flag up and our yellow quarantine flag. A golf cart is here to take Lyman and Randy to immigration.

To their delight...the immigration person was a very lovely Dominicana. Back to the boat...time for cocktails! We are so tired we just go down to *sans clés* with our wine and beer in hand and toast while sitting on the dock. "To our landing in the Dominican Republic!" "Cheers!"

Chapter 16
The Dominican Republic

What A Great Place!

Now we settle in. The first few days, we sleep, clean, and sleep again. Do laundry and provision. We provisioned at La Serena, a big store in Puerto Plata, kinda like a Walmart. As a matter of fact, Walmart owns it or is buying it, I think. Obviously, we rented a car to pile the provisions in. Since *sans clés* will not be here long, we decide to share the rent of a car and go exploring. So, first, we provisioned.

"Let's do the Falls," Terri said. The Falls...the Falls...I read somewhere about the Falls, but I need to refresh my memory. "The **27 Charcos**! It will be fun!" OK! I'm up for anything. I look it up on the internet and it looks really fun. Wonder how hard it is? Oh well...I can handle it. "You hike up the Falls and then slide or jump on the way down." OK. "We will just do 12...not the whole 27." OK.

Off we go. First, we need to find our way there. Driving in the DR is not easy. There don't seem to be many rules...there are a LOT of cars and even MORE motorcycles or scooters and not many rules. Or at least not many that are followed. They do drive on the same side of the road as the US. That's helpful. There's a great deal of faith put into the *"other guy"*. We head to the Falls full of anticipation. Get there…put our swimsuits on…have our Teva sandals on. Now, what do we do? We need helmets and life jackets. OK. We acquire our guide, who brings along a helper. OK. Let's get going. We have to hike for awhile to get to the falls…across a fun, rope bridge, and through streams. "Come on, Momma." They called me 'Momma' and made sure I had sure footing crossing the streams, holding my hand. I appreciated that.

This was sooo fun! It was a beautiful, warm day. The area was gorgeous. The falls were magnificent. You had to fight against the current a few times to go up the Falls, and … you had to climb some pretty 'hairy' spots. And …you had to hold on to ropes to pull yourself up against the rush, rushing water. Climbing up to the 7th fall was the worst. Well…the one where we had to climb a precarious wall was kinda hard, too, but up that 7th fall was definitely the most challenging. The guides had to PULL us up. Not easy. They are very strong, however. And were able to pull up this plus-sized 'momma.' We still had more to go. I decided not to go further. The 8th fall we had to climb was REALLY challenging. You had to act like a monkey to get up while holding on a rope… against the current. I don't want to push my luck. Randy decides to stay with me. Terri and Lyman go on up to the 12th fall while we waited. (They're younger. HA!) It was still hard for them to get up. But they did it and went to the 12th one. They said we really didn't miss much by not going that distance. The other falls weren't any more fun than what we've already done. Good.

So now…down we go! Cool! We start jumping…very, very high, some of them were… and sliding our way down. Water slides! Really fun but a little precarious now and then. Coming down was definitely faster and easier than going up! There was one fall…pretty tall. I look down. Well,…gotta get down somehow! *Kowabunga!* So fun. Great, great, great day. We end the trip with beer and great food at their little restaurant there. This experience was one of the highlights of my life.

The next day... we still have a car... agenda: the top of the mountain and Luperón. Remember Luperón is where we want to end up for the season.

First, we tried to find our way to *Mount Isabel de Torres*, a scientific reserve and a peaceful botanical garden. They have a *teleferico* (gondola) that takes you up, but we decided to drive. I'm glad as you see more country and people that way. Mt. Isabel de Torres is 2600 feet up, and it's gorgeous. We had a wonderful clear morning, and the views were spectacular. There is also a wonderful large statue of Christ similar to the one in Rio de Janeiro. Awesome.

Now we drive on to check out Luperón and see if we can find our friends on *Gravyboat*, *Opal*, and *Wanderlust* there. It's a wonderful drive through the countryside to get there. Luperón is a small, little sleepy town northwest of Puerto Plata. Found the City Dock, and we hailed our friends on *Gravyboat* on the radio to let them know we were in town. They were at anchor there. They dinghy'd in... so fun to see them. We hadn't seen them or Marc on *Opal* since Nassau. Lots of boats anchored here. We went to Capt. Steve's for a beer, where we ran into other fellow cruisers we have met along the way. Marc from *Opal* and the Duncans, the South Africans of *Wanderlust* who were in Rum Cay with us. Capt. Steve's was a fun place... and so fun to see everyone.

Back to our home away from home. Ocean World. Terry and Lyman on *sans clés* are waiting for a weather window to cross the Mona Passage to Puerto Rico. They aren't getting one. They decide to stay. We decide to stay. We like it here. Wonderful people, a pool to use at any time, fresh water delivered, ice delivered, laundry done for you, electricity if we need it, guards 24 hours, restaurants close by, mini-mercados close by... nice. We all go up to talk to James, the marina manager, to see what kind of deal he can give us if we stay for the whole hurricane season. It's a go! James gave us a great price on slip fees, electricity, and water for the 6 months. Excellent. We will stay here for hurricane season. Now... to the pool with our adult beverages! Ahhhhh...

I traveled to CA for a month to spend time with the kids and grandkids. Randy stayed with the boat. Since it is hurricane season, we didn't feel comfortable leaving *Kwanesum* by herself. First season we've weathered in the hurricane zone. So far, so good, but we have 8 more weeks and September is notoriously busy with storms. And there's one sitting out there now that we're watching. We shall see if we made the right decision to stick it out here...in the Dominican Republic. Randy spent his time while I was away with our new friends here at Playa Cofresi and keeping our boat safe from TS/Hurricane Bill that blew through. All at the marina kept a sharp eye on everyone's boats and made sure all had extra spring lines tethered along the docks for extra protection. There was big surge from the storm but all faired the weather well.

Ending our stay in the Dominican Republic was bittersweet. We were ready to sail on. It was time. Hurricane season had ended and we need to get a move on to our next port of call. But we hated leaving new friends behind. We packed in whatever fun we could in those last weeks in the DR. While I was visiting family in California, Randy spent a few days in the capital of the Dominican Republic, Santo Domingo. Our friend Marc, on *Opal*, had taken an apartment in Santo Domingo for a few months while waiting out hurricane season with his boat anchored in Luperón. Randy decided to take advantage of Marc's stay in the capital and see the city Columbus frequented, the Zona Colonial. Taking a pretty decent bus and traveling for

3 hours or so, he arrived and proceeded to partake in festivities Marc lined up and tours of the city. I regret that I didn't get down there to see the sites, but Randy said it was magnificent and so interesting walking the grounds that Columbus walked on.

It is said that Columbus explored and colonized the Dominican Republic on his first voyage in 1492. He named it *"La Hispaniola"* and his son, Diego, was its first governor. Santo Domingo became the site of the first cathedral, hospital, customs house and university in the americas. The town itself was laid out in a grid pattern that became the model for almost all town planners in the New World. Fascinating history everywhere we go.

Because of our lengthy stay in the Dominican Republic, the people we met became very dear to us. I'm afraid it was a teary day for both Randy and I when we left Playa Cofresi, the neighborhood beach area where the Ocean World Marina is located. We said our goodbyes to all our new friends, which was very hard. As it turned out, we had to wait an extra week because the weather turned bad. So we had to say our goodbyes twice. I hurried through them the second time because it was just too sad! They made a mark on our hearts.

And a cast of characters they were:

Our marina family:

JAMES - the stoic, British Marina Operations Manager

ROBERTO - one of the greatest of Harbor Masters that have touched our lives. Always smiling, always appreciative, always there to help. So hard to leave Roberto.

BERNARDO - one of the dock workers. *"¿Qué pasa?!"* he would shout every time we saw him, often driving around in the dock cart. Always smiling, always teasing me. Always ready to get us anything we needed, even if he had to drive into town for it. He didn't always find the right thing but, oh, how we loved him for trying. He would help us with our Spanish. How we cried when we hugged him goodbye.

JOSE - one of the guards. *"¡No ducha!"* (No shower) he would say, teasing us as we sat in the pool every afternoon, Randy with his Orange Julius (Randy's concoction of orange juice and rum) and me with my tropical drink of whatever my mood was that day, splashing him while he pretended he would jump in. *"No ducha... for 20 days!"* he would tease, waving his finger back and forth. *"Pew!"* we would answer back, pinching our noses. So fun. He was so touched by our tears when we hugged him goodbye that he wrote down his name and phone number in case we needed anything. Many of the guards became good friends, but Jose was special.

DANNY & FLORENCIO - the pool dining area waiters.

Always smiling, always helpful and friendly. When you stay in one place for 5 months you get to know everyone. I loved saying Florencio's name. *Flllooorrrennnciiioooo!* It would always make him smile.

EDY - my laundry guy. LOVED having my laundry done, returned perfectly folded and smelling wonderfully clean. I do miss Edy.

IGOR AND CAROLINE - they took over the s/v *Conch Pearl* (you will remember from Rum Cay) when Neil brought her in to Ocean World and then went back home. They were great. They worked so hard on the *Conch Pearl* to get her all ship shape to charter. Hoping to see them down island.

Our Playa Cofresí family:

JUAN - from the mini mercardo. A quiet, gentle, handsome man. Always helping us with our Spanish. Supplied Randy with orange juice and rum for his Orange Julius drink and had the Snickers bars cold in the refrigerator for Randy's sweet tooth.

CHRIS & MADY'S RESTAURANT - our home away from the boat. Chris, Mady, Jennifer, Jason, Christal, Johnny, little Ally and Denise...all family we learned to love. Sweet Shereen and Carlitos, family, too, and always getting us what we needed. Hard to leave these people.

JOHN DOBBS - our VERY special friend. With his perfect Atlanta southern drawl. So hard to leave John. He and Randy became very close friends. John would cook BBQ chicken every Sunday. Soooo gooood. We watched sports and drank Presidentes with John. Love him.

JOE & ANNE - became VERY special friends and hailed from Canada. In charge of fun and frivolity and Tuesday night movies! They were so fun and helpful to us. Picking Randy up from the airport. Taking us to la ferretería. Going above and beyond. They have since moved back to Canada and we hope to do the Calgary Stampede with them some day. Joe and Anne had Canadian 'drawls.' Eh?

PHILLIP - who spent days wrangling with our sewing machine and helping us so much by repairing our dodger and bimini and making new awnings for us. In turn we gave him a stipend, enjoyed lunches with him and drinking Cuba Libres and Bloody Caesars. Phillip had a Tennessee drawl.

MARIANNE AND EDUOARD - from Germany...and their 3 scottie dogs. A fun, interesting couple that we were privileged to see often at the restaurant. We drank their German beer. Eduoard always on the computer, trading stocks. Marianne...so fun to talk to with her German accent.

186

Always a grand time, and good quiet moments, with the gang at Chris & Mady's. We miss them all… a lot.

Desperados Restaurant

KAREN & RANDY JOHNSON - fun, friendly, very generous. Loved the calamari they made there along with their burritos and *queso* dip. YUM! And the Johnson Java! Wonderful, chocolaty, coffee martini. They had the best margaritas in the neighborhood, too.

Las Churros Restaurant

TIM and his wonderful family that put on quite the show on a Sunday night with traditional dancing, serving us mouth watering mango margaritas and tapas.

Ahora Restaurant

SAHEEL and, Charley and Jenny. Eating good burgers at the beach bar with

Presidente beer. Randy is growing his hair like Saheel's ponytail. What a smile Saheel has. Charley, a charming, handsome young Dominicana whom we had good talks with… left before we did to visit his girlfriend in Germany. Never saw him again. He was worried about living in Germany, learning German when we met him, and concerned that her parents might not like him! Hope he's doing well.

A cast of thousands we were so privileged to meet.

We had such fun in the D.R. at Playa Cofresi, partaking in a beach party for Phillip's birthday, Christal's birthday party at the new pool behind the restaurant, Sunday BBQ chicken made by John complete with corn on the cob and football, Tuesday night movies, Canadian Thanksgiving dinner, music put on by Chris which prompted much singing and dancing…. Staying in the D.R. meeting all these wonderful people was truly one of

187

the highlights of our lives. They made us feel so at home. Randy took a brief week to fly to Oregon and visit his mom. Our new friends in the D.R. took great care of me while he was gone. It was nice knowing they were there if I needed them. Very nice.

Because we were delayed a week longer in Playa Cofresi due to weather, we were able to partake in one of the best parties ever! Halloween! Ocean World Marina went all out for Halloween…moving their disco downstairs in the dining room and preparing a cool haunted house that you had to enter to get in. The costumes were unbelievable. Ran and I scrambled around the boat trying to figure out a costume without making complete fools of ourselves. "Ran…what's new with that? We are always making fools of ourselves." Not sure he appreciated my humor.

But first we started the Halloween Crawl at Chris & Mady's restaurant. Festivities began there with great costumes, good beverages, cigars and dancing. So fun. Then we moved down to Ocean World to check out the haunted house and the great costumes. In the meantime, while we were drinking and dancing and carrying on, what turned out to be new friends were entering the harbor. They pulled in Halloween night to all the party festivities in their wonderful sailboat *Allegro*. Camilla and Peter.

We met Camilla and Peter the next day and became fast friends. After a couple more days of weather-waiting, it was time to go. Camilla and Peter decided to leave in the morning. We were going to leave that night, but waiting for night proved to be too frustrating for us. We were already a week overdue. So off we went…waving goodbye to the marina office, turning right and heading into the Mona Passage for Puerto Rico. We were in the Dominican Republic for 5 glorious months. What an experience.

¡Vaya con Dios, Republica Dominicana!

Chapter 17
The Mona Passage

On to Puerto Rico!

The Mona Passage was uneventful for us! We read and read in our cruising guides about the trip across the Mona Passage…when to go, when not to go, what time of day to go, what time not to go, which course to take, which course not to take…. It was sort of a daunting trip hanging in front of us. One of the longer trips and the passage could have its quirks and was noted to be one of the most difficult we would travel. Timing is very important, they say. Sometimes I think we read too much. We like to be über-prepared for our crossings, but after reading and reading you start to worry and worry. And it turned out to be just another day and a half on the water.

Originally we planned to leave with Fernando, a fellow from Uruguay who had his boat next to ours in the Ocean World Marina. He left his boat there for the hurricane season. Randy and I wanted almost perfect weather when we tackled the Mona Passage. We wanted plenty of days to get there and have 2 or 3 places to duck in should we need to because of weather and/or seas. Fernando agreed. We checked all our weather sources and thought we were ready to go. We contacted customs and the DR Navy who must check us before we leave. All set. Each country had their own set of procedures of checking in and checking out of their country. For some reason we had to check with their Navy in the DR. No problem, just one extra thing to do that was a little different than the other countries.

Then a fishing boat came into the marina with his tuna tower banged up. Randy walked over to talk to them. "Don't go out there!" the fisherman said. "The waves are huge and we got banged up."

We shall wait.

Fernando was getting impatient. He wanted to leave soon and he wanted us to go with him. We explained to him, through a little bit of a language barrier, that we weren't going unless the weather met all of our criteria. And it still wasn't matching our specifications. Fernando went ahead. We weren't ready. He made it fine and so did we, about a week later. By then Fernando had moved on as he was meeting his family in Trinidad. He was on a schedule. We were not.

The Mona Passage turned out to be very easy for us. It took us 1.5 days. Our friends on *Allegro*, being a much longer, and therefore much faster boat, made it in less than a day. We met up in Boquerón, Puerto Rico!

¡Hola Puerto Rico!

Boquerón! We are here! Marc on *Opal* was there, too! YAY! Always fun to find the people we have met along the way when we pull into a new port, or when they pull into the port we're in. We're all headed in the same direction, give or take.

We chose Boquerón as our port of entry to Puerto Rico. It was recommended by the cruising guides and it proved to be a good decision. Now we need to check in. We called a phone number or two to see the best way to check into the country. One of the calls we made was to Raul Santiago. Though we can sometimes get worried silly reading so much in our cruising guides, they, more times than not, become invaluable with their information. Obviously these guides are written by those who have gone before us, so they are tried and true bits of information. To call Raul proved to be one our best guide-following decisions.

Raul met us in front of one of the restaurants near the dinghy dock. Fun place, Boquerón. Plenty of neat restaurants near the dinghy dock. (Lots of mosquitoes though! And I mean LOTS of mosquitos.) Raul pulled up in his very used looking van with his daughter riding in the back. OK. Let's do this. Off we go to Mayagüez where the ferries dock. We timed it perfectly to avoid the crowd coming off the ferries. We are met by a nice looking trim, cute, immigration senorita. She led us through all the paperwork and customs. Raul told us he was no longer able to take people to help them through customs and immigration, but he took us anyway. And the immigration gal said for him to call her anytime. That she would help. So nice, these people are.

It was a huge help having Raul take us there. We told him we were in need of a Yamaha outboard engine repairman and a marine store. He found both for us on the way back to the dinghy. Eric, the Yamaha repair guy followed us back to the dock and we immediately arranged for him to take our engine to be repaired. It needed maintenance and the carburetor needed cleaning. Remember our prior frustrations with *Bob*, our dinghy? This was one…now fixed. Perfecto!

Boquerón was quite the happening place…toward the end of the week. Beginning of the week proved to be very quiet. But by Wednesday or so, it got shaking…bands, singing, traffic driving through the little narrow streets, families and friends walking up and down, all hours of the day and night…mounds of fresh oysters and clams piled high at road side stands. With lemons and hot sauce, waiting for you to buy. We hesitantly shied away from them because they were not on ice or being kept cold in any way. It killed us to let these piles of savory goodness go past, but our instincts said no. Instead we found a neat tapas bar with Camilla and Peter. So good! And the music was so LOUD! Got to the point where you could not carry on a conversation anymore. But was fun while it lasted.

Days were spent at Galloways Bar and Restaurant drinking beer and sitting on the computers trying to connect with home. I guess I shouldn't say 'home' as home is our boat, but in this sense 'home' being our family and friends. One of my frustrations, as a computer/internet fan, which I've said before and I'm sure I'll say again, is finding good sources of internet reception. It usually can be done but can be frustrating. I know…not one of my best traits, but it's my connection to friends and family. An instant pick-me-up for me, and an instant way for me to share our pictures and thus our adventures…right away. From the moment I figured out about computers I have loved them, explored them, ruined them, and hollered at them, but it's something I really enjoy. From games, to uploading pictures, to email, to searching for information, to reading the news, to trying to watch programs, to Skyping the family….it's my thing. Sometimes I get cranky, even though I'm in paradise, if I can't be in touch. Not sure if it's good, bad, ok or not ok, it's what I like. Therefore…finding sources of internet connection are part of my program. That and finding great cheeseburgers, great beer….and Painkillers!

We spent 10 days in Boquerón during which time we rented a car and explored Puerto Rico. One of our plans for Puerto Rico was to be hauled out of the water and new bottom paint put on.

While in Boquerón we contacted a fellow name Jose Becerros in Ponce. It was suggested that he was an excellent source for our bottom paint job so we called him and arranged to be pulled out of the water. While we had a rental car we decided to drive to San Juan by way of Ponce so we could talk to Ho Chi, as he is called, in person. We found the place in Ponce, stopped, had lunch and talked with Ho Chi and the person in the office to arrange our haul out. Excellent! All is on the books. From Ponce we drove into Old San Juan and explored this wonderful old town. It was a gorgeous drive. Puerto Rico is just beautiful. And Old San Juan is just as you'd expect. Though it was raining we had a nice day walking around the cobblestone streets. While there...we had to find West Marine! A sailor can't go too long without being in a West Marine Store. We knew there was one in San Juan, but we weren't exactly sure how to get there. And when we called...the message was all in Spanish. Shoot.

While wandering around Old San Juan we of course mosey into a neat little bar and have a beer. While there we ask the bartender to please call West Marine for us so we could understand how to get help on the phone. As it turns out, the bartender knew where West Marine was! YAY! She gave us directions, we finished our beers, and we were on our way. Arrived at West Marine and a few hundred dollars later we were on our way back to Boquerón ...with all the things we needed, and some that we didn't... but I wanted anyway.

Now it's time to head on to Ponce and getting our boat hauled out. We leave Boquerón early on a beautiful November morning. We decided we also want to put on another solar panel to boost our power when at anchor while we are in Ponce. We called Ho Chi about that, and he thought he could do that no problem. Excellent. On our way to Ponce we stop at La Parguera, a little anchorage we can duck into. Another Island Packet, *Marilou*, whom we briefly met before we left Boquerón, also anchored in this little area. It was fun getting to know Ann and Jay on *Marilou*. La Parguera is a sweet little area. We swim a little and take a cocktail cruise in our dinghy to see the neat houses all along the shore. It's like a Caribbean Venice.

We spend one night at La Parguera and are then up early to head to Ponce. "If we get there before noon, maybe they will pull us out today." Randy was hopeful that this would be the case. Particularly since we had it all arranged and they were expecting us. We were scheduled to be pulled out the next morning.

We arrive in Ponce and try to find a place to anchor. The area is full of private mooring balls which makes anchoring a chore. We drive slowly around trying to find a good spot and drop the anchor out near the yellow midchannel marker. There is a *malacón* (boardwalk) nearby and the Ponce Yacht Club. We aren't feeling great about where we are anchored but know that it will just be for one night. "Let's call Ho Chi and see if they can pull us out soon." Randy makes the call to let them know we're here and ready to go when they are. They'll call us back. We wait. Not much to see from this anchorage and we feel we're close to the public dock where a large party-type boat is docked. We wait. No call. Randy calls again. "Oh, let me check and I'll call you back." Ok. Seems as though he forgot about us. We wait. It's now late in the afternoon and obviously they aren't going to pull us out today. That's ok. We should be scheduled for the morning. We can see the travel lift sitting there unused. The travel lift is a structure on wheels with straps they lower in the water and the boat is moved onto the straps in the water and then slowly lifted out of the water and on to stanchions on the dry dock for work. Verrryyyy carefully. It's a bit nail biting watching the process.

We wait. Finally Ho Chi returns our call. "It looks like we won't be able to pull you out until Thursday or Friday. (Today is Tuesday.) The yacht club regatta is this weekend and they need to pull out the committee boat to work on it." "Uh....Ho Chi...we made a special trip over here to schedule the haul out with you and the marina and they said tomorrow morning. We asked you if there was anything going on at the time or any problem with getting hauled out on time and you said there wasn't. Have you checked on ordering the solar panel?" "Uh...no...I'll have to find out about the solar panel. I...." "Ho Chi...forget it! Obviously you aren't worried about accommodating us, we do not like waiting in this very crowded uncomfortable, noisy anchorage, so we'll just weigh anchor in the morning and go. Thanks anyway." Well...so much for prearranged planning! We just didn't have a good feeling about the whole thing. Other cruisers have enjoyed this anchorage and working with the boatyard, but apparently it was not to be for us. We will figure something else out.

Off we go, early the next morning, to Salinas, Puerto Rico. What a great anchorage this is! Lots of room, nice and calm, lots of boats around. We drive *Kwanesum* around the anchorage looking for a good spot to drop the anchor and do so. Not sure it really is a good spot though...we seem too close to one of the boats. We sit and wait to see what we think. In the meantime, in comes Marc on *Opal*! Yay! As it turns out there are several other boats there that Marc knows from Luperón, Dominican Republic. They call themselves the Luperón ex-pats, as they all stayed there for hurricane season. Nice people.

We visit briefly with Marc and then decide we do NOT like where we are anchored. Up comes the anchor and we drive around and around testing the best spots, again. Again, like a dog that circles and circles before he finally lays down. There... we choose a spot that has plenty of room around it and is sort of away from the madding crowd.

Sometimes being farther away is quieter and you know you have plenty of room around you. The more we anchor, the more we are getting used to picking good spots and trusting what we do.

Now I get on the phone. We knew that we could also be hauled out in Puerto del Rey Marina in Fajardo. It's a well recommended boat yard area. I call them and ask for companies that can haul us out and do the work we need. I am given two options and I pick Ken at Island Marine. I call, he answers, I tell him what we want done, he asks me to email him the information and he'll get us a quote. I email him, he immediately sends a quote back. Now this is more like it! I like to see everything in writing and know exactly what's going to happen. The good news is the price is right and he can order the solar panel we need. The bad news is…we have to wait until the first part of December. But this time that is no problem for us. We like where we are anchored, we like Ken and his prompt and diligent responses to us, we can wait. Having good communication is such a key element in reducing stress when you're spending money and having work done such as this. We are feeling good about Ken, his assistant Jenifer and Island Marine boat yard at Puerto del Rey. Excellent. We settle back to enjoy Salinas. We will be here 2 weeks.

At Salinas we enjoy meeting and getting to know the Luperón ex-pats as well as Paul and Lynn on s/v *Kiana* and Sue and Rick on s/v *Orion*. We glean much appreciated information from Paul and Lynn who have been living the cruising lifestyle for 10 years. They have a wonderful big Wauquiez, which is the brand of boat we had in the San Francisco Bay before we moved East and bought *Kwanesum*. We learn a lot about our travels ahead, while enjoying gin and tonics in the cockpit. We learn what to expect, what to see, where to leave our boat during the next hurricane season down in Trinidad, the latitude where we must be to accommodate our insurance restrictions. Randy and I are always in love with this part of our cruising life, meeting new people. Not only do we get to see new countries, but we have the privilege of meeting wonderful, new, interesting people. At least 99% of them are. You know there are always a few that aren't quite as wonderful.

Sue and Rick have their boat in the marina at Salinas and are planning to retire and go cruising soon. They are so great, and Sue is quite the entertainer on her boat. As is Lynn. Many gin and tonics and Sue's famous rum drink she likes, produce wonderful cockpit conversations while the sun sets. I highly recommend this life.

Through Paul and Lynn we were invited to a nice Thanksgiving Day feast at Drakes, a little bar/restaurant near the marina owned by their friends Luis and Nancy. Luis smoked a turkey and we all brought side dishes. Since we couldn't be with our own families this was the next best thing. You just have to remember to bring your mosquito spray with you everywhere you go. The highlight of this wonderful feast were the *tostones*!! Fried Plantains! Oh My Gosh. Soooooo good!!!

On one of our daily walks, we found amazing burritos! We are having fun eating all these great foods here. The burritos were at a little cafe along our walk called La Barkita. They topped their burritos with Franks Hot Sauce, which I HIGHLY recommend and have purchased since, every time I see it in the store. We also sauntered down every other day or so to Cruises Gallery to get on the internet and have lunch and a beer. Always meeting colorful characters along the way. Some more colorful than we need.

And now we are ready to head to Puerto del Rey. It's located quite a distance around the east end of Puerto Rico so we decided to stop for the night at Puerto Patillas along the way. That will break it up into shorter trips. Besides it's fun stopping in these little anchorages. We are up early, which is the best time to leave. And it's always so beautiful in the morning. "Should be a short trip, El. It's not far at all." Love that.

The seas are kind of tumbly, but because it's a short trip it shouldn't be bad. We are going along quite nicely when Randy notices a small fishing boat off to starboard, waving a red flag in distress. One of the codes of being a good sailor is to always stop to help those in need. Randy slows *Kwanesum* and hails the coast guard. "United States Coast Guard, United States Coast Guard this is the sailing vessel Kwanesum, over." "This is the United States Coast Guard, go ahead." "Roger, Coast Guard, we are spotting a small fishing boat in distress at..." Randy gives our latitude and longitude at the time. "Roger, Captain. We request you stand by the vessel until we can be of assistance. We had received notice of flares in this area that we are investigating. Can you get close enough to the vessel to ask if they had released the flares? Over." "Roger, Coast Guard, will do."

We maneuver *Kwanesum* closer to the little fishing boat.

The seas are no help. It's like a washing machine out there. Up, down, up, down, sideways, up, down.... I am hanging on to the stern rail on the starboard side so I can talk to the fishermen, hoping they speak English, and trying to practice my **PPM.** Randy steers the boat close as possible and I try to holler to find their status. I, however, don't hear worth a damn anymore, and I don't wear my hearing aids when I'm on the water, so that's kind of a useless tactic. We switch places. Randy is able to communicate with them, and, yes, they speak English. Their engine quit. They did not send up flares. We relay the information back to the Coast Guard. In the meantime a Coast Guard helicopter has come hovering over. Oh good. They can take care of things. But as it turns out, the helicopter was out only to see why flares were sent up the past early morning. So the helicopter left. Now what?

"Uh....United States Coast Guard, this is the sailing vessel Kwanesum standing by the distressed vessel waiting for further instructions." We did not want to bring these guys onboard unless absolutely necessary. First of all the seas would be very difficult to manage to get near enough to bring them aboard. Second of all, we have heard of situations such as this where it is a setup to get aboard and rob you. Third of all we don't have a ladder available for boarding the side of our boat anyway. "Coast Guard... still standing by..." "Uh roger Captain." "Randy...now what are they doing? They are holding up their oar and it's cracked in half!" They had started to row to shore making hardly any headway at all as the seas were so high and the shore was a long way away. We watch them maneuver their little boat close to a fishing buoy and tie off to that. Well at least they have that available to cling to.

"Uh, Coast Guard, two of the people on the boat donned snorkel gear and jumped over the side." My mind is thinking...Are you kidding me??? What the heck are they doing?? Keep in mind, that while all of this is going on we are circling and going back and forth slowly to stay near them....slowly...*Kwanesum* bobbing and weaving through the big seas...Ellen practicing her **PPM**. Coast Guard hailed us again, "Uh, Captain, can you get close enough and ask them what they are doing?" We circle around and try again to get close enough to talk to them. Randy hollers at them, "What are you doing??!!" "Oh! We're cleaning the bottom of the boat. We figured as long as we're out here waiting we might as well be doing something useful." My mind is still thinking...Are you kidding me???? "United States Coast Guard, this is the sailing vessel Kwanesum." "Go ahead Captain." "Uh, roger, we spoke to the vessel in distress and they have attached themselves to a fishing trap buoy and are in the water cleaning the bottom of their boat." Silence. "Roger, captain. Don't they know it's against regulations to tie themselves to a fishing trap buoy?"

My mind is now shouting at me ...Are you kidding me??? The US Coast Guard is worried about them breaking the regulation for tying to a fishing trap buoy? This is getting weirder by the minute.

The coast guard indicated when we first talked to them that they were sending someone out. No one was coming. Oh great...now what are we supposed to do? We kept standing by to be sure they were ok, by circling and driving back and forth. Well this puts our travel to Puerto Patillas a lot longer than we anticipated! We notice out of nowhere, another little fishing boat come up and throw the distressed vessel a line. Yay! Where did they come from? They are going to tow them to shore. Perfect. Now we can get on our way. "United States Coast Guard, this is the sailing vessel Kwanesum." "Go ahead Captain." "Uh, roger. Another fishing vessel has come along side and is towing the distressed vessel to shore. Requesting permission to go ahead with our plans to Puerto Patillas." "Roger, Kwanesum. Can you continue standing by the vessel for another 20 minutes or so to be sure they will make it to shore?" That mind of mine. You know it is thinking... Are you kidding me??? "Uh, roger. Kwanesum standing by."

Oh well....good Samaritan and all, it's the right thing to do to stand by for a while. We will eventually get to our destination. We slowly drive alongside the two fishing vessels. The guys on the distressed vessel wave at us signaling thanks for standing by them. That made us feel good. We stood by for the additional 20 minutes or so and requested permission again with the coast guard to be on our way. Permission granted. We can now continue on to Puerto Patillas in time for sunset.

Puerto Patillas is a quaint, calm small anchorage. We arrived in the late afternoon. We poured ourselves a nice drink and watched the sunset in our cockpit. Nice. The area is very charming and I take my usual tons of pictures. We are just there

200

for the night so enjoy a nice meal I rustled up and some wine. I'm telling ya people...you gotta try this!

All in all it was a good, somewhat interesting, day.

Up early and on to Puerto del Rey Marina. We are ready to be in a marina. It's a nice change of pace having tons of power and tons of water available. Long, hot showers. Excellent. We have arranged to go in to the marina a couple of days earlier than our haul out time. We arrive on a Friday. They will pull us out Monday. We have a good trip around the east end of Puerto Rico and pull on in. And what to our wondering eyes should appear but *Gravyboat*!! Hooray! Our friends Jack and Marianne who we were berthed next to in Deltaville, VA when we started all this craziness. We knew they had kept their boat on the hard at Puerto del Rey during hurricane season and we knew they had arrived back to Puerto Rico but we weren't sure where they were. And now we find them only 3 berths down from us. How fun. Break out the beer! Oh, wait...Jack is having a serious conversation with a rigger. Beer later. In the meantime Randy eases on in to their conversation and later is able to hire the rigger to go up our mast and check all our rigging, too. A good thing to do now and then. All is well. Excellent. Now, bring out the beer.

While in Puerto del Rey we also found our friends on *Archipelago* that we met in Ocean World. They had stopped by Ocean World Marina on their way to Puerto Rico. Donna and David. They used to work at Puerto del Rey and now are back here working for the owner...designing the new island he bought. Yes...an island! Donna is an architect. What a great job, right? She confirmed our excellent decision to use Ken at Island Marine for our haul out. That made us feel really good about our choice.

We had a good experience with our stop at the marina. We were able to enjoy time with Jack and Marianne. We found a perfect Mexican restaurant per their tour guiding one day as we rented a car. Great margaritas and food! Our haul out went great. We ordered our new Honda generator, from Camping World of all places and it was delivered, after a little fiasco with the shipping, as we were to get it in Salinas originally. We also wanted to get a new, very trustworthy anchor we had heard about on the internet to replace our CQR anchor. I got online and ordered it and the new Rocna anchor was delivered. We steered *Kwanesum* into their travel lift to get hauled out of the water and taken to our new spot in their shop. We will stay on *Kwanesum* up in the air on the travel lift while they work on her. Ken's crew did an excellent job of attaching our new solar panel we ordered and putting on the new Rocna anchor. They were superb with the bottom paint job. It was a really good looking adobe red color. We had blue paint before. I like the red. Makes her look snazzy. We were so glad we made the decision to have the work done by Island Marine.

We took advantage of being in this beautiful area while they worked on our boat. We had a rental car so we drove through the hills one Sunday to find the best pig BBQ ever in the southern rain forest of Puerto Rico; the area Anthony Bourdain and Andrew Zimmern, the chefs extraordinaire from the Travel Channel, recommended. What a beautiful drive that was. We didn't make it to the big rain forest, El Yunque, but we did drive through another little rain forest area which was perfect. At the BBQ, we found the Pina Colada booth (imagine that!) along the main street, grabbed a couple and started walking around. There were so many people there! I guess it's something people do on Sunday after church. They gather here to enjoy the food and music and dance. There was music everywhere and these pig BBQ restaurants to die for! We found the one Andrew Zimmern suggested, El Rancho Original, and got in line for food. You could see the pig roasting on the pit through the window while we waited in line. I wasn't sure exactly what to order when we got up there, so we asked the couple in line ahead of us what they suggested. I'm glad I did, because other than the barbecued pork, I wasn't exactly sure what some of the other dishes were and what would go best with the pork. It was delicious!! People were dancing as others were sitting at their tables eating and watching. We had the best time. Amazing traditional food, perfect Pina Coladas and Heinekens were in our bellies as we watched everyone dance. They are such great dancers, too. Couples that obviously had been dancing the salsa together for many years. We were mesmerized by their smooth sequence of steps and movements. It was a really great day.

We decided to drive up the coast to find a Best Buy. It was important to me to have good music aboard. We found a new Sony car stereo we can install at the chart station. That will give us the music I've been wanting aboard, for down below and in the cockpit. We were disappointed to not find good Bose speakers, but we will keep looking. They only had large speaker packages for a whole theater type set up. We just need 2 small speakers. That can come later. In the meantime, we have a stereo we can hook our iPods to that will give us our tunes while watching the sun set. Some Jimmy Buffett, some Gordon Lightfoot...plus all the choices my iPod carries that are perfect for sailing. All these years....and I do love my music....we have not had music in the cockpit. Just with my standalone Bose docking station for my iPod and that takes electricity. Now we are all set. Happy me! Happy me!

We decide to drag out the heavy, cumbersome Sailrite sewing machine as we AGAIN had to repair our dodger. The StrataGlass had torn on the side panel. Ugh...I thought we had re-enforced it all. Apparently not. I also got the name of a fabulous fabric store in Fajardo that had all the outdoor type material I could ever imagine! I was looking for screening type material to make shade panels for the cockpit. The sun can get very hot out there and we want to be able to put up panels to diffuse the light and keep it cool. This store! I could have spent a fortune in there! It's called ONE, or something like that. Unfortunately, I didn't have a fortune or the time to look at everything. I found the Textaline I needed for my screening and some other things. We repaired the dodger and I made my screens. They work just great. I was extremely proud of myself! HA! We just need to figure out how we want to fasten them to our bimini so they will be easy to put on and off. We will live with them awhile to see what might work best.

We now have additional characters on board:

Rocky - our new anchor we are so excited about!

Hank - our Honda 2000 generator!

Sunny3 - our third solar panel - woohoo!

Blue - our new stereo (named because it lights up blue)

OK...are we ready to hit the Spanish Virgins?

• Bottom paint done?	Check.
• New solar panel?	Check.
• Honda generator?	Check.
• Rocna anchor?	Check.
• New stereo?	Check.
• Dodger repaired?	Check.
• Screens made?	Check.
• $$ at West Marine?	Check.

It's 106 miles to Chicago, we got a full tank of gas, half a pack of cigarettes, it's dark, and we're wearing sunglasses. Hit it.

- The Blues Brothers

Chapter 18
The Virgin Islands

Heaven's Gate

Ok, Captain Ran, we are heading into the beginning of the Virgin Islands. Oh my gosh! Did I ever think in my life before all this that I'd be sailing my own yacht in the Virgin Islands?? This is huge!

Technically the Spanish Virgins belong to Puerto Rico, but they are part of the Virgin Islands to our thinking. *"The Spanish Virgin Islands, formerly called the Passage Islands and also known as the Puerto Rican Virgin Islands, West Virgin Islands, primarily consisting of the islands of Culebra and Vieques, are part of the Commonwealth of Puerto Rico and are located east of the main island of Puerto Rico in the Caribbean."*

Thank you Wikipedia. We think it's always interesting to find out the history of where we are and where we've been and…where we're going!

We head out of Puerto del Rey and into some great winds for sailing. You mean we can finally sail? You betcha. Randy has all 3 sails up: the jib, the staysail, and the mainsail. We are on a beam reach and we are haulin' ! Love it! Our plan is to sail over to Vieques to Green Beach and spend the night. We are heading that direction. *"Kwanesum, Kwanesum,* this is *sans clés.* Over."* Its *sans clés!!!* These are our friends we buddy boated with from Hotel Rum Cay, you will remember, to Ocean World, DR. They left their boat in Ocean World to travel back to Oregon for hurricane season. We departed Ocean World before they returned. It was sooo good to hear from them!

Our plans quickly changed. We wanted to catch up with *sans clés.* The plan is to rendezvous in Puerto Ferro on Vieques. Roger that, we are on our way. Now we're even more excited. We are very compatible with *sans clés* as far as destination choices and daily activity choices. And we don't have a need to be with them all the time...which can be stifling if some folks want to spend all hours of the day with you. It's just a real pleasure traveling with *sans clés.* And we have learned so much from them as sailors. They are really good, experienced cruisers. We can't wait to see them again.

We round the corner of Vieques and go down to Puerto Ferro. Puerto Ferro is one of the bioluminescent areas that we wanted to experience. Like on the Pacific Coast, phosphorescence appears at night when the water is disturbed...as when your hand travels through it, or the dinghy travels through it, or dolphins and other fish travel through it. We will experience that tonight when we get to Puerto Ferro. We travel down the coast and turn into the little harbor.

Lyman, from *sans clés* travels out on his dinghy to greet us and help guide us into the harbor. It's so good to see him. We immediately drop anchor, get settled and dinghy over to *sans clés* for happy hour and appetizers Terri has so thoughtfully prepared! Hooray! We weathered Rum Cay with them, sailed for 3 days with them to Ocean World in the DR, did the 27 Charcos with them, drove around the island of the Dominican

Republic with them, then parted in July when they flew back to Oregon. Now we're together again...on the beautiful island of Vieques! Cheers!

We waited until it was pitch dark, later that night, and headed out in our dinghies to find the bioluminescence. Going back into some of the coves, we thought the water would be *'richer'* with the plankton that cause this spectacular event. As we drove the dinghies, I could see it in the wake the boats made. Like little sparklers going off. We were hoping to see some caused by fish, but we did not. It was still pretty cool and kinda fun running around in the dinghies at night. We spotted a large sailboat back there in the mangroves just sitting, waiting for hurricane season to end. Everything taken off of it, anchored and hunkered down back there all by itself. Someone had obviously trusted that all would be ok when they returned. I don't know how they do that. I couldn't leave my very expensive boat sitting at anchor with no one to watch it. To each their own.

We stayed 2 nights at Puerto Ferro. Terri spotted a great place on the charts for our next destination, Bahía Icacos, a little spot on the North side of Vieques, so off we went on a beautiful December morning. We round the east coast of Vieques and we can see islands off in the distance. "Randy...is that St Thomas?" "By golly, I think it is!" Randy radios *sans clés* to confirm our siting. Terri confirmed by saying, "I think this may be Heaven's Gate." It sure does look like Heaven's Gate. Wow. We are just dumbfounded that we are actually here, on these beautiful waters, in our own sailboat, looking at the Virgin Islands that we had read so much about and longed for. By golly, it pretty much is Heaven's Gate. From our vantage point we could see Puerto Rico, Culebra (the other Spanish Virgin Island), St Thomas and St John. We have made it! It was a milestone for us. This is what we had imagined for many, many years and now here we were, at Heaven's Gate.

We carefully picked our way around the east end of Vieques into Bahia Icacos between the corals on the northeast side. The water was like the Bahamas, wonderfully clear and spectacularly azure. Mother nature never fails to impress me with the colors she chooses to paint things. I loved this anchorage. We swam and snorkeled and visited the tiny island of Isla Yallis where I picked up shells for Abby, our son Kevin's little daughter. She has a shell collection going.

We had fresh lobster! A fisherman came by while we were at anchor and sold us 3 fresh caught lobsters. Oh my.... Randy dispatched them and put them on the barbecue, and it was THE BEST lobster I have ever had.

US and NATO Navys have used the east end of Vieques for land, air and sea-based war games and that was evident everywhere ashore. There were signs prohibiting us from going ashore at Icacos. There is still danger of possible unexploded ordinance on the island. We could, however, go onto the little island of Yallis. At night we could see lights ashore, and black vehicles, sometimes with police type lights glowing, driving around. We were sure they were spying on us. As you know, we do have a former CIA agent aboard. Perhaps they know this and are afraid. They should be very afraid. We were indeed quite curious what they were up to, though. Interesting.

We stayed and relaxed and swam and snorkeled and hunted shells at Icacos for 2 nights. Then on to Culebra, a very short trip. It's still very exciting seeing St Thomas and St John out in the distance. Beckoning to us. So cool. We went into the little harbor of the town of Dewey on Culebra. While here Terri can do some laundry and we can get on the internet again to catch up and upload pictures. It's a cute little town. We find a great grocery store that has wonderful produce and meats. It's fun finding these quirky little stores in the oddest places that are almost gourmet. We picked up quite a bit of things we needed and some that we didn't need but really wanted, like more rum and orange juice. I'm always on the lookout for fresh tomatoes and avocados, onions and potatoes, and good breads.

We need to fill our water tanks while were here so Lyman and Randy schlep water containers from dock to boat. From dock to boat. From dock to boat. Not the most fun thing to do, as it's time consuming and cumbersome schlepping the containers for water from dock to dinghy, from dinghy to the sailboat. Over and over.

We gather with Terri and Lyman at Mamacitas for mucho gin and tonics. They met up with friends from other boats they knew previously. Fun night had by all. Randy felt a little 'scratchy' the next morning, as our Australian friend Peter likes to say.

And now...into the United States Virgin Islands!

Anxiously, we get up early, weigh anchor and depart for St John, USVI. We decided to go directly there first.... bypassing St Thomas. We will go there later. St John is where Terri and Lyman got married so they are very excited to return. We head for Caneel Bay, which is adjacent to Cruz Bay. It's now 23 December so we are planning ahead for where we should have our Christmas dinner. It takes awhile to motor sail past St Thomas, but it's interesting watching the cruise ships come in to Charlotte Amalie, the capitol. Looks like a busy place. We continue to motor sail, as the direction is still with the wind on our nose. But that's ok. We put our mainsail up and our staysail and it makes for really smooth motor sailing and powers us up a bit more.

A milestone has happened here. All along our trip, since Virginia, we have used cruising guides. They are wonderful. As I said previously, they are written by those who have gone before and they give you charts and routes and places to see and places to eat and what to avoid, how and where to check in and out of each country…they've proven invaluable. We have now closed one of the most useful books, **The Gentleman's Guide to Passages South**. We had previously read and re-read this book in anticipation of traveling the Bahamas, the Dominican Republic and Puerto Rico. It's sort of the Bible of cruising this area. And now we have done it! We have traveled down the Intracoastal Waterway, we crossed the Gulf Stream into the Bahamas, we crossed from the Bahamas into the Dominican Republic, we crossed the Mona Passage into Puerto Rico, went through the Spanish Virgins and now into the Virgin Islands themselves! We close the **The Gentleman's Guide** and open the guide to the Virgin Islands. Holy cow. We are here!

We enter Caneel Bay on the island of St John… and there are mooring balls. This is our first mooring ball experience! They are everywhere in the Virgin Islands so we must learn to deal with them. No *problemo*. We have read what the procedure should be to catch the mooring ball and Terri and Lyman gave us good tips, too. So here we go. I'm at the helm and I head *Kwanesum* straight for the mooring ball we have chosen to latch on to and go very slowly. Randy stands on the side of the bow with the boat hook ready to snag the pennant that's attached to the mooring ball. I put the boat in neutral and let her drift slowly forward. Ran snags the pennant, I reversed it to stop the boat, Ran pulls our bow line through the pennant and attaches all to the bow and we're all set! That was easy! Safe Arrival Beer is warranted.

We are now mooring ball qualified.

We settle ourselves, clean up, and dinghy over to the Caneel Bay Resort. Very fancy place, I guess. We are ready for our fancy Virgin Island drinks. Everyone orders Bushwackers, except me. I order a Pina Colada. $10 a pop. OK. But we are celebrating so it is ok. Bushwackers are too ice-creamychocolaty for me. I'm laughingly picky, picky. We toast our arrival and order some appetizers, which are excellent. This is a top-notch resort, after all.

Randy and I and Terri and Lyman buzz over to Cruz Bay the next day in our dinghies, which is just a dinghy ride around the corner of the island from Caneel. Neat area. Ran and I went to the National Parks office to get our senior discount card for the mooring balls in the USVI. SENIOR DISCOUNT!! Are we that old already? Well, Randy is. You get half off the mooring price if you're 62 and over. We were advised of this by our friends Paul and Lynn and we are glad! So instead of paying $15/night, it's only $7.50. Every little bit helps. These moorages in the USVI are run by the National Parks Service so the senior discount card we got is the same one used in the States for National Parks there! We had no idea it could also be used here, on the water. Cool beans. In the meantime, in anticipation of Christmas, while we are here in Cruz Bay, Terri makes reservations for our Christmas dinner at Morgan's Mango. They had eaten there when here on their honeymoon. It sounds perfect.

It's rocky and rolly at anchor in Caneel Bay. There are a lot of ferries that go by lickety-split, and their wakes make for much rolling. We decide to move for the night. We leave that afternoon for Maho Bay, around the other corner of St. John. Also mooring balls. We are prepared… we get half off the price, and we are now mooring ball experts! So pretty here. We spend Christmas Eve, and we have carolers! A wonderful little family from one of the boats came by in their dinghy with their Santa hats on and serenaded us. How perfect! It was so sweet and made missing our family at Christmastime a little easier to deal with.

It's 25 December. Merry Christmas! We spent a leisurely Christmas morning at Maho Bay, then headed back to Caneel Bay to prepare for our Christmas dinner at Cruz Bay.

We've got the BAYS down. Again, the anchorage is rolly here, but it's ok. It's Christmas! We dinghy'd over to Cruz Bay, had drinks and bought some neato wine glasses at a little kiosk bar in Mongoose Junction before dinner, had a wonderful dinner and toasted everyone. Missed our family terribly but was glad to be able to share Christmas Day with Terri and Lyman.

Again we pick up and go around the corner of St. John, past Maho Bay to Leinster Bay and Waterlemon Cay... or Watermelon Cay. We have seen it written both ways in the guidebooks and charts, and we're not sure which is right! Doesn't matter... it's spectacular. (I looked it up, finally, and it is Waterlemon Cay. And now you know.) We stay there for 3 days, swimming, snorkeling, hiking to the sugar plantation ruins. It was a beautiful place. We meet up with *Opal* there! Marc! And he has Amber with him, whom we had met in Nassau. So fun. We have dinner together on *sans clés*. Marc and Amber are headed to Jost Van Dyke, BVI for New Year's. There's a huge party at Foxy's. It's the place to be... unless you don't want to deal with a zillion people all in the dinghies. We opt to wait for the Foxy experience. But we so love Marc and Amber. It's good to see them. Amber is a teacher from Delaware, so she's just out for the holiday. Her goal is to buy her own boat one day. I love that about her!

Lyman and Terri leave a day early, as they had some things they needed to do back on St. Thomas at Red Hook at American Yacht Harbor. We spend the extra day at Waterlemon Cay and then go back to Caneel. I want to see more of Cruz Bay, and we have things we need to pick up at the hardware store there. There are some nice upscale grocery stores and shopping areas there. We do lots of walking around and have a great lunch overlooking the bay.

The next day, Ran and I decide to take the ferry across to Red Hook in St. Thomas and go to the marine store there and have lunch. It's a rainy day. We find Terri and Lyman at the marina and decide we'll all go to Christmas Cove for New Year's Eve. The weather is super lousy... raining all day... and we want a nice calm anchorage. Terri and Lyman leave for Christmas Cove, and we do our chores there, head back to our boat at Caneel, and take off to Christmas Cove. We wanted to see fireworks somewhere but the weather was so bad we just decided to go to this neat cove on St. James Island across from St. Thomas. It was a perfect decision. I LOVED Christmas Cove.

In my opinion, Christmas Cove has the best snorkeling so far. We are well protected from the seas and winds there. It's New Year's Eve! I cook turkey legs and wings in my pressure cooker, Terri makes a great potato salad, I make a cabbage salad, too and we toast in the new year... early... about 2000hrs or so. Cheers! Happy New Year to everyone.

We just enjoy the heck out of Christmas Cove...swimming, snorkeling, having happy hours watching the sunset. We dinghy across to St Thomas to the St Thomas Yacht Club one day where we can get online. Neat club. And of course I buy a St Thomas Yacht Club ball cap. We have lunch, do all our internet stuff and dinghy back making plans to return the next day and hike down to the main road, catch a safari taxi for $1/person and go into Charlotte Amalie, the capitol of St Thomas and the USVI. Randy and I were looking for new computers and we thought we might find some down where the cruise ships come in at the duty free shops. Next day we did as planned, dinghy'd across to the Yacht Club, tied our dinghy up there with permission, and we walked and walked and walked until we found the main road. Whew! Good exercise. But not attractive when you get all sweaty. We grab a safari taxi and head into Charlotte Amalie. We peruse the shops all along the harbor, but they have no computers. Only every other thing you can possibly imagine. We walk along the bay back toward the Yacht Harbor looking for a Radio Shack. Might be a computer possibility. We find it, but no computers. But we find a good place for lunch and Bushwackers…and for me, of course…a Painkiller. I have a wonderful Caesar Salad with calamari. That hit the spot! Charlotte Amalie from the vantage point that we had that day is not worth the trip. Not our kind of spot. But I'm glad we went.

No computers there but we do know where Office Max is in Red Hook on St Thomas. So we jump on the safari taxi back and stop off and buy 2 new computers. Coolness! We safari taxi from there and then walk and walk and walk back to the St Thomas Yacht Club where our dinghies are. This time, carrying a bag with computers. Ugh. We definitely got our exercise that day!

The weather is starting to turn again, and we are starting to rock a lot, so we decided to move across the bay to a better location to anchor. We choose Great Bay on St Thomas. This is where the Ritz Carlton is. Nice little bay and we find a spot along the shore that keeps us turned in the right direction for the winds and seas. Much more comfortable. In the meantime, we watch the patrons of the Ritz enjoy the toys they have: Hobie Cats, kite surfing, and canoes. They're all having fun. Too bad the weather isn't better.

It is decided that we all need to go into the marina at Red Hook the next day. Everyone needs to get supplies, do laundry, get on the internet and get mail. We call American Yacht Harbor and arrange to be in there for two days. We head in there after spending one night at Great Bay. Again…nice to have lots of power and lots of water to take long showers! The

214

Internet isn't what it should be but we at least have it. I do 7 loads of laundry....with HOT water. Sheets and towels need hot water. Everything came out smelling so nice and fresh and clean. They were so nice in the Laundromat. We get all our chores done there...water, fuel, laundry, mail received, new snorkel fins purchased (I LOVE, LOVE my new snorkel fins), Mexican food fix....done deal. Terri and Lyman left the day before to anchor out. Now we are ready to go. Let's hit it!

Chapter 19
British Virgin Islands

We Meet Foxy!

We are departing American Yacht Harbor, Red Hook, St Thomas, USVI at 0945hrs on 8 January 2010. WE ARE HEADED TO THE BRITISH VIRGIN ISLANDS!! Woohoo! This is big. This is the dream. USVI...yes. But BVI??!! That's the beginning of the rest of our trip down island. This is very cool. We talk to *sans clés* on the VHF and decide we are all heading to Jost Van Dyke (named after a Dutch pirate)...to Great Harbor, where the famous Foxy's is! We can go through customs there. It's a perfect day.

Foxy is a legend in the Virgin Islands. We have read in all of our sailing magazines about him for years. To get to Jost Van Dyke and then to Foxy's is huge for Randy and me. I know... it doesn't seem like much in the scheme of things, but it has been part of the dream! And Jost Van Dyke is the island Kenny Chesney sings about... **No Shoes, No Shirt, No Problem**. To semi-quote from Peter Farrell, who wrote about him, Foxy is a delightful, very colorful Caribbean character who has created a unique island paradise. Foxy is an entertainer, entrepreneur, philosopher, community activist, world traveler, conservationist, musician, storyteller, cultural historian, fisherman, comedian, sailor – a true West Indian Renaissance Man. Just this past year, Foxy received a medal as a member of the Order of the British Empire for his exemplary contributions to tourism and preservation of the Territory's culture. Quite the guy. Gotta find Foxy.

We set our anchor in Great Harbor at Jost Van Dyke and wait for the rain to pass. Seems like it's raining a lot here! It's still paradise. The rain finally subsides, and we dinghy in to check into customs. Island customs people are their usual not-friendly-we-don't-smile, surly selves. Not sure why, but they all seem to be like that on these islands. Particularly the women with power. We finish our forms and get it all done with no problem. They charged us 20 cents for the forms. But surly customs people are not the best welcome to a new country. What's so hard about smiling and saying hi? Perhaps, as Terri suggested, if they are friendly they will not command as powerful a presence as their position requires. Perhaps.

We're hungry, so we hunt out a spot along the beach. We find Corsairs… and Vinnie. It looks like our kind of place from the outside. We walk in and are immediately greeted with folks having fun and Vinnie with a big smile. THAT is what we are looking for! We order Red Stripe beers… they're Jamaican, but why not? We haven't had those yet. We ask for a menu as we haven't had lunch. He's sent the chef home. Shoot! But… he says… just walk next door and order something from them. They will bring it down. I do that, at the little shack-like place next door… order chicken and fries, what they said they had… to share with Ran… then back to my beer. No Shoes… No Shirt… No Problem. A great way to start our BVI entrance. Terri and Lyman join us, and we mosey on down to Foxy's! Excellent.

It's just plain a neat area… Great Harbor. I like it a lot. Not sure what I'm expecting at Foxy's but it's about what I thought. Lots of beach, cruiser, island, laid-back, tag-we've-been-here kind of place. I like it. We check out the bar and order our drinks, talking with Hedrick, the bartender. As we stand there drinking and talking, another tourist type rushes in very important-like and orders a beer. It's for Foxy, he says, very self-important and rushed like. All red in the face. Whoa! Cool! Foxy's out back, Hedrick says. Go back and say hi! We grab our drinks and head back there. There is a huge stage area out back, and Foxy is sitting in a chair with all this weird stuff lined up on the lawn below the stage. Lines with tree branches and poofed out black stuff. Foxy is busy poofing out some of the black stuff, and there are 2 tourists hanging all over him for pictures, one being the self-important tourist that came in and got the beer for him. We stand back and watch… while they look overly star-struck fawning all over Foxy. Finally, they're done, and we go up and introduce ourselves, and he asks where we're from. We tell him, and he immediately goes into poetry about the Bay area of California and the Portland area of Oregon. It's so cool! He mentions in his sing/song poetry way all the spots we frequent. He's quite the showman, obviously. We had no idea we would get to see/meet him. That was quite a treat. There is a large wooden ship back there up on stanchions that apparently Foxy has arranged so students can work on it and learn the trade of building boats. How great is that? A great day for us, indeed.

Next up, we are going cruising around, here and there, with *sans clés* checking out all the islands… the British Virgin Islands. From Great Harbor, we did a day anchorage right on the beach at White Bay, still on Jost Van Dyke, in front of the Soggy Dollar Bar, so named because you must swim ashore from your boat and your dollars get wet. Apparently, and from their mouths, they invented the Painkiller drink!! My favorite! But I must say

I'm partial to the Pusser's Rum version that I got accustomed to in Annapolis, Maryland when we lived back East, at the Annapolis Boat Shows.

Pusser's Rum –

SINCE THE DAYS OF WOODEN SHIPS & IRON MEN

Rum Made to the Admiralty's Specifications

Pusser's Painkiller Recipe - for your enjoyment, dear reader.

'A delightful blend of Pusser's Rum, pineapple juice, orange juice, and cream of coconut, served on the rocks with an orange slice and a cherry, then topped off with freshly grated nutmeg.'

Ingredients

2-ounces (60 ml) Pusser's Rum

4-ounces (120 ml) pineapple juice

1-ounce (30 ml) orange juice

1-ounce (30 ml) cream of coconut

Freshly grated nutmeg

Directions

Add liquid ingredients to a cocktail shaker and shake vigorously.

Pour into a big glass or goblet filled with ice. Grate fresh nutmeg on top.

Garnish with an orange slice and cherry.

Be careful–this is a smooth and sneaky drink. Enjoy!

The Pusser's Painkiller® Story

- as told on pussersrum.com

A version of the classic Pusser's Painkiller® had its start at the six-seat Soggy Dollar Bar on a long stretch of white sand beach at White Bay on the island of Jost Van Dyke in the British Virgin Islands. There's no dock, so the usual way in is to swim. Of course, your dollars get wet, hence the name "Soggy Dollar Bar." It was owned by an English lady, Daphne Henderson. Boaters, including Pusser's founder, Charles Tobias, came from distant places to sample her version of the Painkiller for which she'd become locally famous. The fact that Tobias had gone to The Admiralty Board of the Royal Navy and gained permission to commercialize the rum in 1979 made him curious about this deliciously concocted recipe made with Pusser's Rum.

Daphne Henderson and Charles Tobias became good friends, but in spite of their close friendship, and no matter how he tried, she refused to divulge her secret recipe for the cocktail. Two years passed. One late Sunday afternoon, after a morning spent "killing the pain," Tobias somehow managed to get one of her concoctions back through the surf and over the gunwale into his boat, and ultimately into his kitchen on Tortola where he lives. There we went to work trying to match her flavor as closely as possible with his own recipe, which he finally worked out to be a "4-1-1-1" ratio—four parts pineapple, one part cream of coconut and one part orange juice, adding Pusser's Rum to suit.

The following Sunday, Tobias returned to her bar and announced to the patrons on hand that he had finally broken her secret. So he mixed one of his and circulated it for comments. Tobias discerned a slight difference, but thought his mixture to be better, not quite so sweet as hers, and told her so. The ten patrons gathered around the bar unanimously preferred his version to hers, and the rest is history!

Soon after, Tobias started promoting Pusser's Painkillers®, first at the Road Town Pub and then at his restaurants at West

End and on Marina Cay. But he has always given Daphne Henderson credit with a by-line in Pusser's printed media: "AS INSPIRED BY DAPHNE AT THE SOGGY DOLLAR BAR AT WHITE BAY ON JOST VAN DYKE." From this modest beginning, the fame of the Pusser's Painkiller® has not only spread throughout the boating and sailing communities but to the bars, corner pubs, chain restaurants, and some of the finest cocktail venues throughout the world.

And now you know how to enjoy a Painkiller Cocktail!

It's the little things along the cruising path that make the experience.

A beautiful beach here in front of the Soggy Dollar Bar. We found our spot to anchor and jumped in to swim ashore with Terri and Lyman. We all ordered chicken roti for lunch, at the suggestion of Terri, Painkillers for Terri and me, and beer for Randy and Lyman. All was a perfect suggestion to enjoy this island paradise. We played the cruisers' beach game of trying to get the ring on the hook like we played in Rum Cay. We got pretty good at this on Rum Cay... Lyman is still the champ. And we just relaxed. Until a small party boat bringing guests to swim and snorkel decided to park WAY too close to our boat. So close they put a fender out. Randy swam out and told them what a BAD idea that was. "It's ok," the guy said. "We have a fender out." "Look, bub... if you have to put a fender out, you're too damn close! Move!" Ahhhh... the joys of boating. Maybe we are overprotective, but I don't think so.

Since that's just a day anchorage, when we exhausted our memorable time there at the Soggy Dollar, we swam back to our boats and went around the corner to Little Harbor for the night. Small, quiet place... with mooring balls. $25/night. Our US Senior National Park cards don't work in the British Virgin Islands, so we pay the $25. Cynthia comes around in her little boat to collect our fee. She's delightful. Gives us coupons to eat/drink ashore but we're all eat/drink'd out so we will save the coupons for another time.

From Little Harbor, the next day we go to Green Cay where Sandy Spit is on Little Jost Van Dyke. Terri and Lyman know of this place as a great snorkeling area. It's also near Diamond Cay which has Foxy's Taboo, another one of his establishments. It's beautiful here! Randy and I sit on our boat just thinking about how we've dreamed of getting to places like this. And now we're here. On our own sailboat! It's continually surreal to think that we've actually done this! We've actually done what we've dreamed of doing for years. We swam and snorkeled... had a great day. A boat is coming toward us... and now they're honking... it's *Allegro*! Camilla and Peter, our Australian friends we met at Ocean World Marina in the Dominican Republic right before we left. How fun! I had been in touch via email with Camilla so they knew kind of where we would be... and that we wanted to find Sandy Spit because it reminds us of the screensaver we have all had on our computers one time or another. They have 2 of their kids with them, Simon, who's 19, and Lauren, who's 18, I believe. So fun to see them. We all decide to dinghy over to Foxy's Taboo that evening for drinks and dinner. Another great evening.

It started getting really rocky at Sandy Spit, so we decided with *sans clés* to go to Soper's Hole on Tortola, right across the bay. We bid *Allegro* farewell, and we will see them again. Soper's Hole is a great sheltered harbor but has mooring balls, so again $25/night. It's just so much cheaper when you can anchor. Saving here and there helps a lot! But it's fun to be at Soper's Hole and see my first Pusser's Landing in the BVIs and have Painkillers. Sounds like my life revolves around my drinks, but it really doesn't. It's just that these fun drinks are... so... fun! It's like going to Hawaii and having a Mai Tai. You know you've arrived.

We stayed at Soper's Hole one night. Got online at the Jolly Roger Restaurant there so we could upload pictures and check our mail. Then we went back to Little Jost Van Dyke, this time anchoring at East End Harbor which is a little more sheltered. The weather is still pretty brisk and rainy. We anchored ourselves good and solidly in there, also putting out stern anchors to keep us facing the direction that was most comfortable for the weather we were having. This consists of having our main anchor on the front down and holding and then putting a smaller anchor on the stern to hold you in one direction.

We anchored there 2 nights. Mostly just staying down below out of the weather. But it was still really rocky and in checking the weather, it sounds like it's going to last a few more days. We decide to go back into Soper's Hole to wait it out. Fine with me! I can finish my blog and get it uploaded with pictures, I can catch up on my email and Facebook, I can have a Painkiller if I feel like it and I need to buy some beach towels. They have great shops here. I sat down below out of the weather working on the blog and reading books. There's always lots of action when you're in a harbor, no matter where you are. We like to watch the goings-on. Today we watched boats racing for the limited mooring balls to get out of the weather. There are only so many in the harbor, so you have to grab one quickly! We will go over to the Jolly Roger Restaurant later and have a late lunch. That is if the rain lets up a bit.

It's an interesting thing, sailing these Virgin Islands. You longingly look forward to getting here… you arrive… they're wonderful… gorgeous… magnificent … and fun… but now what? We sort of feel like we're partied out! LOVE the snorkeling. I could do that all day every day… well maybe not 'all day every day' but a lot. But not every place has that available. We are staying in and around the USVIs and the BVIs in anticipation of our youngest son and his wife coming to visit.

Skip and Kim. We can't wait to see them and are planning our route for their short stay with us. And we are anxious to show them some of our favorite spots in the short time they're here.

But in the meantime... we've decided these BVI islands are pretty much just tourist islands. That's not a bad thing but... it's interesting for us, as full-time cruisers who live on their boat all the time. We like to find places to explore on the islands and so far it seems these are mostly resorts/ shops/ restaurants/ bars. They are so beautiful, but there are so many charter boats. And all the islands seemed to be geared to charter boats or big cruise ships. I would venture to say there are 8 charter boats for every 2 privately owned boats. Or more. And that's fun. I don't mean to sound negative, but it's sort of an invasive thing. In a way. We are tourists, too, so that's kind of an odd observation, but what I'm getting at is when we go to a new island here, it's about grabbing a mooring ball or an anchor spot before the next guy gets it! Parking lot activity! Then it's party city. And I love that... as most of you know I would, but when we are here all the time, it gets a little much. I don't want to sound like I'm whining, and I actually feel really odd making these statements, but I guess I never realized how MANY charters there would be and how many people on each charter boat. But then again, I would recommend people to do just that, as this is so great and fun and beautiful! I'm just a little worried about the space all these boats take up... particularly the catamarans. We need to take care of what we have as best we can and I guess the number of people startles me a bit. When you snorkel some of these places, you actually run into people! They've just come in on a big fat catamaran, and there are 25 or 30 of them all at once trying to snorkel in a relatively small area. Then that boat calls their people back, and a new boat comes in with the same thing. Interesting.

I'm all for people enjoying seeing all of this and having fun, and, as I said, that's exactly what we're doing, so I shouldn't be worried about it, but I'm wondering what it will be like in a few more years? It feels like you're in line at Disneyland sometimes out here. I don't know the solution… or even if it's a problem, it's just my observation. I guess I didn't expect this. And we can move on… to different islands south, and we will. I think it just caught me by surprise, as I have never been here before.

We've noticed in the BVIs… particularly since we have just reentered the USVIs where the anchorages are run by the parks dept… they cram the mooring buoys into their anchorages. Then they charge you $25/night. In Waterlemon Bay on St John, USVI, the moorings are far apart. You aren't allowed to anchor here unless there are no moorings at all. So it seems more peaceful. They only charge you $15 here or $7.50 if you're over 62 like us. There, it isn't a noisy-I'm-having-too-much-fun restaurant/bar thing going. Trust me, I like those too, but I think this peacefulness is what it's all about.

We ended up weathered in at Soper's Hole, BVIs for 3 days. Awfully glad it's a good protective harbor for not-so-great weather conditions. In the meantime, we got lots of internet work done at the Jolly Roger, where they have a good signal and great pizza and beer. A good combination for us. Finally, the weather turned gorgeous and we were ready to leave. Our next destination will be Norman Island. We filled up with water and provisions and tried to get our propane tank filled but failed to do so. Something about our little propane tank is not compatible with a lot of propane places. Well, that's a pain in the rear. We had trouble in Puerto Rico, too, but they finally figured out how to fill it. We need propane to cook so it's kind of an essential product. Though I guess we could eat out all the time. I'm not much for cooking anyway. But that wouldn't be good. As much as I like having people cook and wait on me, those home-cooked meals can't be beat. So we will try to get it filled when we get to another marina area. After a bit of a George and Gracie morning, we're off. (For those who remember who George and Gracie were.)

Our first stop will be The Indians, just off Pelican Island on the way to Norman Island. I believe it was named so because it looks like the feathers on the Indian's headdress. It's a wonderful snorkel spot. The jutting rocks make cliffs of sort on which the coral has grown. Unfortunately, it's very popular, too. We are still traveling with our friends on *sans clés* and they were able to find a mooring ball right away. We had to drive around and around and wait for one of the other boats to finish before we could snag a mooring. There are only a few moorings available here, and that's a good thing — that way, there are not so many people snorkeling about at one time. So we patiently waited. We noticed a boat making preparations as if to leave so we stationed ourselves near in a position that indicated... *"This is our spot...just TRY to take it from us!"* There were other boats waiting as well. Finally, we can jump in and enjoy. Snorkeling is such a peaceful thing. You are floating and all you hear is your breathing. I like it. And I love seeing the different fish. The coral is interesting, but the fish are what I love. Just watching them.

Now to our final destination, Norman Island in the Sir Francis Drake Channel. To The Bight, which is a well-protected anchorage there. We grab a mooring ball after checking to see if there were places to anchor...and settle in. Norman Island is referred to as Treasure Island. It's beautiful here. Apparently, legend has it that there is sunken treasure about. Perhaps I shall dive and recover doubloons!

We jump in the dinghy and go into the Pirates Bight restaurant for lunch. It's fun to see people at these restaurants as everyone is in a great *'I'm on vacation!'* mood... in their swim wear or shorts and flip flops. My kinda place, 98% of the time.

226

We watched some folks play a game of stacking blocks of wood. Often there are silly games of this sort to challenge you at these places, particularly the more casual spots like this. I guess it's a Jenga game, but we didn't know the name at the time.

Gorgeous day, the next one! I relaxed in the morning on the bow of the boat with my book and watched the goings on in the little harbor. So nice. In the afternoon we dinghy'd over to Treasure Point and snorkeled and explored the caves which were fabulous. We snorkeled a long time. Loved it. Then…a charter company dumped off about 20 people and that was annoying as it stirred up the water too much, but it was still fun.

Chapter 20
The Willy T

Too Much Fun!

We dinghy'd back and had a beer at the *Willy T*, aka the *William Thornton*, a floating restaurant/bar named for the architect of the US Capital building. Our guide book said the vessel is a replica of a topsail lumber schooner and measures 93 feet long. Stories of raucous fun and abandon run rampant about the *Willy T*. It's all pretty much validated by the x-rated slide show that continually plays at the bar showing the antics of past patrons. We decided to come back for dinner later so we made reservations just in case. Dinner was fun. Not the greatest but it didn't matter. People start piling on the *Willy T* as the night goes on. WHAT A GREAT DAY!

Here at the Bight, and also at Cooper and Peter Islands, the supply vessel *Deliverance* makes rounds about 1700hrs to see if you need anything. They have just about everything you might be lacking. And they take your garbage! For a fee of course. But sometimes that's a great service. Looking for places to take your garbage can be a challenge. Some places are free...some charge you a small fee. Also if you need anything special you just hail

Deliverance on the VHF and they will bring it to you. Pretty neat little business. Randy likes it best when the cute girls in their bikinis deliver.

We decided to move closer to the inside of the bay and try to anchor, saving us $25/day. We did find a good spot as did *sans clés*. Excellent. Then it started to rain. We set up our rain catcher, which I made for days such as this. Kinda funky but it works pretty well! It blows around when empty and the wind is going crazy so not sure if that's a good thing. But what a concept, yeah? Catching your own fresh water? We did catch some water in our bucket and in our rain catcher. Pretty cool. Our boat holds 160 gallons of fresh water, which is pretty good. We figure we average maybe 10 gallons of water per day, give or take. So we are good for a long time, but it would be so fun to top off the tank with rain water.

The night was busy! Pirates Bight had music...sort of reggae...wannabe reggae. They weren't very good but they were loud! I had to put earplugs in when we went to bed. They didn't last long. *Willy T* had music, too, but we were far enough away from them to not hear it much. The harbor was busy with dinghies zipping here and there. When you looked out...there was a *'sea'* of anchor lights from all the boats. Pretty cool. Wish I could have captured that on film. We had an early dinner and watched more episodes of *Deadwood*. We bought all 3 seasons in Puerto Rico. We started watching the series when we lived in Virginia, but then we stopped HBO and never finished it. Love that show. Hate when it will be over. We don't watch TV as we have no antenna or cable, so movies it is...or books. We do tons of reading, too. And... Sudoku. And...play cards, dominoes, etc. And...I beat Randy at Scrabble. The wind and rains came up again that night. We caught more water in our bucket and in our rain catcher.

Next day was nice. We piled in our dinghies and went in to the Pirates Bight to have lunch and work on our computers. That is, we tried to work on computers. We can get a small signal from the boat but we wanted to go in and get a strong signal. We were working great when their system went down. Finally Terri asked them to try to reboot it and it was fine. They just aren't tuned into computers like we are. They could care less if the system is working right or not. Made me miss my tech guys from work! Terri and I played Scrabble. She won. Crap. I need to tune up my brain. There was more music that night from the Pirates Bight, but this time the band sounded 100% better and not as LOUD!

We watched more *Deadwood* that night and I finished my book and started another. Saw a topless lady on a Swedish boat today. Randy got all excited until he zoomed in on her with the binoculars. Guess she was older than he was expecting. She piled in a dinghy with 3 other guys…that also looked older…and off they went! Somewhere! Maybe to snorkel? We weren't sure. Hmmmmm….

The next day we departed The Bight on Norman Island. Just as we got outside, our engine overheated. Oops! Part of our routine when motoring is watching the engine rpms, the oil pressure and the temperature. "Good eye, Randy." Ran caught it right away. "Stop the engine, El, while I put up the sails!!" We were heading to Cooper Island and at this point were just off Pelican Island where The Indians snorkel area was. We stopped the engine, Randy pulled up the mainsail and went below to see what was wrong while I manned the helm. It was a fan belt. Randy scrambled around and found the new belt in his spare parts duffel and proceeded to change it. I was monitoring the boat, at sail, in very light winds and felt we were getting too close to Pelican Island. "Uh…Ran. I'm going to tack. I don't like the direction we're going and that we're getting so close to

Pelican Island." "Roger that", Randy mumbled with his head inside the engine compartment. I tacked through the wind to point the boat away from the island. It was a good move. I had to reach through the dodger opening and muscle the boom over to allow the wind to catch the mainsail as there was virtually no wind. It all went well. Randy got the belt changed, we started up the engine and she worked perfectly. Excellent. Love that smart husband of mine that knows how to change fan belts. He's my hero!

We were headed to Salt Bay to snorkel on the shipwreck of the *Rhone* before proceeding on to Cooper Island. According to Wikipedia, the RMS *Rhone* was a British packet ship owned by the Royal Mail Steam Packet Company. She was wrecked off the coast of Salt Island in the British Virgin Islands on 29 October 1867 during a hurricane. We grabbed a mooring ball at the wreck site. The seas were pretty busy but it was fine. It was an interesting snorkel experience. Ran and I swam from the boat to the wreck. Terri and Lyman anchored farther out so they took their dinghy. From there we motored to Cooper's Island at Manchioneel Bay. We grabbed a mooring and relaxed. We missed our first grab which is the first time that happened. I didn't have the boat facing into the wind and the wind pushed us past the pennant grabbing spot. No problem, I turned the boat and we tried again. We relaxed and had lunch and then dinghy'd over to snorkel at Cistern Point.

Now this is quite a feat for me. Dinghying over to snorkel. The dinghy over…I can do. The jumping in the water from the dinghy…I can do. Getting back into the dinghy from the water…not easy for Ellen. Randy rigged up a stirrup on a line across the bow of the dinghy so I can get a leg up. Not an attractive sight but it works. While snorkeling I saw a barracuda so I quickly swam back to the boat hoping that guy wasn't following me. They do like to follow you. And they won't harm you if you leave them alone but they look imposing. I didn't want to look back at him because I didn't know if he saw me and I didn't want to know if he was still there!

After a great day of snorkeling, we went back to the boat and waited for our dinner reservations at the Cooper Island Restaurant while watching everyone come into the anchorage and try to grab mooring balls. It can be very interesting watching other boats. Sometimes Randy and I are really catty and rate them on how well they are doing. We're so perfect, you know. We gussied up and went in for dinner with Lyman and Terri. It was very good. We toasted with Bushwackers and my Painkiller! Randy is letting his hair grow long and he looked extra handsome that night. Very *suavé* and captain-of-the-boat-like. It was another really good evening with Terri and Lyman.

We had a Tania Aebi sighting at Cooper Island. Tania Aebi is a woman who completed a solo circumnavigation of the globe in a 26-foot sailboat between the age of 18 and 21. Most of us cruisers have read her book *Maiden Voyage* about her trip. Quite a feat. Today there are two 16-year-old girls out there on the ocean trying to do the same thing but they've got a lot more equipment they can use now. Still, quite a feat. Tania now, apparently, does training on sailboats and there were 2 charter boats full of women moored there at Cooper Island that she was in charge of. Kind of neat for us to see her.

We left Cooper Island to try to catch a mooring at The Baths on Virgin Gorda. We didn't leave early enough, darn it. There were only yellow buoys left and Randy and I thought they were designated commercial use only. We later found out this was not true at this spot. Terri and Lyman took one and asked about it when they went ashore. Apparently it is ok to grab one of those for the day. I should have researched that better. Rats.

Ran and I took *Kwanesum* on in to Virgin Gorda Yacht Harbor where we had reservations for 2 nights. We can visit The Baths another day. We have time. We easily got into the marina. Nice place, but small. We had lunch and a beer and watched all the Sunsails charter people bring their charter boats back, again rating how they did. We are so tacky! We also watched some apparently wealthy people have lunch on the back of their large yacht. It was odd to us why they had their yacht facing the shore restaurant instead of facing the ocean? As we are sitting there having our burger and beer, they are being served by several crew, a quite fancy meal with wine. Ahhh…the life of the rich and famous. In the marina we got on the internet…so nice to have it on the boat. I need to get my fix on the internet. We relaxed and at happy hour took our cocktails down to *sans clés*, who had since arrived, and sat there for hours analyzing life. Another great day in the Virgin Islands.

Busy day, the next. Had the laundry done. It cost too much, but it was nice having someone else wash/dry/fold while I worked on other chores. I finally mended the dodger. It's like wrestling with a crocodile trying to get that thing in the sewing machine. Stupid dodger/bimini hasn't lasted worth a darn. I keep having to mend it. The threads have rotted out and the canvas, supposedly good quality Sunbrella, has faded terribly. This is about the only thing I'm unhappy with on our boat. I love the style of the dodger/bimini, but for the amount of money we spent it sure hasn't lasted. But then again…the sun is harsh out here on the ocean.

Randy worked on a bridle for the dinghy so we can tow it if we want. We went to the little store to get provisions. Spent too much money on lousy coffee. I miss my Starbucks French Roast! For the life of me I can't figure out why Starbucks hasn't invaded this area yet. The Pottses (Terri and Lyman) came over for happy hour and we again solved the problems of life and reminded ourselves of our favorite movies. Later Ran and I finished watching *Deadwood*. Darn it. I wish they made more seasons. I'm going to miss it. Slept really good. Not always the case.

Off to Gorda Sound today. We sailed a tiny bit, then motored in. It's still really windy. You might say that's good for a sailor, but too much wind in the wrong direction doesn't make for good travel. This area has lots to see: Saba Rock, the Bitter End Yacht Club, Leverick Bay and some other anchorages.

We toured around and found a good spot to anchor off of Prickly Pear Island. We can dinghy in to Saba Rock and the Bitter End and to Leverick Bay from here. This is the last of the BVIs after which we will go on to the Leeward Islands when we're ready. The water doesn't seem as clear at our anchorage but maybe that's because of the winds and currents. But it's a beautiful blue. We watched a gorgeous tall ship come in and another multi masted cruise ship come in. It's nice to have a good anchorage that's close to all we need to see. It's still very windy but not rocky too much. Tonight we watched a *Die Hard* movie. We're running out of movies! There is lots of book trading as we go along but not so much with movies. We trade back and forth with *sans clés* but I think we've about seen all of our inventory.

Today we went in to Saba Rock for lunch, taking our computers to catch up on stuff. It's a beautiful day but it's kind of a choppy ride in the dinghy. And our dinghy engine hasn't been working well…STILL! I'm so sick of that stupid Yamaha 9.9 four stroke piece of crap! The lunch was ok and VERY expensive. Beers were $5.50. (Remember, Dear Reader, this was 2010.) Too much! It was almost $70 for the 2 of us for lunch including drinks. Nice place though. Since we are anchored off of Prickly Pear Island which is a ways out, the trip in with the dinghy got Randy VERY wet. The water always splashes on the side he needs to sit on to run the engine. Should have bought a hard bottom dinghy. Haven't I said this before?! HA!

It was a really windy night so Ran and I were up and down all night, making sure things were ok. We both dove on the anchor this morning just to check and it hadn't budged at all. Love our Rocna anchor! We went into the Bitter End Yacht Club today. Another wet dinghy ride and our engine was really acting up today. The Bitter End is not really a yacht club, but a resort. It's beautiful, but we were a little disappointed in the place. It's very expensive. I guess that's to be expected. They only had a buffet to offer at the main restaurant for $28 per person. Didn't look like what we wanted. We ate lunch at their pub instead. We had quesadillas that we shared. They were pretty good but, again, it's not enough for the price.

But the place is just gorgeous.

Terri and I found some lounge chairs overlooking the beach and sat and talked all afternoon while Lyman and Randy did the hike of the island. That was fun. Now we've decided to dinghy across to Leverick Bay thinking we would hit their happy hour and therefore cheaper drinks! But when we got there, their happy hour didn't start until 5! Ugh! It was only 1600hrs! At the Bitter End and Saba Rock the happy hours started at 1600hrs. Doggoneit! Well…we're here…we need to order drinks. What the heck. Bushwackers and my Painkiller ordered up. $8 each. And they're too small for that price. Ugh. Oh well! We still had a lovely time with a lovely view. Tomorrow off to Trellis Bay.

Off we go the next morning to Trellis Bay on Tortola. We sailed but it was hard. The wind was behind us and the seas were following but choppy. It's hard to hold the boat steady and keep from accidentally jibing. To explain the jibe, here is a blurb from the web: *"A jibe or gybe is a sailing maneuver where a sailing vessel turns its stern through the wind, such that the wind direction changes from one side of the boat to the other. Because of the inherent dangers in jibing (uncontrolled, the boom can travel almost 180° with great speed and lethal force), communication with the crew is important."* It's also important for the helmsman (me) to pay attention! We did an accidental jibe once. I wasn't paying attention. Damn. But it was ok. I concentrated much harder the rest of the journey. We are finding our auto helm, aka Max Headroom, doesn't seem to be holding right. But then with the wind behind us and following seas it's more of a challenge for Max, too. We will have that checked when we get to the marina in Red Hook at the end of February.

We made our way into Trellis Bay and we see our friend Marc on *Opal*! Yay! Fun to see him here. It was very busy in there with several boats trying to find a mooring, though there were plenty to be had at this time of day. It gets a little more crazy toward the end of the day when people try to find moorings that are no longer available. I avoided banging into a couple of boats milling around the mooring, but it was ok. This weekend is the Full Moon Party here. Saturday night. That should be fun! Marc dinghy'd over when we were settled and we visited with him and then made plans with Marc, Terri and Lyman for dinner at the Last Resort, the restaurant that sits on the little island at the head of Trellis Bay. We got to the Last Resort by Happy Hour and had Painkillers…two for one. Yay! Really cute place. Had a wonderful dinner and conversations. First really great meal I can say we have had around here…particularly for the prices they charge in the BVIs. We had a cute little waitress from South Africa that Marc had already befriended. Of course.

Then the entertainment started setting up. We thought we might not stay…probably will be too loud and with lots of reggae songs. The guy started playing. He was unbelievable! So good! He was not only an excellent musician but quite the personality. They were to have name-that-tune contests where the winners got to go on stage and have a shot of tequila and help sing the song. Oh great…this sounds a little corny. When he started playing *Dock Of the Bay*, he asked us all to whistle with him. OK…. But it was good! And Randy got to go up and have a shot because he's such a good whistler! Ha! That Randy is so talented, you know. Then the entertainer guy…it would be nice if I could remember his name…started the name-that-tune stuff. OK…we may want to go now. But …again…it was good! The songs he chose were great. And the renditions he and a key board player did were OUTSTANDING. By now, I know I can do this.

I know I can guess at least one of these songs. Five notes in…I've got it! "Come Together by the Beatles!" YAY! I won! Lyman guessed it, too, but he let me win. I go up, get my shot of tequila, entertainer guy says, "This is going to be the upbeat version." Ohhh kayyyy. I stand there and they begin. And they're playing fast. This is not normally a fast song. I can't even think of the words at that speed so I mostly just dance around and sing the chorus when I hear it. They played an 8… minute… long version of that song. I stood up there for 8… …minutes making a fool of myself! But they are such good musicians, it was so fun. (The reason I know it was 8 minutes was because Terri video'd the whole frickin' thing!) Goodness! What a fun, fun, fun night.

Next day the weather was kind of crummy. We dinghy'd to shore and had a burger at Da Loose Mongoose. Good burger. We planned on going back over for the Full Moon Party that night but the weather was awful. Rainy, windy, so we stayed in. We would have been sopped by the time we made it to shore from riding in the dinghies. I hated to miss this once a month traditional party. Marc, of course, did manage to go and said it was great! This was his second Full Moon Party. The first one he attended was on New Years Eve. Marc KNOWS where the parties are. It's ok…we had such a great time the night before that made up for missing this one. Randy and I ended up watching the movie *Serenity*…the ending movie of the *Firefly* series we had borrowed from Terri and Lyman. We liked the series but not really the movie.

The next day was STILL windy but now at least the sun was out. We all decided to stay another day at Trellis. I wanted to visit Marina Cay, just across the bay, but the weather wasn't great to take the boats over. So Terri got us all together and we took a ferry to Marina Cay. And it was free! We just had to call for them to pick us up. We figured that out after we stood and waited for awhile. Duh. It was really pretty over there. We walked around, had lunch, and I got another Pusser's cup for my collection from the Pusser's Restaurant. Of course it was filled with a Painkiller. Fun day.

A rainy, windy, ugly morning. What's the deal? We paid for sunshine…always! We left Trellis Bay and put the sails up. We are headed back to Norman Island. Terri and Lyman needed to get back to the USVIs as Terri's mom and son were coming to visit. We also need to get back as we've been in the BVIs for most of the 30 days we are allowed and we are also expecting company the end of the month. So we're working our way back to the USVIs together. It ended up being a nice peaceful sail. The rain went away and the winds died down a little. We again anchored in The Bight, about where we were before. And what should we see but *Opal*! Marc decided to head that way, too. Yay!

I always want to get in the water when we reach spots so I immediately donned my attractive snorkel paraphernalia and snorkeled on the anchor to check it and then around the edge of the bay. It felt good to be back in the water. Trellis Bay wasn't conducive for snorkeling. After a bit we decided to move our anchor. We felt we were too close to the cement dock that was there… if the boat were to turn and swing that way. That's better. The new spot is better. Marc stops by and he's headed to the *Willy T* for drinks about 5-ish. "OK…sounds good, but just drinks. We'll have dinner when we get back." Off we dinghy. Five hours later…. Holy Cow! I must have had a zillion Painkillers! We met so many fun people and they were buying us drinks and we were talking and laughing and dancing and….whoa! It's time to go! And the place hadn't even really started to rock and roll! We were taking our dinghy back to the boat as many others were dinghying on to the *Willy T*. Holy Cow! I can't keep up with that bunch. Marc, of course, stayed. He's younger, you know. It was sooooo fun. But we hadn't eaten…ugh. That doesn't bode well for the rest of the evening. Memorable, though! It was memorable! We did the tourist/party thing that night. Yes…we…did.

Ugh…slept in. I'm sure you were expecting me to say that! Headache/stomachache. Can't do that anymore! But it was such fun. It's a windy day (windy all night, too) but the sun is out. Everyone just sort of hunkered down on their boats today. We read books… played Sudoku. I made spaghetti and found out I can get online from the boat. Good. We had a nice quiet night and the wind was quiet, too.

Up and at 'em, we left Norman Island to check out of the BVIs at Sopers Hole. Marc's engine was overheating…again…so he headed out to Roadtown where he had mechanics work on his engine before. Randy started to check the engine oil, as is routine, and there was oil all on bottom of engine compartment. Oops! Not sure what that was. Randy mopped it up and checked the oil. It looked ok but needed a little more. Then he tightened the oil filter. We'll just keep an eye on that. She started fine and was ok all the way to Soper's. We had an early dinner with Terri and Lyman at the Jolly Roger. Pizza and beer. I had them put anchovies on my half of the pizza. As long as they don't touch Randy's half. Nice evening. Nice sunset.

Checked out of BVIs the next morning...easily. The guys were nice, and efficient, for a change. We said goodbye to the Lyman and Terri as they were heading into Red Hook to get their new cockpit cushions they were having made. They then were headed to Christmas Cove in anticipation of their family coming on Saturday. We are kinda having separation anxiety! We've been together with *sans clés* most of the time for the last 2 months. We decided to head to Waterlemon Bay. One of our favorite spots on St John. That's where we spent Christmas Eve. It's so nice here. Very peaceful. And very close to Soper's Hole so it was an easy motor over. Got a mooring no problem. Went snorkeling. Relaxed. Met the couple that are volunteers for this little bay for the parks dept. So nice. Ran into another couple we met through Terri and Lyman at Ocean World in the DR. Connie and Keith. They spent hurricane season at Luperon. They are both now working in Charlotte Amalie to build up their coffers. We had a very nice quiet evening. But didn't sleep well! Maybe it was too quiet and still.

It's so peaceful here. This is a very protected area with tall mountains all around. The area reminds Randy of the Pacific Northwest. With the green hills. The next day Randy worked hard on waxing the transom and the port side of *Kwanesum*. I worked on the blog out in the cockpit. Lots of fish around. We saw an iguana swimming across the anchorage. Not sure what he was doing! I guess just swimming from the tiny island to shore. Silly iguana. There is lots of fish activity, jumping all around and little fish swarming. We saw a shark, too. A nurse shark. Randy saw it later sitting under our boat. As we know, nurse sharks aren't known to be aggressive. But I didn't jump in that day... just in case it was the shark's day to go against that rule. Our mooring neighbors on a boat called *Hanco* stopped by and chatted from their dinghy and invited us over for cocktails at 1630hrs. They also invited us to ride with them into Cruz Bay in their large tender for lunch but we declined.

We're trying to save some money and we had work we were in the middle of. We did take them up on the cocktails on their boat. I made some tortilla chips and a dip and we took our drinks over. Very fun. Very nice people. From Ohio. Of course when we left their boat we had trouble starting the damn Yamaha! Finally... got it started. Ugh. YAMAHA FOR SALE!!!

Woke up and decided to move on. We left Waterlemon Bay and motor sailed to Christmas Cove. Found a good spot to anchor. It is more rolly over here but so nice. The weather was good. We did have to ask a boat to move as they anchored too close for an overnight anchorage. You never know which way you will swing during the night and they were too close. They were very nice and moved. They seemed to have trouble anchoring. They were on an Island Packet that was chartered out of Red Hook. We snorkeled for an hour or so on the reefs near our boat. Love it! Randy decided he was going to work on the dinghy engine. OK. Good idea! When we were in Soper's Hole Lyman and Randy took off the cowling and did a lot of cleaning and checking. (Terri and I played Scrabble. She beat me then, too, dammit.) So today...Ran decided to take apart the carburetor. Not an easy job! He checked everything and cleaned it out with gasoline. And he got it all back together! First time he's done that.

OK...the engine seems to run well now, according to his test run. Yay. Hope it stays that way. We had a dinner of hash and salad and we sat in the cockpit until dark. Saw some neato phosphorescence in the water from fish. We weren't expecting to see that here. Loved it. Nice evening. Breeze started coming in from the West which is different. Turned our boat the opposite way. Hope the anchor knows that. Randy slept in the cockpit, which he loves to do when there are no mosquitos or noseeums. I got online! Someone in the anchorage had wifi. Perfect.

The next day we decided we are not comfortable at this anchorage. The boat turned almost completely around during the night which meant the anchor twisted around, too. It looks ok, Randy dove on it, but we aren't comfortable with it. And it's rolly here. I think we're going to leave. We wanted to stay and wait for *sans clés* and meet Terri's mom and son, but we're not sure when they'll be here. We decided to just head over to Caneel Bay. We found a mooring just to the left of the entrance to the Caneel Bay Resort. It's a perfect spot. And…tah dahhh…I have GREAT internet! Three bars! The weather turned out to be great this day. We are making lots of power with our solar in this sunshine. Now that we have that 3rd solar panel our power has been excellent at anchor. So nice not to have to worry about that. Ran and I decided to dinghy over to the resort for a fancy drink and share a quesadilla. They were having a super bowl party that evening but it was going to be $30/person and then …you buy your drinks on top of that. Cheap beer was offered, but it still seemed too expensive. Last year we were in Lucaya and watched the super bowl there with our friends from New Zealand, Robin and Peter. But this year we weren't sure we wanted to spend the money. We walked around the resort, it's beautiful, and then went back to the boat and had our own drinks in the cockpit. We will probably stay here a few days. It's nice.

Another nice, relaxing day. The weather was beautiful. The water was calm. We had a nice late breakfast and I put the computer in the cockpit and started back on the blog. That is exactly what I had pictured myself doing before we left on this adventure. It was so nice. Sometimes people look at us funny when we lug our computers in…specially in the BVIs where there are a lot of charter people on vacation. They're wondering why these people bring their computers on vacation. Terri got an odd look one day from a guy. The deal is…this is our life, so we have to get our internet where we can…to check our banking, to check email, to check the weather, to search websites for various things we're looking for or need information on, or to Skype our families. It just happens that most places that offer internet are bars/restaurants. Oh well. They can just think either we're very busy business people…or we're weird. Steaks for dinner tonight, with my rice recipe that I love and tomatoes and avocados drizzled with olive oil and balsamic vinegar, feta cheese and walnuts sprinkled on top.!Dinner in the cockpit with an ocean view. Doesn't get much better than that.

We will probably stay at this location another night or so. It's a good spot. We are waiting until the 21st when our son Skip and his wife Kim will arrive on St Thomas, which is just right across the bay from here. I've got cleaning and provisioning to do prior to their arrival and we've already visited just about all the spots in this area so we're just enjoying being at anchor…or on a mooring.

Chapter 21
Movin' On Down

Are We Having Fun Yet?

SPOILER ALERT! At risk of repeating myself and sounding self-indulgent I'm beginning this with a little whining of sorts. This book is about our travels but also about our *life* as we travel and therefore…I tell it like it is. Or …like I'm experiencing right now. Some people want, or need, to know how it *really* is. So…if you don't want to read the rant jump down a bit to **RANT DONE**. And if you continue to read here…thanks for listening.

Sometimes this life isn't the greatest. Often times this life isn't the greatest! It sounds glamorous and romantic and like a dream come true (and it is)…but oft… it's not ….in the real world. Everything seems to be a hassle.

Has·sle (noun): a source or the experience of aggravation or annoying difficulty. EXACTLY!

Hassle > doing the dishes…usually in cold water. (Which prompted this rant-like carrying-on).

Hassle > because you have to try to SAVE water, you therefore are always recycling the dishwater. Yuck.

Hassle > taking a shower…99% in cold water.

Hassle > getting the laundry done…most often in only cold water. (Sheets and towels need HOT water!) And so… laundry doesn't get done often and…you wear clothes over and over until someone starts to look at you funny.

Hassle > *getting*…cold water!

Hassle > lugging groceries from the store; particularly a case of beer. Randy has to carry the beer. We have collected a random selection of bags to use for our groceries, which really work great. And are necessary. A lot of the stores don't have bags to put groceries in. If you have to get a lot of stuff…they get heavy. And the store may be a mile or more away from where you can park the dinghy.

(**Hassle** > trying to find a place to PARK the dinghy.) Or you may need to get on one of the local buses that are hot and crowded with people so you have everything piled on your lap. I need to find a folding pull cart to help us. I should have already bought one as I've seen them here or there, but it never seemed important at the time. When you're trying to lug your groceries back to the dinghy, then to the boat…it's important then! (UPDATE…I found one! YAY!)

Hassle > finding what you *need* at the store. Makes me miss the wonderful grocery stores at home. I've been trying to find Velveeta Cheese for a few islands, now. Just an odd thing that I want to have on board. I use it for a really yummy dip when we have guests over for cocktails… 'sundowners' they call them in the cruising lingo. Always need to have snacks on hand for that. And Velveeta can last for years! I should have purchased a case when we were in the states. And corn tortillas. I find flour, but not corn. Silly things but I want them. Marc used to bring over his CheeseWiz as a munchy.

Love that! Creative dining.

Hassle > finding a bank to get cash and then figuring how much you need (you may not find an ATM handy at your next spot. So glad they have ATMs now!) Must figure out what currency you need and what the dollar is worth in that country.

Hassle > getting in and out of the dinghy, getting wet on the way, trying to look nice, but failing by the time you get where you're going. My legs carry an assortment of bruises most of the time from dinghydom.

Hassle > trying to find an internet source.

Hassle > trying to call your family, but you need an internet source. Glad to be traveling in this day and age of internet!

Hassle > watching your power usage all the time. I know it's a good thing to do anyway, but essential on a boat running on its own little power source. I believe I mentioned before that now we have replaced most all our inside lights with LEDs (my cousin Deb will be glad to hear that!) so we can use them freely at anchor and not eat in the dark with candles. Well, maybe not freely, but we can use them. And candles are nice, but on a boat...sometimes not the best. In Puerto Rico we did get more power: one more solar panel and *Hank*...our Honda 2000 generator. God Bless solar and God Bless *Hank*.

Hassle > constant repairs... Randy's job. Always working on the stainless. Salt water makes for rust. Trying to keep ahead of maintenance.

Hassle > cooking, when the boat's rolling all over the place....

You get the picture. And I'm sure you might be saying... 'what is she complaining about'? They are in wonderful warm places having a lifetime of experiences...and she's complaining?!'

Is it worth it? Absolutely! I wouldn't change this experience for anything. But it does get to me once in a while. (Can you tell?) If we were to do this, perhaps, for six months... then take a six month break...and do six more months, where everything is shiny and a new experience again....maybe it wouldn't hang there so ominously how much a hassle it all is. Insert smile here. As it stands right now it's been 9 months since we've been off the boat. It will be a year by the time we fly home to the states for a break. I just like a little more convenience. Like being plugged into a marina with electricity and water and TV reception!

As an end result of total contemplation...Ran and I have decided we aren't cut out to do this forever. Our kids will be glad to hear that. Some people do. And we actually thought we might want to carry on. We continually meet people, more so as we get into these southern islands, that are living/have lived this lifestyle for many, many years. Only taking short breaks from the boat. Traveling to wonderful places, always living on their boat. Most, not in marinas. They may change their boat, but they continue to travel from island to island. Some find an island they like and stay for months or years. Then decide to travel on. Some just decide to stay anchored out in one island permanently. Most of these I've found are men, by themselves. That might be telling. It's definitely a cheap way to live, *on the hook*, but it's not exactly luxury living. It's just not easy. I'm not opposed to *'not easy.'* Sometimes *'not easy'* spurs me on. But Ran and I miss our family. And I just plain like convenience! This life is really interesting. LOVE the adventure. LOVE the challenge (sometimes.) LOVE meeting the people. LOVE seeing the new islands we land on. LOVE the experience of sailing on the water and overnight excursions. But we have decided it's not what we want to do for a long, long time.

Our aim was to sell our boat we had in California, buy a new boat in Virginia, the boat we've always wanted, and sail it home

247

to California where our family and friends are when we retire. This is our retirement adventure. And we're doing that and living a lifetime full of experiences along the way. We won't look back and say, *'we should have done that!'* Something we will talk about and relish for the rest of our lives. Stories we can share with our grandchildren. Let our kids and grandkids know that there's a lot of life to live and only a short time to do it. So go for it!

When we say we're headed home, *cruising* people often say, *'but your boat IS your home!'* That's true. And we love this home. But, at this time in our life, *'home'* to us is closer to our family and friends, and if still on the boat, plugged into a marina. And there's something about the familiarity of a home town or at least a home state or at least a home coast! I miss that. I miss the connection. By the time we get back to California I think it will have been about 9 years since we've been permanently *'home.'* Five of them living back East in Virginia. That's way longer than I anticipated we'd be gone. I like grabbing life as it comes and taking advantage of opportunities. And that's certainly what we've done. Moving back to Washington DC for a stint back there, retiring, buying the boat of our dreams and sailing it home. Check that off our Bucket List. But it's time to go home.

The plan right now is to continue to live on our boat when we get back, happily plugged in at our yacht club marina in Alameda. Perhaps we will make more excursions of the shorter variety, there are wonderful trips to take just around the Bay, and we want to get our grandkids sailing... but now we're headed home.

RANT DONE.

Itchy Feet

We were so excited for Skip and Kim to arrive. We wanted to show this life to our family so they can see what it is like, at least a little bit. And we hadn't spent much time with just Skip and Kim, so this was very exciting for us.

The weeks prior to their arrival seemed to go… so…..slowly. You know how it is when you're excited to have someone come visit or when you're going to visit them? We tried to stay busy working on boat projects but knew they would be much easier when we moved into the marina. There we would have unlimited power and water; essential cleaning tools.

We hung around Caneel Bay (St John, USVI) awhile prior to heading into the marina to prepare the boat for guests. To keep our so-called 'budget' in line, we didn't want to go into the marina too soon. Staying on a mooring ball or at anchor is hugely cheaper. Seeing parts of the world and traveling from a private boat gives you a unique perspective and is fairly inexpensive if you don't buy t-shirts and hats at every stop (which I am wont to do) and if you don't eat out all the time and order the foo foo drinks (which I am wont to do.) This, all considering your boat is ship shape and large expensive repairs aren't needed, knock on wood.

Caneel has been one of our favorite spots. Not that it's the best anchorage in the world, but it's very convenient and it's pretty there and if this girl wants to get a foo foo drink and break the budget we can dinghy in and spend too much money on one drink. And look at the beautiful view. It's a good location, easy to get to Cruz Bay, St John and easy to get to some of our favorite anchorages, plus Red Hook where the marina is on St Thomas where we will pull in. We found a good mooring ball that's strategically located so we get decent internet coverage and isn't too rolly…at least most of the time. We liked Cruz Bay. Found a good optometrist there to fix Randy's sunglasses. They worked very hard to repair the screws on the frames that the optometrist in Oregon said could never be fixed. So now Randy has 2 great pair of prescription sunglasses. It's just one of those little towns that you felt comfortable in and were able to find what you need.

Because we still had a few days to wait until we headed into the marina, we buzzed back around to one of our favorite anchorages, Maho Bay. Such pretty anchorages there are in the Virgins. We relaxed there and went exploring ashore to their campground we hiked up to. Neat place. Very rustic.

Now it's finally time to go into the marina at Red Hook and prepare for Skip and Kim. We wanted to do some big time cleaning and laundry. Nothing like having guests come visit to get things done around the *'house.'*

All is ship shape and we left for the airport so excited to see the kids. We left too early. We weren't sure how long it would take to get there because the airport was on the other side of the island. We had everything done so we left giving ourselves plenty of time. Our taxi driver asked when the kids were arriving and whistled when he realized how long we'd be waiting. Oh well…we'll just have a drink and relax while we wait. And we brought our books to read.

We were practically the ONLY people at the airport. Good grief. It was night, the plane wasn't due in until 9 something. NOTHING was open. There were a few people working, but not many. So we sit…and wait…and read our books. I had enough time to literally memorize all of the advertisements that were rotating on the signs all around the airport.

Finally they arrive! Yay! It was so good to see them walking toward us down the hallway. Yay! Off we go. Back to the boat to get them acclimated to life on the water. Skip had been on our boat in Virginia but Kim had no idea what to expect. We gave them a quick briefing on boat living and relaxed and talked. So good to see them! I miss them just writing about it!

We had SUCH a good time. The weather wasn't as good as Randy and I wanted, but it didn't matter. We headed out to some of our favorite places. First to Sandy Spit on Jost Van Dyke. Our last visit there was so beautiful and warm and calm. But of course this visit was not. It wasn't bad, but it wasn't nice enough to spend the night. We donned our snorkel gear and swam around awhile, but then decided to go on to Norman Island and spend the night at The Bight. The kids didn't have a long time to be with us so we couldn't waste valuable time.

It's nearly always nice at The Bight as long as you can get a mooring. And we found one in a good spot. We got all snuggled in and opened some beer and relaxed. Talking about all kinds of things. That's so fun. Randy noticed a couple of guys trying to anchor in the middle of the mooring field. Oh, oh…that's not going to work. Following the lead of another friend of ours from another mooring experience, Randy went forward to tell them they were not supposed to anchor in the middle of a mooring field; there's not enough room, which is true. There are plenty of places to anchor outside the mooring field. They weren't happy with his interference and said so. "We did NOT pay $25 for this mooring to worry about running into you in the middle of the night because you're anchored too close! Now MOVE!" said Randy with a few expletives added in. (He's getting good at these encounters, right? HA! I guess we seem to be the anchoring Nazis! *"No anchoring for you!!"*) A few expletives received back from them…and they moved. Well that's ONE way of having your new daughter-in-law get to know you!

We donned our little-bit-nicer attire and went into the Pirates Bight for dinner. It was a beautiful evening. After dinner we headed over to the *Willy T* for drinks. Skip was trying all the fancy drinks: Painkillers, Bushwackers. I think he preferred beer. But you need to try them while you're there. It was a fun, fun evening.

251

The next morning we had a nice breakfast in the cockpit and went over to the Caves to snorkel. It was sort of a windy, choppy day but not bad. The good thing about that ... there weren't many people there. This is the place I mentioned in my last post that we snorkeled and a big load of people were dumped off at one time by a catamaran. That wasn't fun. Getting elbowed while you're trying to enjoy the ocean life isn't what I had in mind. This time it was perfect. Just a few of us there. And it was spectacular. We saw more and the sea was clearer. And Kim spotted a turtle eating on the bottom! So cool! What a fun day. I could do that over and over again. But it had to come to an end. It was still early in the day so we decided to head over to Soper's Hole on Tortola to have a late lunch with Terri and Lyman our buddy boaters from *sans clés*. I wanted the kids to meet them. And they could do a little shopping there. After lunch we unfortunately had to head back to the marina in anticipation of their flight home early the next morning. Too short a visit! We did dinghy over to Latitude 18° for a great dinner and some nice entertainment.

Up early, early and put the kids in a taxi for their ride back to the airport. Pooh! Too short a visit but so fun. It's so good to spend close, quality time like this with your kids. I need more.

Now it's time to get going. We have been in the Virgins a long time. We pointed the boat back to Sopers Hole on Tortola to do a 72-hour check-in/check-out of the BVIs. That should give us enough time to get down to Gorda Sound and head out the Anegada Passage to St Martin. We did our check in/out and headed to Coopers Island. We wanted to try to get to the Baths on Virgin Gorda before we headed out. We spent the night on the mooring at Coopers and got up early to head to the Baths. But it was not a good day. Very, very windy and the mooring was very choppy at the Baths. We decided not to stay. We weren't comfortable leaving our boat on the mooring in such choppy seas. Oh well, you can't see everything. We headed on around to Gorda Sound and anchored off Prickly Pear where we had been before. This gives us a great spot to get going to St Martin.

Because we had the kids visit, we hadn't been traveling with Terri and Lyman the last week or so. We caught up with them at Gorda Sound to make our future travel plans. Randy and I wanted to start going more quickly down the islands. Terri and Lyman wanted to go to Anegada first. So we decided to meet up in St Martin. Terri and Lyman have guests coming aboard in St Martin, but we told them we would wait there so we could see them one more time before we start going faster. We have been with Terri and Lyman since May 2009, so it's going to be very hard to say goodbye to them. The good thing is, they live in the Pacific Northwest so we know we will see them again.

Just as our 72 hours was about up...who should appear at our anchorage in Gorda Sound but the immigration guys! Holy Cow! First time of all our travel that we've had them come to our boat. Fortunately for us, we had done the 72 hour in/out. And we had planned to leave that afternoon for the overnight to St Martin. Whew!

About 1500hrs we up anchor and head down the Anegada Passage, passing Richard Branson's Necker Island as we go out. What a spot that is. Imagine owning your own island! He was hosting a whole slew of kite boarders that weekend apparently. Fun to watch them.

The weather was perfect, but there was no wind. But that's ok in this case. We would be going against the wind anyway. So we motored with calm seas, a beautiful sunset and a beautiful full moon. Nice.

Early morning arrival in St Martin. We are now in the Leeward Islands. We put down the **Virgin Islands Cruising**

Guide and pick up the **Leeward Islands Guide**. We decided to go to the Dutch side, St Maarten. There is also the French side, St Martin. We anchored in Simpson Bay. There is a lagoon inside this island but you must pass under a bridge at appointed hours to get inside and find an anchorage. For a couple of reasons, we decided to stay outside in Simpson Bay even though it was pretty rolly. Actually, it was very rolly. The main reason for staying in Simpson Bay was the Regatta. While we were there the St Maarten Yacht Club was hosting the Heineken Regatta which was spectacular. We discovered that the yachts came out of the lagoon and into Simpson Bay every day to practice, and the finale of the race was next to where we were anchored. And there were some very large yachts anchored out where we were. Always something to see when you live on a boat. Your back porch is a window to the world. We did put up with those big rolly seas, but we thought it was worth it.

We took *Bob* the dinghy inside to the lagoon to provision and get on the internet and go to Budget Marine and Island Water World, the big chandleries. We took the dinghy over to the French side which was very quaint with bistros. It was hot that day and we stopped for a beer at one of the bistros and had the best Stella Artois beer on tap in a frosty mug. So cold and refreshing. When you're hot, that's when beer tastes best.

We visited the St Maarten Yacht Club now and then and mingled with the racers just a bit. Of course having Heineken beer. Low and behold....Ran and I are sitting at the yacht club drinking our beer and we spot Igor!! Igor whom we met in the Dominican Republic! Unbelievable. He was crewing on a race boat. How fun was that!? It's such a small world. Igor invited Randy down to the boat he was racing on. Very sparsely fitted out, with no extra incidentals in order to keep weight low and the boat fast, but with all the best racing gear you can imagine.

Quite the deal. Caroline was there, too, so we got a really nice visit in.

We stayed at St Martin for a week so we could see Terri and Lyman before we departed. They came in just as the regatta was ending. We spent quality time with them and then had to say goodbye. They were waiting for friends to visit and Randy and I decided we wanted to move on down island. A gloomy wet morning, Ran and I pulled up the anchor but not before giving a sad, sad goodbye to Terri and Lyman. We will miss them terribly. As we drove off the anchorage we went by their boat and Randy blew the conch horn. I think I cried most of the day. We had gotten to be really good friends.

Chapter 22
St. Barths to Grenada

Headin' Down Island

On we go to St Barths. On to a new experience.

Itchy feet.

It only took us 3 hours to St Barths but it was a gloomy trip. Ugly, rainy voyage. Just as we pull in, though, the sun started shining and we saw a whale spouting. And it smelled like flowers. How lovely. There was the weirdest looking yacht anchored outside the bay. I'm talking futuristic looking and huge. We do see the darnedest things out in the wild blue yonder. We learned later this boat was called '*A*' and is named after the man and woman who own her, whose names begin with A. They are Russian. There are some very rich Russians with yachts around. But this yacht was really different. Like a space ship!

I had been waiting to go to St Barths. In search of Jimmy Buffett!! St Barths, or St Barts, or Saint Barthélemy, is where Jimmy Buffett supposedly wrote the song *Margaritaville* at the Le Select Bar. OK...I'm on a deep search. Hoping J Buffett is in residence. I read all his books and of course love his music and lifestyle, and he did spend a lot of time in these waters. I had heard about St Barths years ago. At that time it all seemed so far away and mysterious. Little did I know that one day I would be sailing my own boat into St Barths. Amazing.

Jimmy didn't show. Well, rats. I can't believe he stood me up. I waited a long time, drinking adult beverages with my sailor, but…no show. Oh well. It was a cool destination to sit and wait. I guess if you have to wait somewhere, Le Select in St Barths is not a bad place! Cheers!

What a quaint little town. I loved it. I wish my daughter Lacey had been with me. We would have had a great time there. Of course we would need an unlimited credit card. Very expensive. But very classy. The shopping there was…oooo la la! All the wonderful classy clothing stores and more. Maybe in my next life.

When you enter a new island, it's usually a new country, so you have to check in. As usual you fly your yellow quarantine flag until you have completed check in. We found the spot where we needed to be to check in, according to our cruising guide for this island. This is where the cruising guides we accumulated for our journey come in extremely handy. We found the spot and were directed to a computer to do the check in. Being a French island, it was a French computer. Really? There's a difference? Yes, it's different than our computers in the USofA. And everywhere else for that matter. It's actually an easy way of filling out the forms, on a computer, but you have to be careful because some of the keys are in different spots on these French computers, for some only-the-French-know-why reason. Interesting. And… the French use very little English on their forms and signage. *Pourquoi*? Everywhere else we go, and have been, has English translation…but not the French it seems. *Mon Dieu*. Gladly and gratefully, the people there at check in were very nice and helped us when needed. As I've said many times, and you'll probably hear it from me many times more, checking in and out of a country can be tedious at best, so having nice people there to help you is invaluable.

We found a sweet place after checking in to have croissants and cappuccinos and then wandered around the town walking up and down the hills and into the neighborhoods. We then had a wonderful lunch with a perfect glass of wine, overlooking the harbor. We didn't stay long. Only 2 nights.

Itchy feet.

Now on to Nevis. I like to keep moving. I like stopping, too, but there's something really neat about picking up anchor and traveling on to the next spot. A new adventure. We left St Barths at 0430hrs and arrived in Nevis at 1245hrs. We took a mooring at Penney Beach. Nice anchorage, but a little rolly. Pretty island though. We checked in at the Police Department which was a hoot. I guess the normal person wasn't there so another official looking gal looked through their desk to see how to stamp the passports and figured out how to do ours. OK! Whatever it takes. The people checking us in were really nice. We filled out all of our paperwork at the customs place but needed to go to the police department to have our passports stamped. Our passports are looking pretty fun with all the stamps of the different places we've been. It's always a new adventure going through customs and immigration at each spot.

While we were at the appointed area for customs/immigration check-in, we decided to reserve a taxi to take us around the island the next day. We found Sarge. He will be our driver. What we have discovered on our island treks is that there seems to be a lot of the same stuff. Different island but old forts and old sugar plantations. They're really very neat, though. The jury was out whether it was worth the price of the cab ride. We ended up going to a lot of resorts that were made from old sugar plantations and are of course gorgeous and very exclusive. We didn't get to see the monkeys. We didn't get to a couple of other spots I thought we should see. But we did get to go around the island.

We also walked around the area near our boat and saw some old churches. We heard some wonderful singing coming out of one church and we got closer to peak in and listen a bit. It was so neat. Such wonderful singing. A newly learned fact unknown to us about Nevis is that Alexander Hamilton was born there. I did not know that! An interesting story. And of course Horatio Nelson was there. Horatio was all over these islands out here. Horatio was married on Nevis. It's very cool to think you've sailed the same waters as some of these famous people.

We spent 4 days in Nevis then up early and on to Antigua. Jolly Harbour will be our first stop there. It's a nice protected area, but I was disappointed in what they had to offer. Often on these islands there are a lot of places that look like they were 'hopping' at one time but now you see a lot of them closed up. This was the case here. The mooring was nice and calm, particularly after the rolly one in Nevis, but the town of Jolly Harbour didn't offer much.

We did provision and filled fuel and water at a decent price. We also had our laundry done...at an ok price. And they did have hot water! While in Jolly Harbour we ran into some people we met in Deltaville...Roy and Doon from New Zealand. Before we left Virginia they had their boat at Deltaville. Doon was a traveling nurse and she used those skills as they traveled to beef up their coffers. Again...so fun to run into people you know...in this small world of ours. We spent a nice evening with them.

Now we are ready to head to English Harbour. We check the weather and decide to get up and go. We head out and turn left. Everything seems ok but it's a bit breezy. We go along down the island at a pretty decent pace and start our turn toward English Harbour. To do that we poke our heads out at the southern end of the island and it's blowing like crazy! In the wrong direction! We have our engine running, our main sail and staysail up and we are only doing 1knot!! OK…this ain't gonna work! We decide to turn around and try it again another day. It's not that far and we have time and we would have been ready to kill someone by the time we got there if we had continued at that snail like pace against those winds and seas.

OK…next morning…let's try this again. It looks much better weather wise according to our weather sources, so off we go, peeking out again to see how it is outside the Harbour. Here we go, trying to get to the other side of Antigua and to English Harbour, where Lord Nelson held court. We were looking forward to that stop. I mean…Lord (Admiral) Nelson was THE guy!! The tales we've read about his life certainly spurred our interest here. Randy is a real history lover and we both read many books while sailing and some contained stories of THE Lord Nelson. Cool factor is large, thinking of this next stop.

This time we got there lickety-split, no problem. I liked this town much better, too. Very quaint and charming. Nice anchorage. Neat little town to walk to. Lots of historic buildings here. We planned to stay at English Harbour for 5 days. And who should we find in the anchorage??? Igor and Caroline on the s/v *Conch Pearl!* Remember we saw Igor in St Barths, too, along with Caroline. We were sort of taking the same track down island, I guess. They brought the *Conch Pearl* from the Dominican Republic to Antigua. You may or may not remember, Dear Reader, that the *Pearl* is owned by our friend Neil whom we met in Rum Cay in the Bahamas. At the Hotel

Rum Cay that struggled to let us go. We traveled from Rum Cay to the DR with *Conch Pearl* but Neil peeled off and went to the Turks and Caicos and we went on to the DR with Terri and Lyman on *san clès*.

Neil met Igor and Caroline when he was in the Turks and Caicos and they all traveled together later to the DR. Neil brought the *Pearl* to Ocean World where we were staying and hired Igor and Caroline to clean her up and take her on down the islands. They got as far as Antigua, but the *Pearl* needs some extra work I'm afraid before she goes much further. It was fun seeing Igor and Caroline again, though. Not sure what their future plans will be.

In English Harbour we were told of a great BBQ that is held on Sundays up at Berkeley Heights. So....being who we are...we took the challenge to hike up there. After all, we have no vehicle to drive up there, and if we want to go, we need to hike. Quite a hike up hill, I must say, but we took our time and it was well worth it. The view was spectacular! We could overlook the whole harbor and see our boat anchored out there. And... the ribs were fabulous! The steel drum music was fabulous! And we met some wonderful people. The hike back down in the dark was a wee bit more of a challenge, yes it was. But we worked off our great dinner and made it fine. Thanks to my Indian scout Randy.

One of the spectacular highlights we experienced while at English Harbour was the event of what we learned was the Woodvale Atlantic Rowing Race. We didn't realize at all what this was until these row boats...very modern and well equipped row boats... started trickling into the harbor under much fanfare. Flares going off! Horns going off! Racing cannons going off! My goodness! It was definitely a site to see. And since we were anchored in the harbor we had front row seats. We learned that they rowed from the Canary Islands all the way to Antigua. The first guy that made it in had been rowing for 75 days! And they continued to trickle in to the harbor for days after that. A couple of women teams, too. And some that were single handed. Amazing. It was quite something to see their boats and to think about what they had done in seas that had to have been much more of a challenge than what we've been through. So glad we were there to see this event.

The weather looks good and we're ready to head on down the islands. We've decided to do the next few islands more quickly. We will just anchor out at the next island and not check in. Then we will leave first thing in the morning. We want to quicken our pace a bit. And, as I've said, these islands seem to be the same in a lot of ways. Interesting but the same. Same relics of churches, forts and sugar plantations. We decide we don't need to see them all. The next island down is Guadeloupe.

It was nice and still the morning we departed Antigua. We motored out beyond the island and caught a wonderful wind out there so we sailed the whole way to Guadeloupe, doing 6 knots mostly which is pretty good for our boat at sail. Nice. Very, very nice. We pulled into Des Haies at a sweet, quiet anchorage. As we are stowing après sail things a skiff approaches and asks if we'd like baguettes in the morning. Oh man!! Of course we do! But...we are leaving too early. Darn it. We enjoy a wonderful sunset, briefly flying our Guadeloupe courtesy flag along with the yellow quarantine flag.

Itchy feet.

Up early, early and we're heading to Dominica. We are bypassing Sainte Kitts, just below Guadeloupe, which are fabulous islands according to friends who have been. We hate to miss that but we just don't want to take that much time. Our goal now is to get over to Panama by late May early June. Originally we were going to head to Trinidad and leave our boat there for the hurricane season. But we have decided to step it up a bit and get closer to home before then. So Dominica is another island we just anchored off.

We steered *Kwanesum* into Prince Rupert Bay. We had big winds along the way down to Dominica so we sailed half way, but then had to turn into the wind to approach the island. I lost my favorite Island Packet hat along the way! Darn it! Randy wouldn't turn around for it. I thought we could practice our man overboard drills. Oh well. I have a zillion other hats but that was my favorite to wear while traveling. I have a clip to put on it, but obviously I didn't use it. Got settled into Pr Rupert Bay and were immediately approached by boats wanting to sell things. But we didn't need any of their wares. Again we put up our quarantine flag and the Dominica flag and watch the beautiful sunset. It got a little chilly that evening.

Next day, we did a short sail down to Roseau, Dominica for overnight. Again anchored off shore. Again we were approached by boats selling things. And '"Did you pay for the mooring?" which we had to take there in Roseau. "No we haven't paid." "I'd be glad to take the money for you." "Thank you. That would be nice. Would you please bring us a receipt?" "No problem." Never saw him again, as you probably guessed. Roseau was not the greatest spot we had anchored. Not a pretty shoreline and the fellow in the skiff made us uncomfortable. Oh well…we are leaving mañana. That sort of encounter was not unusual, unfortunately.

Up early, early, again and off to Martinique, destination Fort de France. It's a nice, still morning. Had a big but short squall along the way. Found a great spot to anchor along the pretty city front. Again, I could smell flowers as we approached the island. We are now in the Windward Islands. Close the **Leeward Guide Book** and open the **Windward Guide Book**. We are makin' time.

I liked Martinique. It was very French, which I loved. The check in on the French islands is Simple Simon, once you figure out their computer. Nice. We again checked with our great guide book on the area to find out the best place to check in here. In Fort de France, we checked in at Sea Services, a chandlery on the main road. It is owned by folks that speak perfect English. Excellent. And they had good wares in their shop, including St James apparel which I love. Ciarla, who is from Canada originally, even let us collect a FedEx package there at her business. So nice and so helpful. Because our health coverage is Kaiser we can only receive 90 days of medication at a time. This is not helpful when you're traveling around like we are. But we like our health coverage and don't want to change so we put up with having to receive a package every 3 months or so. You can get medication easily in Martinique, and some other countries, so we both have stocked up a bit on what we need in case there's a delay in a package being received wherever we are. Our daughter Lacey packed us a package to receive in Martinique.

When Randy and I were in St Maarten we decided to buy an unlocked iPhone to use:

a) We can use it to get internet when ashore.
b) We can buy a local sim card to make local calls which comes in handy if we are in a port for a long time.

In Martinique we set off to find a sim card for the area. We found Orange, which is a cell phone store there and on other islands. Of course not many speak English, or they pretend to not speak English…(constantly surprises us when the main business on these islands is tourism) so we had to find someone we could communicate with. We found a very handsome young man that spoke pretty good English. Excellent. However, $80 USD later…we figure we bought the wrong thing. Oh well! We also thought it would be cheaper when calling home. In St Maarten it was. In Fort de France it was not. Oh well…live and learn. Back to Skype.

There was not a good internet source from the boat in Fort de France so we had to find internet cafes. We have a booster antenna on our boat and can often find unsecured internet sources that don't require passwords from there. But there were none to be had in our location in Martinique. So we packed up our computers and took them for a dinghy ride into town. We found a little bar upstairs on the main road that had internet. Beer and email go together. We found an even better source a few days later. It was a wonderful bistro a little off the beaten path that had a great, secure internet and wonderful salads! And, of course, beer.

We stayed in Martinique at Fort de France for 5 days. The plan now was to head to St Lucia, then Bequia in the Grenadines, the Tobago Cays and on to Grenada. We started out early, early which we like to do. We got past the island and had really great wind and were sailing along beautifully. We were making good time.

"Hey, El, since we're going along so well…want to just keep going?" "Sounds good to me!" So we decided not to stop in St Lucia, not to stop in Bequia and not to stop in Tobago Cays. We went all the way to Grenada in one fell swoop of a really nice sail. We weren't able to sail the whole way but we had the great full moon and the seas were good. I know we missed visiting some nice places, but that's ok. We loved this sail we were on from Martinique and we have been lucky to have seen so much already.

Itchy feet.

We arrived at the bottom of Grenada, Prickly Bay, at 1100hrs the next morning on 3 April. It's very dry here! Not what we expected at all. I thought it would be lush and green.

It seems that many of these islands are having a drought. We found a good spot to anchor. We decided to rest all that day and check into the country the next day, Sunday. We are now at the end of the Windward Islands!

The customs and immigration folks were wonderful here. As you now know that is not always the case. But these guys made us feel so welcome and glad that we are there. After checking in we went over to the little outdoor restaurant off the anchorage to see about something to eat. That's when we met Beryl and Claus. They had just arrived after sailing from South Africa for 53 days straight! They had a 50-foot something catamaran. Oh my! Beryl was having a hard time being on land. I guess so! And she was so fun and smiley and laughing a lot. I would have been ready to kill someone after 53 days at sea! I later told Randy…I'm changing my attitude. I need to be more glad. What an inspiration she was in only the short time we had known her. Needless to say we spent some wonderful days in Grenada with Beryl and Claus.

We learned to take the bus in Grenada. Had to get downtown to the chandlery and to the store and to explore. We didn't do too much exploring. Seemed like we were doing more chores than exploring. But the buses were a hoot. "Look for the little buses with the ONE on the front. That's the one to take to town and get back here." OK. We walk up the street a bit to the rotunda and find the bus. They are like a really small van with a million seats packed inside. There is a driver and there is a guy that sits near the sliding door and hangs out trying to find more passengers. They holler at anybody they see that might possibly ride in their bus. Some were very aggressive at finding passengers. Quite the trip. They pack you in there and you hope they understand where you want to get off. And it's hot.

The most memorable bus run was when Ran and I went downtown to the cruise terminals to their outside market.

Looking, looking for fresh vegetables, fruit, and then finding the regular market for some extra stuff we needed. We bought our wares and then walked and hauled them down to the bus depot. Not a short haul on foot. We finally get there and they piled us on the little bus. We had to stack everything on our laps, hoping not to crush the fresh bread we bought. Thank heaven I'm not claustrophobic and they had windows to open. I was really glad to get off that bus, even though we had to walk and haul what in my mind has become our crap, another half mile or so back to the place we parked our dinghy. Our arms were falling off by the time we got there. So we stopped for a beer first. Of course we did!

On some of the islands where we have been there has been a cruisers' net on the VHF radio. This was the case here in Grenada. The other instance was in Georgetown, Bahamas. It's actually quite a good thing. Every morning at 0730hrs, or whatever appointed hour they choose, on a particular channel...for Grenada it was 68...they broadcast what is going on in the area that cruisers might be interested in. And remember, the word cruisers means those of us who are living and traveling on our sailboats, and perhaps a few power boats, but mostly sail. On the Channel 68 morning chat they ask who is new to the area or who might be leaving. Also they'll ask if you have anything you need or anything you want to get rid of, they give you the weather, and the businesses around announce any news they might have...like happy hours or specials in their restaurant or tours they are offering of the island. It's very helpful. You can put in a 'query' if you need to know, for instance, where to get water or fuel or have your laundry done. If anyone is heading the direction you are going and want to travel together you can put that query in. Or maybe ask if anyone wants to go together and rent a car, etc. Often, too, the cruisers group does things for the island people, like volunteer in their schools or do a cleanup of their beaches, etc.

It's quite a nice idea and comforting to know there's help if you need it.

We ended up staying in Grenada for almost 3 weeks. Our original plan was to head to Trinidad and put our boat there for hurricane season and fly home. Hurricane season remember is from 1 June to 30 November. That's 6 months. We would store *Kwanesum* there and return and carry on our sailing travels the end of November. That's a long time to leave our boat. I researched a lot to find the best and safest places in Trinidad to take our boat to store. After much investigation on the internet, I decided on one marina that sounded good. I contacted them via email and made our plans. In the meantime, a few days later, through chatter on our radios aboard, we heard there was a bit of suspected pirate activity on the sea between Grenada and Trinidad, which is located right off of Venezuela. Not exactly the information to make us feel confident about this decision. We took a bit of time to rethink this. It was all making me a bit weary. Plus… the thought of leaving our *Kwanesum* in Trinidad for that length of time was not sitting well with me, not to mention the trip to get there, worrying about possible trouble. We made the decision. Let's squash that idea. We need to make another plan.

And another plan was made. We are going to head to Panama. Panama, and traveling that direction, is not in the hurricane zone. Therefore, we would not be at the mercy of our insurance company and planning around those dates. Good. I like that idea very much! And it's closer to home. I'm getting to the point where I need to feel like we are getting closer to home.

It's decided the next leg of our trip will be to Bonaire in the Dutch Antilles. It will be a 3 or 4 day trip so we need to watch the weather closely. We put notice on the VHF channel that we intended to head to Bonaire in case there were others interested in heading that direction. While we were still at anchor planning our next leg, a young man approached our boat in his dinghy with 2 little kids. He heard via Channel 68, we were heading to Bonaire. They were going that way, too, and wanted to travel with another boat. We like that idea as well, especially on the longer trips. We chatted a bit and decided on a date to leave. What a lovely little family. The Vrenkens. Roel is Dutch but lived in France. He is a teacher. Isabelle is French and she is a doctor. Tessa is 7 years old and Yoan is 22 months. Though they are from France they now live in New Caledonia! Roel has sailed for many years and found the boat he wanted in Europe so they are taking it back home to New Caledonia. In France, when you have a baby you can take 3 years off and still get your job back. You don't get paid for the time off but your job is there when you return. So they are taking this time to travel home. Their life in New Caledonia sounds fascinating. Not sure if it will happen but it would be wonderful to visit them there. But I'll fly…not take our boat.

Chapter 23

The ABCs

The Dutch Antilles

We leave at 0800hrs on 22 April after filling with fuel and water the day before. We will be able to sail for the first time most of the way, if not all of the way. The wind and the seas will be behind us. We will sail wing and wing. We scooted along very nicely. Randy made a preventer for our mainsail. If the wind makes a shift at all the mainsail can let go and jibe. This is not what you want to happen. The preventer will help with that. Roel's boat, *Quic en grogne,* is longer and faster so he had to hold back a bit so we could stay together.

It took us 3 days to get to Bonaire. We did pretty well, sailing along. But Randy worked hard to keep our sails full. We did have some problems and of course they all happen at night when you can't see. But they were minor…just annoying. It's a sail position I like, but when the seas are big…as they were many times…it's VERY rolly. Good thing we had everything nailed down below. We did have a time in the middle of the night when the winds got big and the preventer broke. WHAM! Sounded like the whole mast had come down! I was down below trying to sleep. Woohoo! Randy brought down the sails and started the engine to get control of the boat. Took a deep breath and decided to just motor sail until morning when we could see to figure things out. There's never a dull moment when you're sailing. Well…that's not true. There are tons of dull moments when you're just drifting along. But you know what I mean.

We saw some neat stuff on this trip. We saw the green flash which was amazing! It occurs just as the sun sets on the water. Poof! A flash of green just as the sun goes below the water. Like a green splash. I thought it was just a myth but it's true! It's very fleeting and goes very quickly. But it's very cool. I wasn't able to take a picture but I found one online. We saw some Portuguese Man o' War floating by…looking like bathtub toys. We didn't know what they were at the time but found out later. Weird looking and not very big for being such mean things. We had dolphins playing beside us for quite awhile. Dolphins are the best. They have such fun. They jump and dive and race with your boat. Unfortunately it was after dark, but we had a full moon. I was hoping they would make phosphorescence but they didn't. This water was apparently not conducive to that at the time. Dolphins just make you feel good and we hadn't seen some for awhile.

We arrived in Bonaire, in the Dutch Antilles, and tied to a mooring, at 0645hrs on 25 April. We actually arrived around 0300hrs with me, very tired, at the helm. I caught myself having very sleepy eyes and looked up just in time to see a big ship going across out bow! Or that's how it seemed. He wasn't that close but it sure woke me up in a hurry, knowing I had gotten that unaware with sleepy eyes! We hung around outside until daybreak as we were not familiar with the area. We follow the rule of not going into any new area in the dark. The mooring was along the city front. Kralendijk (don't ask me how to pronounce it) was the name of the town. The water was crystal clear. I just love that. That's what I loved most about the Bahamas. The water there was spectacular. We could snorkel here in Bonaire from our boat and see more fish and coral than when we were in the water in the Virgin Islands! Loved it.

We stayed in Bonaire for a week. The first night we were there we were invited for drinks and wonderful, majorly yummy Korean hors d'oeuvres on a catamaran, *Slow Mocean,* two moorings down from us. Blake, Sunny and Eileen. They noticed our Seattle, Washington hailing port on the back of our boat and invited us over. Fun! They are from Seattle. Nice people. Then…to top it off… Roel and Isabelle invited us over for dinner to have a fish they caught on the way. No…we have not caught any fish yet. No…we are not trying very hard. Yes…we should try harder because they're so good! Not sure what recipe Isabelle used but it was like sashimi. Soooooo good. Good food, good wine, good people. Love this part of this life. A nice way to start our stay in Bonaire.

The highlight of Bonaire….the Harley ride. So fun! Roel stopped by the boat one day and said he found a place to rent Harleys. Do we want to go with them and tour the island? Are you kidding? YES! Randy used to own a motorcycle back in the day, so he was more than ready to rent a Harley. Randy went with Roel downtown and reserved one for us. Roel had to reserve a trike because they had the whole family. What an absolutely fun day! We drove all over the island and ended up at a perfect beach where they do a lot of sail boarding. We had some of the best calamari and a wonderful salad for lunch. The beach was perfect for the little ones as there was a nice shallow area where they could play. The sand was like powder. It was a long, hot, fun, fun day. Randy and I had always wanted to rent a Harley and ride. Now we have done it! And on the island of Bonaire in the Dutch Antilles.

Now it's time to go on to Curaçao. Just a short trip. We departed Kralendijk (I still don't know how to pronounce it, but it looks good doesn't it?) at 0810hrs on 2 May. Again, sailing wing and wing. The seas got a bit big, but at least they're behind us. No way could we have gone if we were beating into the seas. We had no cruising guide for Curaçao. We had a brief one for Bonaire that included Venezuela, but none for Curaçao. We got online and on our charts and found where we wanted to go and headed out...again with *Quic en grogne*. BTW...that's pronounced sort of like this: *keek in groi-ña*. Roughly, according to Roel, it means *'others may grumble, I don't care'*. It's apparently old French, Roel said - older than the 19th century.

We arrived and anchored in Spanish Waters, Curaçao (or Spaanse Water, the Dutch spelling) at 1500hrs. Kind of breezy in here and very crowded. But we were able to find spots to anchor together. It's good holding and it's not rolly. Two important things to me.

Unfortunately the water is not as nice and clear here as in Bonaire. There are people swimming in it but I don't think I will. As we got settled, I checked online for an internet source and found one available for yachts. It also had all the information about the area we needed available. That was extremely helpful as we needed to know where to go to check in! We again decided to check in the next day. You usually have 24 hours in which you can check in but you need to put up your yellow quarantine flag in the meantime.

Up the next day we go off with Roel to check in to the country. We knew there was a bus scheduled to go by near the dinghy dock, and we had heard of small buses like in Grenada that also stop by. Unfortunately we missed the early morning bus but knew there would be another around 1030hrs. It was now 0930hrs. Ugh. Hopefully one of the small buses will come by. They didn't. We walked up the road a bit thinking we might see one. We did see a couple, but they did not stop. Certainly wasn't at all like Grenada where they were hanging out of the small buses trying to drum up customers!

We finally get on a large, very nice bus and head into town. We told the bus driver to take us to customs. And that happened to be near the bus station so that worked out well. We asked a few people where it was and along our way we came to the floating market we had heard about. So neat! Boats from Venezuela come in and tie up together and sell the most wonderful fruits and vegetables. I loved it. We decided to buy some on our way back.

First, we need to find customs. Finally found it...big yellow building on the water. We fill out our paperwork there, no problem. In the meantime we run into people we had met in Bonaire; the crew from *Slow Mocean* and another catamaran that was in Bonaire. They had left early in the morning and were just getting to customs. What happened? They were told to go to immigration first, which was on the other side of the waterway. But when they got to immigration and after waiting in line over there, they were told they must go to customs first! Oh dear. We lucked out I guess and blindly went to customs first. Phew! Now we had to cross over the water and try to find immigration.

They have a floating bridge you use to cross the water but it was being moved aside for ship traffic. Kind of cool! We were able to take the ferry across which was just leaving. Another lucky move. On the other side we again ask directions and walk up to immigration. We had to show a gentleman our passports to get down by the water where immigration was. Now we wait in line. It is finally our turn and Roel goes first. They are very slow here. They told Roel his whole family must come in. What?! The standard rule is that the captain checks everyone in. Brings in their passports, etc. That way there aren't a million

274

people waiting around. And there was no problem in that regard with customs. But this lady said he must bring in his whole family. And it must be done today. What??!! Roel is not happy. Randy is not happy that Roel must go through that. I usually go in with Randy because I have better printing than he does to fill out the forms and I always want to take pictures etc and see everything. But for Roel, he would have to drag in the little ones and put them through what can become a very long process.

And today was one of those long process days.

When Randy and I had finished, Roel again asked if he could please just get it all done now. They wanted him to bring his family back when they reopen at 2000hrs which would have been very late and dark. No way. Finally, another woman, who appeared to be the one in charge, decided he could complete the transaction. Thank heavens. This was the most time consuming and difficult check in we had encountered. Bonaire was a breeze! Now we had to go to the Port Captain's office to again fill out paperwork and pay for anchoring in one of their ports. Just a minor fee. But...the office was closed for lunch. We had to wait. Finally...we got it all done and were now starving.

Roel was concerned that Isabelle was probably worried about us all since it had been so long! But we did stop for lunch and a beer. It wasn't much of a lunch, but it was food. We stopped by the floating market and got some produce, then we waited at the bus station for the bus back. We made it back to the dinghy dock and finally got back to the boat. My goodness! That was a long day. The good part about the day was seeing the neat buildings downtown and the floating market. I want to go back and see those again. Of course we have to go back anyway to check out of the country. Hopefully that will go more swiftly. I suppose another hassle rant could be added here but I'm not gonna do it. I do appreciate this experience good, bad or ugly. And my self indulgence has been spoken for.

We are now waiting to move on. We want to continue to travel with *Quic en grogne*. I think we will go to Cartagena and then on to the San Blas Islands. That will be about a 4 or 5 day trip. But we are waiting for weather. Nothing new there! We need a good weather window to continue on. In the meantime we are enjoying Curaçao.

We are waiting for weather in Curaçao. In retrospect, all of us would rather have spent more time in Bonaire. By 'all of us' I mean Ran and I and the crew of *Quic en grogne*: Isabelle, Roel, Tessa and Yoan. We all liked Bonaire better. (Tessa found some friends on another boat in Curaçao, so she was quite happy here.) It was a much simpler place in Bonaire and the water was crystal clear. You loved snorkeling right off the boat seeing tons of fish. And we could dinghy in and walk right to where you wanted to be. In Curaçao things were far away from the anchorage in Spaanse (Spanish) Waters. And it was a kind of rolly and always windy.

But we had fun, too. We bought yummy ice cream bars from the ladies on the ice cream boat. The same lady goes around and fills your water ranks if you hire her to do that, which we did. Very convenient. We met great people, which is such a plus in this life adventure. Blake and Sunny and their daughter, whom we met in Bonaire, were here. Nathalie and Art. Nathalie is French and an artist...Art is ...Art, just a great guy. They were taking their boat, *Fanta Sea* back to Florida for a while.

Gatherings were enjoyed at Fisherman's Marina, the dinghy dock, and at the little club off of our anchorage. We celebrated my birthday aboard *Kwanesum* with the crew of *Quic en grogne*. I made my favorite dinner, macaroni and cheese, and cupcakes for dessert, Tessa drew me a picture of *Kwanesum* and they brought a cake, too. And..a couple of days later, *Quic en grogne* invited us over for dinner and Roel made crepes.

So yummy! Crepes made by a Dutch/French person! Can't beat that! And they always served great wine on *Quic en grogne*, in nondescript, small glass cups. Very European and enjoyable.

Ah, yes...in Curaçao we were also boarded by the Coast Guard. Seems they targeted the US boats. We had no problem with them. We invited them on board and showed them all of our papers. (Another US boat didn't have a good experience, I guess. But they were very resistant to letting them on board for some reason.) However, we did later find a paper from our check-in process was missing. When we went to check out...again walking hither and yon to all the spots we needed to visit to check out, one paper they asked for was not there. Ugh! Do not make this process worse than it is! We wondered if the Coast Guard had inadvertently taken that paper with them. There are so many that you must fill out, and then keep, and then show authorities when they ask for them...the 'paper shuffle'. It's a wonder more papers don't go missing. But Randy is very good at keeping all in order. That's why we were so surprised to find one was not there. We actually weren't sure what to do about that missing document, except...the people in the office had a COPY of the same paper. Hellooo? Must you hassle us if you already have a copy? This checking in and out of countries is getting old. Anyhoo...got 'er done. Thank heaven.

And now, we were ready to go. *Kwanesum* and *Quic en grogne* are anxious to get underway to the next destination. Hoping the weather would cooperate, we were also determining what our next destination would be. The closest spot was Aruba. And then there was Cartagena, Colombia. And then Panama. We could go to Aruba and hang out there and then determine if it would be Cartagena or Panama next. We could go straight to Cartagena. We could go straight to Panama. After sitting awhile at Curaçao we were anxious to get going farther than Aruba. When the weather window opens we need to get going while the gettin' is good. Weather is always the huge determining factor. So the next question was... straight to Panama or to Cartagena first? Cartagena was a bit of a challenge to decide because of tales from other cruisers and because our insurance company would charge us extra to go there. The charge was only $100 so that was not a big factor. The scuttlebutt was that it was *'unsafe'*, *'dirty water'*, *'the marina was all torn apart'*, *'you have to use an agent to check in'*, *'it's gorgeous'*, *'do NOT miss it'*....we ignored the first part and concentrated on the latter. And when are we ever going to get to Colombia again? If ever!

"All those in favor of Cartagena say, Aye." "AYE!!!" "All those opposed..."(silence). To Cartagena it is! The trip there will not be easy. They say it is the 5th hardest passage, apparently. (I found that out after the fact.) Not sure what the others are, but I have an inkling. We will wait for a good weather window and the wind and seas will be behind us. These are good things to concentrate on.

Well, it was definitely Mr Toad's wild ride. We were wing and wing, with the wind and seas behind us, able to sail, but the winds were big and the seas were big and the **Proactive Puking Management** that I thought was no longer needed proved to be necessary. Thought I could do it, but I was wrong. I tried really hard, but the body was in charge. Oh well, back to the **PPM**. Whatever it takes. Rocking and rolling are here to stay for awhile on this leg of the trip.

The first 24 hours we made 170 nautical miles. Hello??!!! We were cookin'! We wore our life jackets the whole trip. Normally we wear them only at night and clip ourselves on when in the cockpit. But with this wild ride, we kept them on the whole time. We obviously had a current with us and there were waves we were surfing down at times but our speed at one time was 10kts!! That's HUGE for *Kwanesum*! With a good current we can do 7.5 – 8kts sometimes, but not often. Usually we do 5 – 6.5kts, depending on the elements. It took us 3 complete days/nights to get to Cartagena. And it wasn't much fun. Our preventer broke a couple of times… WHAM/BANG/UGLY! Always at night, of course, like I mentioned before, when things seem to get a little livelier…like the seas slamming us around and the wind slamming us around. KAPLOWEY!!! "Holy crap what was that??" I hollered, having been blasted out of a sort-of sleep down below. "The damn preventer broke. Grab the helm and hold the boat steady, El, while I try to secure the mainsail." "Uhhh, roger Ran, I'm trying but she's not cooperating very well. We seem to be going back the way we started. Man, I'm glad we're not going THIS direction in these waves! Yeee Haww!"

It's hard to see at night. At this point Randy is forward, always hooked on to the jack lines which hold you on board, wrestling away with the boom and the lines. I turned on the deck light so he could kind of see. "Screw this shit, El, start the engine. I'm pulling in the sails. We will deal with this in the morning when I can see. As per usual." Again our common sense decision. Wait until morning. Our beloved Yanmar engine which is soooo good to us, started right up. We motored the rest of the night pounding through the seas that were like a washing machine. Next morning, we discovered the boom vang had pulled out of the mast. The boom vang's job is to hold down the boom of the head sail. Lovely. Not crucial, fortunately, but not exactly the greatest thing you want to happen. Randy jury rigged it and we'll fix it later. This was one of a couple of times that we had drama in the night on this leg of the trip…and …again…always at night. Must be the sea gods' revenge. Are we having fun yet?

Chapter 24

Cartagena

We are Actually in Colombia!

Arrived at Cartagena, early, early and had to wait around before we could call to get permission to go in. It was not a pretty site. I began to have doubts about our decision. The skyline was of tall buildings and there seemed to be smog! I guess I was expecting green hills with a quaint village tucked inside. And the water was green/brown. Ugh. We got permission to go in. *Quic en grogne* had a hard time being understood. Their boat name is not easy, particularly if you don't speak the language well. Roel was tired and becoming frustrated. It had been a long journey. Isabelle speaks fluent Spanish and finally got on the radio but the harbor patrol still could not understand their boat name. We went ahead in. Their patrol boat came out and checked with *Quic en grogne* and all was well. Now into the anchorage. So glad to be here! Yay! We made it!

Not lovely. Lots of garbage in the brown water. Ahhh…this is what people were talking about. I really didn't expect such a 'city', city! Tall apartment buildings and I assume some business buildings on the peninsula surrounding the bay. You could see bits of the old town peaking through on the mainland. OK...we'll give this a try but right now...I'm not impressed. We decide not to check into the country until the following day as we all need to sleep and rest a bit. We leave our yellow quarantine flag up and hit the hay after finding decent anchorages in the harbor.

The guide books say you need an agent to check in to the country and they suggest 2 names: Manfred and David. Roel, Yoan, Randy and I dinghy in to Club Nautico, the socalled marina there. NOT what you'd expect... however, we were forewarned by *Noonsite* (the website, by and for cruisers) that it was a little roughshod. They were very nice at the marina. Apparently, as it was being built, the mayor of the city decided to put a halt to the progress as there was a question of ownership. So it is a partially built marina with lots of rebar and boards and whatever to hold it together and planks to walk on from the dinghy to the covered area and a little building that acts as an office. Hmmmmm.... One of the agents, Manfred, said to meet him at the grocery store down the street. That sounds a little odd. The other agent, David, happened to be in the office when we got there. I read on *Noonsite* that David was the better agent. In hindsight I'm not sure that was true, but you gotta go by some reasoning, so we decided to go with David. Long story short, it ended up being a *'give me your passports, I'll take care of it'* (which is always scary but necessary, I guess)...wait...   *'come   with   me   here'*....wait... wait...wait...finally done. Then to check out...same thing...David was never on time... wait...wait...but he's got your passports so what can you do? Then pay him $50 for all of that...waiting. But it got done. Thank heaven.

We fell in love with Cartagena. Once we got off the boat and into the town, we loved their grocery store/coffee

282

shop/internet café/laundry that was just up the street. Quaint town. Nice people. Ran and I walked across the bridge into old town and just loved it! We were hungry and had our eyes out for a little cantina that held the promise of a great lunch. We were not disappointed. We peeked into doorways here and there and chose one that had a wonderful narrow courtyard with little tables. We thought we might eat inside, but their air conditioning had gone out so they recommended outside. It was perfect. Our waiter was amazing. So amazing, in fact, that we became Facebook friends! The food was spectacular. And we met a couple at another table who were there on their honeymoon. It was a beautiful, charming late morning lunch.

In old town Cartagena a wonderful celebration was taking place during our stay. How fortunate for all of us! *Por la Ruta de los Galeones, El Caribe se Llenara de Velas: "On the route of the Galleons, the Caribbean is full of sails."* A celebration of tall ships!! And, lo...we were able to watch the parade of the tall ships from over 6 countries from *Kwanesum* at anchor. I have to use the overused word awesome here, because that is what describes this experience best. It was just awesome! Never in our wildest dreams would we have imagined we would have been able to experience a parade of tall ships while at anchor in our own sailboat in Cartagena, Colombia, of all places. Magnificent! They came into the harbor as in a parade with proud pomp and circumstance, the numerous uniformed sailors standing on the yardarms, flags flying, some even had music of their country blaring from the ship. Our vantage point was spectacular. A special unexpected touch to our Cartagena visit. Along with the tall ships, there were grand celebrations in old town, too. Costumes, flags, wonderful vendors with candies and fruits and bites to eat. And bands playing and dancers dancing in their colorful costumes all along the cobblestone streets. My heart is so full thinking of what a magnificent experience that was, and it was so unexpected.

We felt very safe there. Never felt uneasy. And it was so wonderfully charming. More than I could have ever imagined. We strolled around the old town taking a zillion pictures of the beautiful buildings and flowers and cobblestone streets. We visited The Castillo San Felipe de Barajas, a fortress that is actually an old castle built in 1536. It's located on the Hill of San Lazaro in a strategic location, dominating approaches to the city by land or sea. There was a lot of pirate activity in those ancient years and Cartagena was much valued because of this strategic layout. We toured the top and then a web of tunnels underneath that were amazing! Apparently you can go clear from point A to point B under there, but we were not keen on being in those tunnels and going too far. I was afraid we'd get lost. Kinda claustrophobic down in those tunnels, too.

Ran and I celebrated our anniversary in Cartagena and Roel, Isabelle, Tessa and Yoan wanted to take us to dinner. We walked around the old town to find the perfect restaurant and one that would take reservations. We found the quaintest of spots but the reservation was not until around 2200hrs. Well that was a new experience for us! But Isabelle and Roel were not shocked at all about the time. It's very common to eat that late in Europe. It did make it a wonderfully different experience for us. And our waiter made us a special cocktail using fresh, juicy mangos and rum. Fresh, fresh mango. What an enjoyable night with Roel, Isabelle, Tessa and Yoan. It was so nice and so special.

We stayed in Cartagena 5 days. Memorable, memorable, memorable. You MUST see Cartagena.

Now…to the San Blas!

Itchy Feet

The San Blas Islands are on the Caribbean side of Panama. I had not heard of them before but we learned about them when we were still in Virginia. And now this is one spot Ran and I had been waiting for. When we were still in Deltaville, fitting out our boat and preparing for our adventure, we came across a boat in the yard from San Francisco. The couple that owned her were working away repainting the bottom and polishing the boat preparing to store her while they went home for a while. We always like to talk to folks that have *'been there and done that'* to glean any bits of information that might help us on our trip. One of the questions we asked them was what their favorite spot was along the way. "The Swimming Pool in the San Blas Islands." This was the spot they said was so gorgeous and clear and wonderful. And now we were about to get there! Goosebumps as to how lucky we are.

This journey from Cartagena to the San Blas was excellent. Ellen kind of excellent. Well, almost. It would have been more excellent if we could have sailed, with smooth seas, but barring that happening, we motor-sailed on smooth seas. With a full moon. I'll take it! It was an easy 207 nautical mile trip that took us a day and a half. A nice way to come into this beautiful spot. We got to Porvenir, the Port of Entry for the Comarca of San Blas, about 0800hrs to check in. Comarca means it's an independent country, not part of the Republic of Panama. The indigenous Kuna people have resisted outside government for 400 years. In fact, the Kunas call this area Kuna Yala. They do not like the name San Blas as it was given the name by the Spanish invaders. Porvenir is not a great place to stay so we just anchored there for the duration of our check-in process. And of course we were too early for the officials. So we wait....wandering around the island to check things out. There were a couple of restaurants and what I think was a hotel and a landing strip, of sorts.

The San Blas Islands are mostly small islands of coral and sand, some densely populated. The Kunas create and sell *molas* which are unique 3, 4 or 5 layer fabric panels decorated with reverse appliqué designs and embroidery. I loved them, but I'm not sure what to do with them. Actually we did purchased one from Vernancio, a master *mola* artist. It was gorgeous. You can see the wonderful hand sewing that is done. It was expensive for this area but worth it. It will remind us of our trip to the San Blas and it will produce nice décor on the boat. Some people make pillows out of them. The Kuna women make identical *mola* panels and use them for a blouse by adding a yoke and puffy sleeves out of whatever fabric, not always matching. Kinda funky. Here, again, the need to have cash on hand came to the forefront. I wanted to buy more than two *molas* as they were so unique and I pictured framing some and making pillows out of others. But…we only had so much cash on hand and there are no ATMs when you need them. Again, that lack of planning foiled my desire for souvenirs of our adventure. But, then again…that might have been for the best.

The Kuna women also wear gold through their ears and nose and wrap beads around their arms and legs. Lots of beads and bracelets. While we were waiting to check in to the country, and before we left Porvenir, I had one of the older women put 'wini' beads on my arm. She methodically wrapped them around and around and secured each wrap, twisting the string around each row. Then carefully and securely tying it off. She was darling. But they don't like you to take their picture. I would have loved to have gotten very close to her wonderful face for a picture. I treasure it. And of course everyone had tattoos. It's apparently a matriarchal society. The women are well respected. They control the money and the men move into the women's family compound. In fact many men dress as women and act as women here. Some of them very prominent in their village.

From Porvenir we decided to go to the West Lemmon Cay in the San Blas, which was close, to anchor for a couple of days.

286

There are many, many islands here to explore. But we weren't going to take too much time, so we needed to chose carefully those we did see. We found a nice little anchorage at the West Lemmons. Stayed there for 3 days. There were several other boats anchored here, some appeared to have been here for quite some time. VHF channel 72 was the voice of the cruisers net in this area. More useful information available on the nets. *Quic en grogne* only stayed for 1 day and then were off to explore other islands. We decided to go our separate ways and meet up again in a couple of weeks. While at the Lemmons we had, of course, the vendors. The Kuna Indians selling their wares. In their dugout canoes called *ulus* they would paddle up to *Kwanesum* with a pig in the front, a couple of children, an older grandmother, the son, perhaps, and a dog with pups. All in one canoe! They were so charming. They were selling *molas*. I did buy one, for $10. We had a sense of the price from the shop at Porvenir. Then Vernancio came along as I said above with his really wonderful *molas*. This is where I purchased one for $100. It's wonderful. Concern for money was the cause to pause at one purchase. But that one was a beauty.

Now our mission was to find the "Swimming Pool" we had heard so much about and been dreaming to see. It's in the East Holandes Cays. We set out for there, found it and anchored in 9 feet of crystal clear, fabulously azure water! OK...this is the spot!! There were about 17 boats spread around. Apparently during the busy season they get about 8 times that! Glad we weren't there during that time. There were boats from S. Africa, France, Ireland, Spain, Germany and of course America. Plenty of room. So beautiful. And the weather was perfect. We immediately jumped in the water. We were in the water constantly here.

As we set our anchor and have our safe-arrival beer, which has become a tradition, Randy decided to don his Speedo (just kidding!) and dive in and check out the anchor. It's so clear you can see it really easily. As he was snorkeling about I heard our bilge go off and saw it spurting water out the back. Hmmmm....wonder why it wants to do that? "Uh, Ran! Why's our bilge going off?" "What??!!!" he says as he's climbing up the stern ladder. "Holy shit we're sinking!!!" "Huh???" (Well I wouldn't go that dramatic, but that's what he said.) In a flurry of arms and legs and dripping all over the inside of the boat Randy starts pulling things apart...checking the through-hulls...looking everywhere...finally rips off the mattress of the aft berth, flinging it into the main saloon area (which is not easy to do) and checks the water pump. I'm standing around watching him in awe and wondering what the heck I can do to help. "Aha! That's it! We're saved! A hose came off the water pump." Randy, my hero, fixes it after another flurry of finding the right tools. "The good news is...we are no longer sinking. The bad news is...there goes all our fresh water." "Huh???" "Well...not all of our fresh water, but we're going to have to watch it until we get a good rain storm." Phew...not all is lost. And we can bathe off the back of the boat. No *problemo*. And we did get a good rainstorm while we were there that filled us right back up with fresh water. Did I tell you how we did that? Catch the rainwater? We jury-rigged a rain catcher! Is this not the greatest? We are getting power from the sun and the wind and water from rain. We could be completely self sustainable if we had to be. This rain catcher was not just buckets. It consisted of a piece of Sunbrella fabric that we had left over. Randy attached it alongside our deck on the handrails and the outside stanchions and lifelines, above our water tank opening and attached a hose to a hole in the center. It worked famously! Crazy fun resourceful thinking.

We spent the most wonderful, relaxing 2 weeks at the East Holandes. We snorkeled and snorkeled and cleaned the bottom of the boat while we were down there. Which is a good thing to do! Tiny critters like to attach themselves to the bottom of the boat along the way and at anchor, and it's best to get them off when you can for smoother/faster sailing. Makes sense, right?

We met some wonderful people also on their sailboats. Exchanged books. Had an appetizer exchange on the beach. We had Kunas come out in their *ulus* to sell us vegetables, rum, beer, cookies, lobsters (which we BBQ'd), whatever we needed. We gave them some gasoline, which they always ask for, and treats *por los niños*, which they also always ask for, as well as dollars. The US dollar is the currency used here and in Panama. One enterprising young Kuna wanted to sell Randy a doll that was supposed to be useful like Viagra! "Ahhhh...no gracias. Don't need no stinking Viagra doll." Too funny! *Quic en grogne* joined us for the last couple of days at the anchorage and then we were all off to Porvenir again, this time to check out of the San Blas.

Then ...on to Panama and *'le canal'*, as Isabelle says.

To step back a minute....remember I said there was plenty of room at this anchorage. Well...it never fails...that some boat wants to anchor right next to you! Have I said that before? Well, I'm saying it again. This particular boat was anchored a nice bit away from us originally and for some unknown reason decided to move...right next to us. OK. We've gotten a little more relaxed about that, but please...with all this room, why right next to us?? And this guy was weird. I figure he was about our age. His wife seemed ok, but this guy liked to be in the nude a lot. Lovely. And he had a duck decoy he put out behind the boat. Lovely. And he liked to wear his camouflage jacket (yes JACKET) and floppy hat...with nothing else. Lovely. And he decided to fly a kite one day off the back of the boat...in the nude. Lovely. "Uhhh...Randy...it might be getting close to time to leave this spot." Do you think he was trying to get us to leave??? I don't think that was his *raison d'etre* but....lovely. We're leaving.

We arrived at Porvenir, anchored and went in to check out of the San Blas Islands only to find ...they were at lunch. We wait.... Decided to try lunch at the little restaurant while we were waiting. There was a French film crew there that Roel and Isabelle recognized from French TV. Apparently they were doing a documentary of the San Blas. That was kind of cool. They had the head Kuna honcho there on the island to film. The Kuna Indians are VERY small people and this man was VERY small and unassuming. That was kinda neat to see.

At the restaurant, we were waited on by little Kuna young ladies with their piercings and tattoos and beaded arms and legs. And I don't think they knew what to do. We ordered. We wait... We had beer that smelled of fish. They brought out one...lunch...at....a... time. Not sure why. You can imagine how long that took! Waiting.... And it ended up Randy never did get his lunch! By that time they had forgotten him, I think, and he told them to forget it. This made for a grumpy Randy, as you can imagine. Kind of a weird way to run a restaurant but we've learned not to expect much on some of these trips. But we at least thought we'd all get served our lunch! And we were very hungry. Poor Randy.

We finally get back to the immigration office on the little island, go through all the paper rigmarole, give them more money, and we're outta there. I tell ya...one thing we will NOT miss is checking in to and out of countries. I know....I've said that before. By checking into Panama at the San Blas we got our cruising permit until the end of July. That covers us for all of Panama. (But when we got to Panama proper, we found we would need to check with immigration again, but this time we paid the marina where we stayed to do that for us.)

We motored over off the island of Porvenir to a nicer anchorage and spent the night amongst some heavily populated Kuna islands. We arose early in the morning to leave and watched the Kunas row to work in their *ulus* or sail in their *cayucos*. Commuter traffic. Amazing. On we went to Isla Linton where we planned to stop for the night on our way to Colon. It was a nice anchorage tucked inside a little bay. Lots of sailboats here. Some of them we recognized from other anchorages. You start to remember boat names. We noticed a lot of debris in the water, mostly logs, on this leg of the trip. So we had to keep a good watch to avoid banging things up. Again we are up early and off…to Colon! The Panama Canal awaits. Holy cow. This is huge. We can't believe we have come this far.

Traveling with *Quic en grogne* along the Atlantic side of Panama we start to see the big boys anchored, the big ships waiting to go through the canal. This is very exciting. We have heard so many stories and read so much about the Panama Canal and now here we are in person! It was…awesome. That's the only word that described our feelings upon arrival. Again, I have to use that word because it completes the feeling we had getting close to THE…PANAMA…CANAL!

Chapter 25
The Panama Canal

To The Pacific, Captain Ran!

Our destination on this side of the canal, in Colon, was Shelter Bay Marina, as suggested from reading our cruising guides. Shelter Bay Marina is located quite far outside the city of Colon in a National Park. The surrounding buildings and airstrip are part of Ft Sherman US Military Reserve. It is a very secure area. Colon itself is notoriously NOT secure. This is where we will stay while we make arrangements to go through the Panama Canal. Again...we used our cruising guides, our valuable, valuable, very informative cruising guides to decide how to proceed with the process of going through the canal; where to stay, what to avoid, a good procedure to secure your boat, etc.

The stories and advice and cruising guide information about transiting the canal is overwhelming. It is a BIG, BIG deal. And you want it to go well. Our senses are on high alert to glean every bit of information from whatever source we run into about making a successful canal transit. While we were in Cartagena I made the attempt to contact via email several suggested agents to use to deal with the bureaucracy of going through the canal. An agent isn't necessary, but all the people we knew that have gone through the canal used one. On the advice of s/v *Ocean Pearl*, whom we met in Grenada, we tried contacting Tina McBride as our agent. She had been recommended by others on *Noonsite* and in one of our cruising guides as well. She was delightful, answered right away, but said she was going to be on vacation during the time of our expected arrival. She immediately gave me 2 other names to try: Enrique and Stanley. I had read not good things about Stanley, but Enrique was used by Terri and Lyman our buddy boaters on *sans clés* so I emailed him. I'm sure Stanley is also a good agent, as others have alluded to when we got through the canal. It's just that once something is written about you that's not good, it's hard to overcome that. So Enrique it was. We actually researched early and our agent was decided and contacted before we left Cartagena.

On arrival at the marina, and after checking in , we noticed on the office bulletin board an ad for line handlers on a sailboat transiting the canal. . When you transit the canal you have to have line handlers on board to deal with the large lines used to tie you to the canal. They can't be yourself because you will be at the helm. In my case I was choosing whether to be a line handler or at the helm. We decided I would do the helm so Randy immediately volunteered to go with the boat needing line handlers. Roel, too, decided to make the trip. This will give them a good indication of how the whole process works. It's actually recommended that you go on another boat first as a line handler. I decided not to go as we had just arrived and I had tons to do aboard to get us ship shape. As long as one of us got the experience that was ok.

The agent you hire deals directly with the canal and all the bureaucracy/paperwork for our transit. The cost for the agent was $400. For me that provided a lot of reassurance. If you do it yourself, everything has to be in cash. That was another deterrent for me but didn't seem to be a problem for others. I didn't want to locate a bank and take out $850 cash which you have to give the canal as a buffer, plus the $800 cash or so you need for the transit fee. The buffer you are supposed to get back in 3 months or so, and I'm sure you do but I'm not sure where or when. Anyway...following the advice of our friends who had previously gone through the canal, we opted to pay for an agent. Hiring an agent saved us time, money, worry and aggravation. This was a big decision for all of us to make. Agent...yes? or no? *Quic en grogne* opted not to hire an agent. Our trip, including the transit fees and agent, cost us about $1400.

Enrique was not the most on-time agent in the world, though we have found that to be the case with most people we have dealt with in the Latin countries, but he was thorough and all went well. He scheduled the Admeasurer for a Sunday, which we thought was odd, and that proved to be true. We waited all day for him and of course he did not come...because it was Sunday! We told Enrique Monday morning we would not be at the boat as we were scheduled to take the bus into Colon for provisions. "No problem." The Admeasurer came on Monday, while we were gone, after we told Enrique we would not be there...of course. He did come by later that evening to finish up the paperwork. He was extremely nice. The Admeasurer...measures your boat. He boards your yacht with a pile of paperwork, a tape measure, and lots of questions. He also fills out all the paperwork for the transit including how fast your boat can go and where you want to be in the canal chamber during the transit. They want you to say you can go 8 knots. We cannot go 8 knots under power unless we have a current with us. A big current. In fact, there aren't too many boats our size that can go 8 knots under power so it's kind of a moot question. He said, no problem. And it wasn't...but it's weird. However, the canal will charge you more if you say you cannot go 8 knots, so 8 knots it is. As far as position in the canal, we were told to say center chamber, if possible. The other choices are along the wall and tug tied. Center chamber is the least likely to have any damage. Well THERE'S a good idea! Damage??? I'm starting to get a little nervous about all of this. The Admeasurer said you do not always get what you request as the Lock Master makes the decision within minutes of your approach to the locks. Well... we'll just hope for the best I guess. All of our paperwork, and there's a lot, was held by Enrique for us.

Enrique said we're scheduled to go through on Thursday. He gave us very specific instructions. I am getting more nervous by the minute. I have not been nervous about anything on this whole trip, but this canal business made be nervous. You read in the guide books all about the transit and they specify exactly what you do. They also let you know all the things that can happen. Great. I know we need to know this but it just kept my nerves a rollin'. The boat berthed next to us at Shelter Bay had not had a good experience coming through from the Pacific. They had been tied to another boat in the chamber and they were tied too tightly together. A tug in the chamber reversed its engines, which creates a lot of water wash turbulence, and caused the boats both to move about erratically fighting against each other. The sailboat couldn't release their line fast enough and one of their cleats tore off. Fortunately it didn't hit anyone! That could have been very dangerous. It takes a lot to pull off a cleat! Oh good...nerves are getting worse. Randy wasn't as worried because he had taken that trip through the canal as a line handler. I'm so glad he did that.

We got our heavy 125', large diameter lines, 4 of them, from Enrique. That was another plus of having an agent. They get the lines you need for you and they will also get line handlers, if you need them. But they cost $60/day. We hoped to avoid having to pay for line handlers, so Randy went scouting. John, who was on a boat down the dock from us, said he would go with us as a line handler. What a great guy he was. He had gone with Randy and Roel on the sailboat that went through the canal earlier. Then we found Paul Cahill and Tamar Lowell, who are from our yacht club in Alameda! They had been traveling down the Pacific coast and through Central America and were moored on the Pacific side of the canal. Rick, a guy who had a boat at Shelter Bay near us was talking about the boat *Xanadu* one day, and we immediately perked up our ears, hoping that it might be Paul and Tamar from Alameda. Sure enough. So Randy called them to see if they wanted to be line handlers for us. And bless their hearts they said yes. Excellent. We have a good crew. That helps. That worry is dealt with.

My job was to make sure we had all the provisions we needed and all the meals for the crew. And places set up for them to sleep. It's a 2-day trip to go through the canal for our size boat. From the Atlantic side you go through the Gatun Locks first, then spend the night out on Gatun Lake. Then, up early the next day and travel down the lake and through the Miraflores Locks to the Pacific. So...I needed to have lots of snacks, lunch, a good dinner and something for breakfast. OK...got it down. John and Randy said the guy on the boat they helped crew did not have good food. John said he would go only if I had good food. HA! And you have to feed your advisor, too. I'll get to that in a minute.

Preparing the boat's sleeping quarters and food provisions helped keep my nerves at bay. I'm usually not a nervous person, but this definitely had all my nerves on edge. It's the unknown, I think. And then all the info I over-read about the trips through the canal on a fairly small sailboat, comparatively. I mean, there are HUGE ships that go through the canal at the same time! We count on the canal manager to make sure we are not in the locks with the huge ships. Imagination runs rampant.

Tires....we had to have tires tied alongside our boat to defend it from damage. (Everything seems to be there to defend from damage! Arrghh! Worry, worry...) Some folks use the fenders they have, but we don't have that many fenders and the tires are recommended as they're tough. We've heard of fenders being torn up badly. (Worry...worry) We acquired 10 tires. You can usually get them off a boat that has finished their transit or you can find one of the guys on the dock to hunt them up for you for $1/ tire. We used 10 tires...5 on each side. The tires are covered with garbage bags so they don't mark up the boat.

Now, we need to cover our solar panels. It's recommended that you do this, too. The linemen in the lock chambers throw their large lines with monkey fists tied on the ends at our boat, and those are then tied to the big lines we rented, that were already secured on our boat. These thrown lines have monkey-fists on the ends so they can be easily thrown and grabbed. Now, in my nervous mind, I'm envisioning HUGE monkey fists that will really put dents in our boat! I was adamant that Randy cover the solar panels. We put our cushions on top of them and then covered that with our shade tarp. Then all was tied down well. Looking more and more like the Clampetts every day! Randy assured me that the monkey-fists and lines weren't as big as I imagined, not even as big as the lines from Enrique, but I still thought the worst.

OK...I think we're ready to go. Paul and Tamar come over from Balboa Yacht Club on the Pacific side on Wednesday late afternoon. That way they are all settled and ready to go the next day. That was fun. Getting to know them again and talking about all our travels here and there. They are great, great people. John was ready to go the next day. I've got my food prepared. Now we relax (not easy for me) and wait. We are to call Enrique at exactly noon on Thursday to get our time to meet our advisor out on the Flats. We are also to call the Port Captain and let him know when we are out on the Flats ready to receive our advisor. There are heavy fines involved if you miss your time or if your engine fails you and you can't make it through, etc, etc. (Worry…worry.)

The Flats is an area out near the mouth of the Gatun Locks. This is where a pilot boat will bring out our Transit Advisor. If you are under 65′ you will have an advisor. If you are over 65′ you need to have a Pilot. We left Shelter Bay with all our crew at 1400hrs to go out to the Flats and pick up our advisor. Jorge, our advisor, arrives, gets on the boat and starts telling us what to expect and, inspects our lines to be sure they are laid out cleanly, and checks our cleats and chocks. The advisor gives helm instructions and coordinates all transit activities by radio with the people in charge of the canal. But he does not drive the boat. The pilots, however, do drive the large ships. They are very professional. Jorge gets word that we are to wait for another sailboat that we will raft up with for our trip through the canal. The great news is that we will be in the center chamber and there will be no other ships in the chamber with us. This is really, really good news. Having the big ships in the chamber with you is worrisome (I don't need more worry) in that they create a lot of turbulence when they begin to move in or out of the chambers. You are very, very close to the ships in the chambers since they are so big. Hooray for us that we can avoid that experience. So far, so good! So now we wait for *NorthFork*, the sailboat we will raft up with.

They are late. And we wait. Apparently, they had to wait for some paperwork before they could depart Shelter Bay. Jorge radios the advisor on *NorthFork* and tells them we are prepared to have them raft up on our port side. "Uhhh…be advised that

298

NorthFork needs to raft up to Kwanesum on her starboard side. NorthFork has their outboard engine on their starboard side so that will not work." Uhhh...excuse me? We are waiting, waiting for them and now they want to call the shots? We prepared by taking our outboard off! (Ok...the nerves are making me cranky.) We move our extra fenders to the starboard side to prepare for their arrival. Finally, they arrive and start rafting up to us. And start telling us what to do! Helloooo!!! ???(Ok, Ellen...calm down.) The little gal on *NorthFork*, Dana, was really being pushy by ordering all of us around. She was concerned about the spring lines holding the boats together being too tight. And rightly so because of the incident, I mentioned earlier. But our crew decided to vote her off the island. She was too bossy, particularly after we had to wait and wait for them. We knew what to do and didn't need her telling us and bossing us around. Her husband was delightful, just manning the helm and asking Randy if everything was ok. They were on their honeymoon! She later told us they had gone through as line handlers and had a horrible experience where the spring lines were too tight and the 2 advisors were arguing about what to do. So, she had reason to be a little uptight about it all. But it didn't fit right with the *Kwanesum* crew, meaning me. But, as you can tell, I was on edge. Majorly on edge, so every little thing....

But it was a good trip. The Gatun Locks are the easiest of the locks to transit. Each chamber is 110 feet wide and 1000 feet long. (Interesting to note, the tidal range on the Atlantic side is 3 feet. On the Pacific side, it averages 18 feet!) We pull into the first chamber, rafted up with *NorthFork*. Since *NorthFork* is the bigger boat, they were the power and steerage for both of us. You just need to heed all the spring lines and try to keep the boats steady together so there will be no damage bumping together. We did really well with that. We were a good team. We're in the center chamber and the canal line handlers throw the monkey-fists on board. Here's an example of part of my worry, a quote from one of our cruising guides: *"In spite of stories, they don't deliberately knock out windows and spotlights, but it does happen. You could be knocked senseless by a monkey-fist if you don't pay attention."* (Worry...worry.) Since we are rafted to another boat we only need to have line handlers on the port side. Therefore, Randy manned our helm and I took pictures and worried! Yay! Tamar also took pictures and Paul and John were our line handlers. Jorge made sure we were doing everything properly and Roy the advisor on *NorthFork* did the same on their side.

The monkey-fists are thrown. John grabs one on the bow and Paul grabs one for the stern line. They quickly tie one of our big canal lines with the loop end onto the monkeyfist and the canal line handlers pull the tied loop up to the chamber side. The canal line handlers then hook our loops to the bollards of the chamber. Bollards are basically giant cleats up on the canal side. Our line handlers then adjust the lines going through the chocks, and then the cleats for better leverage and safety. Our boats need to stay centered in the chamber and parallel to the side walls. Everyone must constantly adjust the lines to factor this and keep our yachts centered. The advisors we had were excellent. They were nice, vigilant, helpful, and non-argumentative with each other. So far, so good.

The canal gates are locked behind us, and 52 million gallons of fresh water begins to rush in from below us. The fresh water mixing with the saltwater causes a little extra turbulence, but it's not bad. It's doable. We begin to ascend. The line handlers are constantly hauling in the lines as they begin to slacken, trying to keep everything coordinated. The advisors are vigilantly watching to be sure both boats are synchronized with their lines. It takes about 15 minutes to fill the lock. Here is where we were really lucky not to have a large ship in front of us. When it's time to exit the lock, a big ship, which, by the way, is pulled by little trains (mules) along the canal, often has to apply power to get going out of the lock. That power creates massive turbulence that, if you are behind them, will set your boat straining to stay center and safe. I'm so glad we didn't have that to deal with. (Less worry...yay!)

We go through two more locks with the canal line handlers walking us through, then tying off again onto the bollards. We now enter Gatun Lake, the man-made freshwater lake 85 feet above sea level. Here, we will spend the night. Our advisor, Jorge, guides us to a large mooring that we will secure for the night while *NorthFork* ties up to a mooring on the opposite side. Our advisors are picked up, and we prepare to spend the night.

I made spaghetti, salad, French bread, and with some red wine, we are very content. It's Tamar's birthday! So we have cupcakes, too. How many guys do you know who would take you through the Panama Canal for your birthday? (Inside joke from Paul.) Mark and Dana from *NorthFork* come over for a chat with the guys while Tamar and I sit below, relax, and chat away. It's a nice evening, even though it's rainy. It rained a lot during the day, but it did not deter any of the crew.

This is an exciting experience. My worries are starting to fade. We did really well. So far, so good.

We are up early, serenaded by howler monkeys, to accept another advisor, and it's Roy! He was the advisor on *NorthFork* the day before, and he's great! Yay! *NorthFork* also gets their advisor, and his name is Roy too. So off we go with the two Roys to cross the lake and head to the next locks leading to the Pacific. We do not raft up with *NorthFork* until just prior to the locks, so we go our separate ways, but we follow them.

Gatun Lake is over 20 miles wide, and it takes us more than 3 hours to cross it. Along the way, we pass several massive ships, particularly those carrying cars. They are enormous, and we feel like peewees next to them. I actually think we timed this transit well. I believe canal traffic is lower this time of year compared to the high season. For that, I am grateful.

We cross Gatun Lake and reach the Gaillard Cut, the narrowest part of the canal. According to my sources, Eric Bauhaus and Pat Rains, the Gaillard Cut was carved through the Continental Divide. We travel about 7 miles through it and prepare to raft up again with *NorthFork* for the final lock transits. We enter the locks, again in the center chamber, and prepare the lines for the canal line handlers. We are waiting, and we now see we will have another boat with us in the chamber. But it's not big...it's a canal tour boat. Cool! Just the right size. This first lock is called the Pedro Miguel Lock. There is apparently a geological weakness on the Pacific side, so they have separated the down locks. The people on the tour boat are very curious and are taking our pictures. We must be quite a site as we are so small in these big chambers. We feel like celebrities. We wave, pose and smile for their pictures! (Worry is going away by the second now.)

Downward lockages are easier, not as much turbulence. You just need to remember to feed out your lines as the chamber sides get taller and taller! We now cross Miraflores Lake to the Miraflores Locks. There are two of them. This will take us down 54 feet. The last chamber of these locks is the highest due to that large tidal variation I mentioned before in the Pacific. Holy cow, we are almost done! (Worry is almost completely gone!) The chamber gates open and there is the Pacific! High 5's all around. Beer for everyone! I take a picture of the crew. I forget to have them take a picture of me. We were all too excited.

We separate from *NorthFork* and wait for the pilot boat to pick up our advisor, Roy. While traveling with Roy, we learned that working for the canal, especially as an advisor or a pilot, is considered a great privilege. It's a highly sought-after job in the area. Roy thoroughly enjoyed his work, and although pilots may earn more, their schedules are often in high demand. Roy was eager to finish our transit because he had plans to meet his family for pizza and to watch the new **Toy Story** movie. He kindly declined my offer of lunch, snacks, and beer. Both Roy and Jorge made our journey through the canal incredibly relaxing and easy. We felt fortunate to have such favorable circumstances for our transit.

Chapter 26
We Have Arrived!

We're In the Pacific

We now pass under the Bridge of Americas...in the Pacific... Ran, we made it to the Pacific! We took our crew to the Balboa Yacht Club, where they will depart. As we pull up to the dock, we pay the guys there $1/tire to take them off our hands. We say goodbye to our crew and head out around the Amador Causeway to Las Brisas, where we will anchor for a few days. On our way around to the anchorage we definitely notice there are what seem like a zillion big ships anchored all over out here. Waiting to go through the canal, I guess, or be loaded or unloaded at the big ship dock just prior to the canal on the Pacific side. Quite a site. Paul and Tamar have their boat moored there at Balboa Yacht Club but it's pretty expensive. Paul said it costs him $1/hour to stay there. But they are having engine problems and need to be there to get it fixed. We will go around to the free anchorage. We find a spot to anchor as the skies grow very dark. We can see the Panama City skyline and there are very dark clouds there with thunder in the background. Our first try at anchoring doesn't work so we decide to go farther out and let the boat anchor itself and have plenty of room to swing. That worked perfectly. We have heard of a number of boats dragging anchor here at Las Brisas, it is very soft mud, so we were prepared to anchor a couple of times until we felt secure. Time for a safe arrival beer! What an experience. Memorable, memorable, memorable. And my worries were for naught. Yay!

Now, we are relaxing and regrouping. We stayed at Las Brisas anchorage for 3 weeks. We met up again with Paul and Tamar at the Balboa Yacht Club at the Monday night book exchange there. On Tuesday nights the book exchange was at the Las Brisas area. Pizza and book exchange. We enjoy this for the obvious reason of exchanging books but also for the camaraderie. Channel 74 on the VHF radio was the go-to net that brought cruising folks together and told of what was going on. If you had something to sell or needed anything, or needed line handlers, Channel 74 was the place. One of the major perks of cruising, as I've said before and will say again, is the people. We met with Paul and Tamar frequently during our stay there. We met Howard and Donna on *Nintai*. They were a hoot. Donna ran one of the nets on certain days, as did Paul. Cracks me up that Donna used to be a Private Investigator. I just love all these people we meet. She told us of a time her granddaughter or grandson had her go into their school to talk about her occupation. And what they said was...' *Grandma...tell them how old you are!'* She's a hoot.

We took cabs into town and went to Albrook Mall, which was the first mall we had seen in quite some time. Bought some new prescription glasses for Ran. I bought some reading glasses that were $5 each. Love that! I had my hair colored and cut...sorely needed. The natural color...now too dark for my liking...had grown back completely and I hated it. Now I feel like a new woman...young and sassy. We relaxed at Las Brisas and read. It was nice. Ran and I decided to treat ourselves to a dinner out and chose a restaurant close to the dinghy dock at

Las Brisas. It was a wonderful dinner that we shared. The dinner had a large plate with different meats on it and I ordered *yuca frita* (fried yucca) and *patacones* (fried plantains) (in Puerto Rico, they were called *tostones*) to go along with the dinner. It was so wonderful. And only $23. For the two of us. But…since we decided to have chardonnay with our dinner, and ended up having 3 glasses a piece throughout the evening…at $5/glass…our dinner ended up being quite a bit more. Oh well…it was so worth it and was such an enjoyable, relaxing evening. Our waiter was perfect.

We had to say goodbye to *Quic en grogne!* So sad! After traveling with them for months…from Grenada to Panama they were traveling on to their home, New Caledonia. They must travel a long way across the Pacific to get there and they will have some wonderful stops along the way. They had a successful transit through the canal then prepared for their LONG voyage. They will have long spells at sea. They have a companion with them now who will help man the helm. Isabelle has a good routine for everyone: Tessa does her lessons everyday, Yoan…causes trouble (as Roel says) and Roel keeps everything shipshape. We will miss them very much. They have been a wonderful part of our lives. The picture I have of Randy waving goodbye to them from the bow of our boat, with *Quic en grogne* in the background, still brings tears to my eyes whenever I see it.

Now, it was time to move. We decided to start heading to Costa Rica, where we will leave our boat while we travel home for a much-needed break and a good long visit with family and friends. We miss our family so much… especially those grandkids. Time to go home for a while. Hurricane season is from July through November. Panama and Costa Rica are not in the hurricane zone. We decided to leave our boat in Costa Rica. We researched everything and decided on Land Sea

306

Marina in Golfito, Costa Rica, which is just past the border of Panama. While in Shelter Bay Marina, I contacted them and made all the arrangements to leave our boat there and our flight arrangements for home. The big stickler for that is that we cannot leave our boat in Costa Rica for more than 90 days. After that, we would have to have the boat bonded, which is a dog and pony show and expense…and if bonded, you can't use the boat during that time. OK… can't do that. We need to be back in Costa Rica before our 90 days is up. That cut our trip short by a couple of weeks. It's just that we would have liked to have visited more of Costa Rica while we were here. We'll just have to come back.

We first checked into leaving our boat in El Salvador, which is closer to the border of Mexico but still out of the hurricane zone. But El Salvador has an even stricter rule. You cannot leave your boat past 60 days or they will charge you a value-added tax of 10% the value of your boat based on what THEY think is the value of your boat. I DON'T THINK SO!!! Why these countries want to shoot themselves in the foot with these restrictions is beyond me. We are more than willing to stay awhile in their country and spend money. But these costly restrictions deter us from making that decision. As you can imagine, the marinas there are not happy.

So it's off to Land Sea at Golfito, Costa Rica. Enrique checked us out of Panama and brought all of our papers to us and we said goodbye. Because we cannot get to Golfito much before August 1, we head out to Taboga, an island off of Panama. Randy had called Chuy (Chewie), who is in charge of the moorings over there and told him our plans to come over for a few days. There are only a few moorings, so we wanted to be sure there was one available. There are many boaters that leave their boats with Chuy, as we are leaving ours at Land Sea, while they travel home. Therefore, a lot of the moorings are already taken up. But he saved us one and we headed out. First to fuel up and fill up our water tanks at Flamenco Marina near Las Brisas. Then traveling through the parking lot of huge ships waiting to go through the canal. Quite a site to see. And, of course, it's raining.

Taboga was a sweet island and Chuy and his girlfriend Susan were delightful and as helpful as can be. We stayed at Taboga for 8 days. The weather was holding us back. And the seas. We needed to have decent conditions to get around Punta Mala, one of the tips of Panama. The weather in Las Brisas wasn't all that good either. But then…it's the rainy season here. And that's what we got. Lots of rain and thunderstorms. We hunker down when that happens and, read our books and do Sudoku and play SkipBo. And if I can get online…that's where I am. We toured the little island. So clean and nice. Had good meals and met interesting people. We had lunch with a family from Spain, the father is American, who are planning to move to Panama. They were delightful. *Xanadu*, Paul and Tamar, got their engine fixed and needed to put hours on it so they motored over to Taboga for a few days. During our time at Taboga, we had some fun with them. Rum cocktails in the cockpit in the evening, exploring the town, including the graveyard, in the daytime. (That is, when we weren't being rained-in and rocking and rolling on the mooring). They say that they're running out of room in the graveyard, so often they dump the bodies behind the cemetery into the sea. We crept around through the graves and peeked back there at the edge of the island, and yep, there is proof of that happening. Pew! The smell was telling, too.

While we were at Taboga, there was a saints celebration. Not as much pomp and circumstance as we imagined might be going on but lots of fireworks/firecrackers and a parade of boats. The church on the island is, of course, the center of all that happens. It is said that it is the second oldest church in the hemisphere! That's pretty special! Taboga is also known for the hospital that during the building of the canal housed those that were overcome with tuberculosis or malaria or other such communicable diseases. Gauguin was said to have stayed there for a time. There were traces of his presence on the island.

Finally, the weather cooperates. We say goodbye to *Xanadu* and to Chuy, and we head to Naranjo, which is around the corner of Punta Mala. We decided to sail overnight all the way there. We want to make sure we position ourselves so that we can easily make it into Golfito when the time comes. We got pointers from other cruisers and checked the cruising guides to see which spots were best for anchoring along the way. As we go, the weather wasn't bad, and the seas weren't bad, just a little confused, which makes it slightly uncomfortable but not bad at all. We spot our destination and maneuver ourselves into the anchorage. Nobody there but us, but we were expecting that. This isn't the time of year most folks travel along here, and they usually aren't going in this direction.

We did have a bit of trouble on the way to Naranjo, now that I think about it. The alternator kept coming loose. We had a larger alternator than would normally come with a boat our size due to the battery bank we had, which is a good thing to have when you're living on a boat. Randy tightened it down before we left Taboga. As we were traveling to Naranjo, just prior to coming around Punta Mala and still in the shipping lanes, Ran and I were changing shifts at midnight. (Yep...everything happens at night...when it's dark.) He's coming up...I'm going down to sleep. He checked the engine first and "Damn! The alternator's loose again. Shut the engine off and let me tighten it, El." "This is not a good time, Randy! There is a ship coming up behind us. The AIS says it will be within a mile of us. And the rip tides are extreme right here. I don't want to get any closer to the shore." "Well, I have to tighten it. I'll try to be quick." Randy starts throwing things around down below to get his tools and into the engine compartment. I shut off the engine and try to hold the boat as steady as possible and not allow us to get further into the shipping lanes or closer to the shore. Not easy when there's no wind to help along and there's a really strong current goin' on. Fortunately, the sea gods were with us and we hung tight right where we were. Yay!! Alternator is all snug. Randy comes up for his watch. I go down below for my sleep time. It's now about 0200hrs.

Oops! "El, need to come up here. We just broke the alternator belt." Oh great. Ran turns the engine off quickly. Up I go and Randy starts tearing things apart again down below. Fortunately, the belt is a spare part we have...but it's our last one. My Captain Ran was really good about keeping all the spare parts he could possibly think of that we might need. We had a special duffle bag for those spare parts. A blessing indeed when they're in need. Apparently, when the alternator gets loose enough it rubs on the belt. That'll do it every time. This is easy and quickly fixed so we're back on the road again. Randy tells me to go back down to sleep and he'll take it until 0600hrs. He's all wound up. Then I'll come up and take over. Roger that. And of course now I can't sleep at all. But...at least I'm resting.

Seems like a nice anchorage, here at Naranjo, with clean brown beaches. No one there. Signs of life on the beach, but we see no one. The water is slightly rocky but not bad. We had some pretty rocky nights at Taboga so we were glad to have it quiet and still here. I made us a great dinner of fried chicken and rice and salad and we enjoyed the evening. But not for long. The weather started becoming squally and the water started becoming rolly. Oh great. Then it started becoming MORE of everything. Oh great. Randy checked our chart plotter to see if we had moved and he thought we had! It looked as if we had moved a few feet and were getting closer to the shore. "We'd better reset the anchor El or just leave and slowly make our way to the next spot." By now it's REALLY getting rolly and the thunderstorm is very loud and boisterous. But I got to thinking. "Let me look at the chart plotter Ran. Ahhh…I marked our anchor spot with a little martini glass symbol this time. The spot you're looking and measuring from with the anchor symbol is the original way point to anchor from the guidebook. No wonder you thought we had moved. Sorrryyyyy!!!" We hadn't moved at all. Phew! I thought a martini glass icon was quite appropriate to mark our anchorage.

But …we were still VERY uncomfortable. Sleep was hard coming. Having traveled all night the night before we had taken big naps on arrival at this anchorage. It's a good thing! Everything possible in the galley was banging around. Despite my attempts to secure it all. We had decided to sleep in the salon area as it's more comfortable when we're rocking around, but you hear everything in the galley a lot more. Just as I would get one thing secure…another banging would start up. Secure that…then something is rolling back and forth. Not very loudly but just enough to drive you nuts. Arrrrgggghhh!!! Finally I got everything quiet. By now it's about 0300hrs….early, early morning. The storm settled down but the seas did not. Rock….roll…rock…roll….BIG   rock….BIG   roll….BIG rock…BIG   roll…medium   rock…medium roll…rock….roll…rock…roll. All … night…long….

OK…let's blow this joint!! We were up and outta there so fast you couldn't even see us. Faster than the speed of light. On to Bahia Honda. "At least it looks like Bahia Honda anchorage is back in a nice bay. Hopefully, it's quiet back there." I made much needed coffee (we had not had any the day before because it's too hard to make coffee while traveling and the seas are big) and we actually had a nice day of travel. We are motorsailing going this direction. We don't want to, but we have to. We are heading directly into the wind, if there's any wind at all. But bless our engine, it's working great.

Heading into Bahia Honda was a nice day of travel. The seas weren't bad at all. And because we were traveling along the coast, there are green mountains all around. And we saw whales! Not sure what kind but Randy spotted them swimming quite far from us. And then again …we saw them breaching! That was exciting! Unfortunately (or fortunately) they were quite a ways away but we could definitely see them and I was able to get some pictures with my zoom lens. Quite spectacular to watch.

We are here, anchored, and I'm having one of those moments! One of those moments when I want to beam everyone I know right to where I am. We are now in the most beautiful anchorage at Bahia Honda, Panama. Drinking martinis in the cockpit, (with a tiny martini glass marking our anchorage position, right?!) overlooking tranquil waters and beautiful mountains. The beaches are brown but pristine. The mountains are jungle… thick jungle that ends at the brown beach with palm trees. You can imagine the velociraptors parting their way through the jungle to get to their prey. You can hear the howler monkeys which is eerie, but actual…and cool. It's like a lake here…but it is a bay off of the Pacific Ocean. This is a much needed anchorage for us. We're alone…no other boats. Only those that live on the island. The extreme contrast when compared to what we experienced at the last anchorage being one of the worst nights on our trip. But where we are right this minute… wipes all of that out, and with a martini in hand and my best friend with me in the cockpit…analyzing life and what we want to do in the future…life is perfect. And I wish you were all here with us.

Itchy feet!

As I reflected back on the past months, we covered some territory; checked some things off our Bucket List. We like to keep moving. We like to get there, see stuff, then, keep moving. Or... we like to get there...and do nothing for a while. Or... we will get there, see stuff, do a little boat work, and do nothing for a while...then keep moving. Many times, we arrive after a long passage, which we've done a few times lately, and the down time is greatly appreciated. And the views while you're having that glass of wine or martini or rum drink...are priceless.

Let's see: Curacao to Cartagena...Cartagena to San Blas...San Blas to Colon...through THE Canal...the Pacific!... Las Brisas to Taboga...Taboga to right now, anchored at Bahia Honda.

Bahia Honda, Panama, is about halfway from our departure point in Panama City to Golfito, Costa Rica. Anchoring at Bahia Honda was wonderful. Nothing really to do there, but it was a good place to stop and do a little boat prep/maintenance in anticipation of leaving the boat for 2.5 months and, relaxing in the peace and quiet of lake-still waters. We anchored back in the bay at what is called Domingo anchorage because Domingo owns the land there. Fitting. And Domingo is wonderful. As we set our anchor, he rowed up in his dugout canoe. He speaks no English and we speak little Spanish but we managed to communicate with smiles all around! Later, on that day, Domingo brought us some wonderful vegetables and fruits from his garden! Limes, spinach (unlike the kind we're used to), bananas (unlike the kind we're used to), cilantro (that...we're used to), all kinds of produce. In return we gave him canned goods. We had heard that people on the islands like to receive canned goods and school supplies.

Bahia Honda is a remote village in Panama with almost no development. There are no paved roads into this little village. There is a very nice sport fishing lodge on the shore near where we anchored that has been built but we saw little action there. It looked like perhaps there were some staff staying there and maintaining it, but the sport fishing boats we did see only came into the northern part of the bay and anchored over night as if they were on their way somewhere else.

We also got to know Domingo's adult son Kennedy. Of course fishing is one of the mainstays of the island and Kennedy stopped to ask one day if we had any fishing gear we did not need. And we did. Randy went through his box of fishing paraphernalia and found several things that he could give to Kennedy. Kennedy spoke a little English. He also asked if we had any old backpacks for the kids at school, but we didn't. I gave him several pencils and pens and a few tablets, but we wish we had known about the need for backpacks. We could have easily picked some up along our trip.

Now Randy gets down to work. First up, careening through the lazarettes ...tossing things hither and yon to get all out and purged. The lazarettes, by the way...not sure I have explained this term...are the lockers in the cockpit under the seating. They are big and hold everything you can think of and then some. You could get lost in there! One time I had to help Randy pull himself out as he was so far in headfirst he couldn't get a grip! Get a grip, Randy! Organizational skills are a plus in the lazarette management department, but it often goes to the way side as we travel along. Yes...all this going on as I sit and sip my cool drink while eating bonbons.

Next up...the cleaning of *Bob*. *Bob* the dinghy. Again a Randy chore. Ooooo weee! That made your eyes water. Ran pulled out the inflatable floor and practically gagged! Hadn't been done in quite some time. I mean...quite some time. I do believe there were a few flying fish skeletons in there! I'm not kidding! Scrub, scrub, scrub and scrub some more. Then, turn *Bob* over and scrub the bottom. Now, sparkling clean, the *Bob* machine!

314

But don't think all was well just because Randy thought he was Mr. Clean. A tragedy unfolded in the form of my favorite little yellow bucket. "Oh no!" I hear as I put down my glass of champagne and scamper up the companion way. "What, what, what??" "There goes the yellow bucket!" "Well, jump in and get it!" "No!" "Well, grab something to hook it with!" "Too late!" "It can't be that deep Ran." "It's deep, El. Let me get the look bucket and I'll take *Bob* out and see if I can see where it is on the bottom." "Doggone-it! I liked that little yellow bucket!" "Well, if I can't find it, we'll get another." (Update: we have NOT found another bucket like my little yellow bucket.)

After 4 days relaxing and doing boat chores in Bahia Honda, we headed on up for our next leg of the trip to Costa Rica - destination Isla Secas. We departed on a nice, still morning traveling only 6 hours to get there.

Isla Secas is a group of three wooded islands that form kind of a triangle. It will be a good place to stop for a couple of nights on our way to Costa Rica. We can't get to Costa Rica too early because of the 90-day rule. And we will be gone off the boat most of that time. We need to time our arrival at the last possible moment to still give us time to prepare the boat for leaving and catching our flight out of town.

We found a nice place to anchor within the triangle. A little rolly but not bad at all. And the view was beautiful. The biggest island has a fancy private eco-resort on it, but not like you'd expect. It is, as you might imagine, built to mimic what the Chiriqui Indians might have lived in. The rooms are yurts (I had to look it up), which are constructed of natural materials, wood and cloth, like fancy huts. Quite *chi chi*, I'd say.

And we keep moving.

Next stop was Punta Balsa. We stayed one night but it was *mucho* eventful! We got in there and anchored in like...45 feet or so, which is deeper than our usual anchorage experience. This is the border of Panama and Costa Rica. We knew it was just for one night, so no problem. We settled in. It was a little rolly but not bad at all. I went down below doing something and Randy called me up topside. "El, I think there's a whale up here!" Cool! I thought. We lost our good camera that took videos and my good Nikon wasn't happy either. I lost one of my lenses. It wouldn't move. The one that that took the closest pictures, so I brought up the Vivatar camera we had as a backup. "It's a baby whale, I think," Randy said. Then...up comes the mom. OK. This is different. There is a baby whale with a mom. They say you should never come between a baby whale and its mom. We are good...we are not between them but she is definitely checking us out. And she's huge! The baby is very curious. The mom is just watching. She comes up now and then and snorts. "I hope she likes us," I say to Ran. "Me, too!" We were worried that the baby might become entangled in our chain since we have a lot out due to the depth we're anchored. But so far...so good. It was actually an amazing experience. We were hoping she didn't get agitated and aggressive. Momma whales are known to be aggressive if they felt their baby was threatened. Understandable! We were very quiet and still. They swam around us slowly, with interest, but displayed no aggression. Then, after awhile...they moved on. It was so wonderful! We were holding our breath but it was such a perfect experience!

Chapter 27

You Say Costa, I'll Say Rica!

Costa...Rica! Costa...Rica!

How many times have you ever wanted to say, let's go to Costa Rica?!

We left Punta Balsa at 0530hrs on 27 July 2010 in the pouring rain. Oh yay. Rain. We pointed *Kwanesum* to Golfo Dulce, Costa Rica. Took us about 10 hours of rainy motor sailing. We arrived at the anchorage location that was recommended, off the town of Puerto Jimenez in Golfo Dulce, in the late afternoon and we were relieved to know it was nice and still in there. This anchorage is directly across the gulf from Golfito Bay, which is our destination, so it will be an easy trip across when it's time to go in. Every time we get into a new country, we feel...so accomplished! It's a huge thing for us! Safe Arrival Beer! Our continued routine: drop the anchor, mark its spot on the chart plotter with my martini icon, open two beers and let the boat and anchor settle while we drink them. Perfect settling amount of time. Now, we slowly back down on the anchor to make sure it's tucked in tight. Perfect. Again *Kwanesum* delivers us safely to our destination, so there's always a toast to her.

We are now a bit anxious to get home... to see the kids...finally to the States…and, we are very excited about that prospect! Being in Costa Rica means we are flying home for a bit. We have been away for a year from our family and friends and it feels too long. This is the first time it's been a whole year since we've seen anyone. We did see Skip and Kim in the US Virgins and we're so glad we did, but it's been too long since we've flown home. We are extremely excited, though a little nervous about the leaving *Kwanesum* for so long. First time we've done that, too. Cue the *Ellen Worry System*. Ugh.

We stayed anchored in Puerto Jiminez for 2 nights. Not checking into the country, just out at anchor. Again we were waiting until the last possible day to check into Costa Rica so we would have a good amount of time before we left. It was a nice anchorage. Gave us time to relax a little before going into Golfito. The Golfo Dulce is a gulf off the Pacific and Golfito is a bay and town within this gulf. So it's a good, safe place inside to leave *Kwanesum,* they say. We hope.

It's getting toward the end of July. We have 90 days can leave the boat in Costa Rica without making arrangements to bond the boat. To refresh your memory, if you bond the boat, you have to keep it in a marina here that does bonding and the marinas are not cheap in Costa Rica. Then, once bonded, you are not allowed to use the boat for 90 days. That would not be a problem if we had lots of money. But we are trying to do this the less expensive way and the timeliest way. We don't want to spend that much time here. We want to keep moving. We need to cross 2 fairly difficult passages on the way to Mexico: Costa Rica's Golfo de Papagallo and Mexico's Golfo de Tehuantepec. *"The two terrors of Central America,"* according to **Ocean**

Navigator Magazine and web page. That information does not set well with me, but we have faced difficult passages before and have had no problem, so....I'm keeping that thought at the forefront of my overactive brain.

"All right! Let's do it, Ran! Up and at 'em! Man, the helm and take us in to Golfito." It was 0900hrs on a cloudy but not rainy day; we weighed anchor and headed into Golfito Bay to our destination, Land Sea Services or *Servicios Tierra Mar*. We did our research to find the best spot to leave Kwanesum that would be safe and yet not cost us an arm and a leg. Land Sea came highly recommended by the cruising community. We motored in on very calm serene waters, listening to the howler monkeys and taking in all the lush green hills. A few houses were spotted up in those pretty hills, few and far between, which makes for a very nice homestead, I would assume, overlooking the bay. I liked it in here. I liked the calm. It seemed very protected inside. And it smelled so nice.

So far, we felt really good about this decision. Lots of boats, powerboats and sailboats are settled in here. There are several marinas to choose from. Our decision is based mostly on cost and protection while we are away. Land Sea is well respected for taking care of your boat. Good deal. Glad we decided on here to leave the boat for that length of time. We hailed Land Sea, told them we were near, and asked how they wanted us to proceed. They directed us to the mooring ball they had reserved for us. Right in front of their funky marina. It's so cute! It's like a place you'd expect to see Jimmy Buffett. Kinda tiki looking. I love it. Very Costa Rica like, in my opinion. My worry-busy mind was very relaxed knowing that this place looked like a good home for our girl *Kwanesum* while we trek back to the States for a break.

Tim Leachman, co-owner and co-founder of Land Sea met us at our mooring and helped us tie up. A nice greeting for our arrival. We settled in and got the boat ship shape down below for our stay. Things tend to shift around when you're moving on the water, no matter how still the water is. We had our yellow quarantine flag up when we pulled in and also flew the Costa Rica flag. The quarantine flag will come down, as always, after we check in to the country. We decided to do all that checking in business tomorrow. We will get the scuttlebutt on how to go about checking in here in Golfito from Tim and his mate Katie Duncan, who is also a co-owner and co-founder. "Gotta get *Bob* down so we can head in and fill out paperwork, El." "I'm ready, Ran! It's been 5 days since we've been on land. Gotta get my land legs back. Should be interesting to see if our legs will be wobbly." Our stainless dinghy davits for *Bob*, that we had put on in Deltaville, VA, have been a God send. Plus, they look good. It makes us look like real cruisers having *Bob* perched back there while we travel. And, our stainless lift for our unreliable Yahama engine for *Bob*. It's good to look good.

We go to the funky Land Sea Services to fill out paperwork and pay for our stay. They have the neatest porch for sitting and relaxing. We made sure to ask them for the steps we must go through in Golfito to check into the country. Writing down everything they told us about Golfito, checking in to the country, and good places to eat, because my brain is untrustworthy at times, we finished up with them and realized how hungry we were. Next door, we were told by these wise persons at Land Sea, was a great place for a beer and a burger. And that sounds absolutely perfect! Off we go to Banana Bay Marina… *"Bar, Restaurant, Diesel Fuel, Clean"*, the sign says …appears to be our kinda place! Clean is always good. We found a great seat at a long counter overlooking the water and a lot of really nice fishing boats, ordered the beer popular in Costa Rica, Imperial, and had a great burger. A great burger is always a good sign of a good restaurant, in my opinion, and it hit the spot perfectly as we toasted our arrival in Golfito.

Up the next morning...let's get the Costa Rica check in done. It's cloudy and a bit drizzly. And we are walking. I think we got 20,000 steps in that day. Maybe more! The first stop was not too far. "Walk down about a half a mile to this old building you'll see on the right, next to a gas station and there's a lady at a window. That's the Immigration Office and she'll give you the rest of the steps you'll need to finish off your check in process." That's the directions we got from Land Sea that I carefully wrote down. A little sketchier than I was anticipating, but what the heck. We'll go down there and find it and feel our way through the rest of it. We have all our necessary paperwork with us: crew list, passports, boat documentation, insurance papers, port clearance from checking out of the last stop... I think that was it. Oh, yes...we had to have photocopies of a lot of this in case they asked for that.

We found the Immigration Office and got going. We walked here, we walked there, we walked across a bridge, it's raining, we need to find the *Aduana* (customs) office, we can't find it. We were told it was in the *Zona Libre* (free zone). We did find the *Zona Libre* which is a huge marketplace with lots of shops and restaurants, but we can't find the *Aduana* office. UGH. Finally we walk by a policeman and ask him where it is. It's so tiny we walked right passed it! We are getting tired and cranky but we finally found it. We go in, and start the customs process, and they tell us they need a photocopy of EVERY page of the captain's passport. Every page? Every other country just needed copies of the front pages with our info on them. "Well, do you have a copy machine here that you could copy the pages?" "No." "Well, where can we get copies made? Is there a place here in the Zona Libre?" "You might try the bank around the corner." "OK, thanks, we'll be back." We find the bank around the corner. Their copy machine wasn't working. "Well, do you know WHERE we can get copies made?" They tell us we can go back into town and there's one there. "Ran...let's take a taxi this time! We've already walked all over 'tarnation!"

We find a taxi, we find a place to make copies, and we go back to the *Aduana to* finish up with them. Now we go to *Banco National*, which is also in the *Zona Libre*, and show them our paperwork and give them money for a receipt to show to the Port Captain when we find him to get our permit to be in the country. Port Captain is our last stop. We walk to the Port Captain's Office and give him the receipt he needs and we are done! YAY! We are now legally in Costa Rica for 90 days. "Let's hike back to the marina but stop at Banana Bay again for a much-needed beer, El." "Roger that, Captain." That beer tasted really, really good. And by now, it's pouring rain. We are glad that day was done.

Basically, we were in Costa Rica to leave the boat, secure the boat with extra lines, and clean the boat for our time away to the States. We took a week to make sure we had the right length of time in Costa Rica for of all this, with some leeway before we left, and then allowing for leeway when we got back. Land Sea helped us make our plane reservations from Golfito to *terra firma* in the States. We took a puddle jumper from Golfito to the bigger airport in San Jose. Had to squeeze my stuff for two and a half months on that puddle jumper and squeeze my body through the seats to sit down! But it was a neat flight out of the lush, green area. When we got to the airport in San Jose, a bit of drama unfolded. We wanted to carry on our bags to be sure everything arrived with us on time. We got our tickets at the counter, and are now going through security, when the young man noticed from the Xray that I had shells in my suitcase. "Why yes...I have shells that I got in Rum Cay, Bahamas that I was saving to give our granddaughter Abby because she saves shells. Is that a problem?" "Yes, I'm afraid it is. You are not allowed to take shells out of the country." "But I've been carrying these shells for months on our boat! I got them in the Bahamas, not here." "I'm sorry, madam, I cannot let you take the shells." I start to cry. Seriously. I was stressed already, as long flights are won't to do, and these shells were for Abby! "Look", he said, "you still have time, if you hurry, to check your bag and then it will be ok." "I can check my bag with the shells?" "Yep. Then you can get them to your granddaughter." I gave him a huge hug and ran to the counter to tell them I changed my mind and wanted to check my bag. It worked. My bag was checked, and it was there when we landed in San Francisco on 6 August for our two-month stay with family and friends. And the shells got to Abby.

You know...what a life this is! I can say that again...now...but...when we got back from being away, I have to admit it took me awhile to readjust. We got back to a very green, dirty boat. Actually, not as bad as we thought it would be but still...very bad. And alas...I regret that I did not take any pictures. Which, as the roaming reporter that I've been...is very odd for me. I think, to be honest, I wasn't quite sure I wanted to be back and dealing with a boat. Being on a sailboat sounds glamorous but it's not. And leaving family and getting back to a boat that needs a lot of cleaning up......ok...it took me awhile to get with the program. Time out...step back two steps...it's not glamorous, but it's really kinda cool. It's just a lot of damn work. But then, life in general is a lot of work so doing it on a sailboat is not so bad. But in Costa Rica...when we returned...it was raining. Rain, rain, rain, rain. Which is why it's so damn beautiful! Scratch the complaining...on with the story.

It's the third week in October and we came back to that green boat. I'm not kidding. Welcome home to the Pirate's Life! Rum at 5 o'clock! You can imagine the weather Costa Rica has to make it so lush and green. Well, for your boat, left on a mooring for 2.5 months, it makes for a rather lush green on it, too. The price you pay, apparently. Not sure why we were a bit surprised by that, but there it is - *Kwanesum*, the green. "Well, I guess we have our work cut out for us the next few days! Oooo, weeee!" So, cleaning it is. "Get in the lazarette and dig out all the cleaning products, Ran. We're going to have a cleaning marathon party!" We had labeled duffles with spare parts, cleaning products, whatever you need to store, and we kept a book on where on the boat those duffles were so finding them was not a problem. Just don't get stuck in that big, deep lazarette.

Now we need to provision for the next leg of our trip. Destination - Nicaragua. We made our list of what we needed and headed to the Zona Libre. This time, we took a taxi. I also bought a couple of bed pillows while we were there. I always like to have lots of pillows and ours were getting a bit flat. They were a funky kind of pillow, quite different than I was used to, but they worked. We got all we needed, got a taxi back, and took 99 trips in the dinghy from the dock to the boat, back and forth, until all was loaded on *Kwanesum*. And we started to laugh. "Just look at this, Ran!" There in our cockpit is the important part of our buying trip: 6 bottles of rum, 3 bottles of Tanqueray gin, 3 bottles of Cutty Sark scotch, and 9 bottles of wine. Yes, I took a picture of that. Cheers! We just had one more thing to do - check out, which our last stop was again at the Port Captain's office to get our Zarpe. The *Capitania De Puerto*. Then we are ready to leave. I plan meals we can have at sea...usually fried chicken we can easily eat cold, Aram sandwiches, tuna sandwiches, hard-boiled eggs...things that are easy to get to in our refrigerator. We filled up with water and filled our extra jugs with water we keep on deck, and we will get fuel on our way.

Right before our last day, we went to Banana Bay Marina for our last hamburger and beer and there was a bit of a crowd and obvious signs of something going on. We asked what was happening and they said there's a sailboat docked out front that will be doing an acrobatic show on their boat. No kidding?! We thought the best vantage point to watch this would be in the water on our dinghy so we finished our burger and beer and raced back to get the dinghy and head next door for the show. It was amazing and so unusual to see. A very handsome, fit couple that did quite a performance while dangling from the shrouds of their boat. It was a lovely and fitting departing scene from Costa Rica for us to experience.

Chapter 28
On to El Salvador

We Have to Cross a Bar?

This next leg of our trip took 3 days. I wrote on my Facebook page that day, "Heading out early tomorrow morning. Finally! First goal, Nicaragua, but if the weather is good, we shall keep moving. I think I might have linked our SPOT GPS here on Facebook! If it works, it will post on here and you should all be able to see where we are each day on the map. We send this religiously out to our kids via our email sources on SPOT. See you in a few days!"

We are discovering that sailing on the Pacific out here is a lot rougher and more challenging than sailing in the Caribbean, or even the Atlantic. A lot more weather and a lot more sea action. We, of course, as part of our routine, check with our weather apps. Our rule is checking all 3 and if any of them show anything detrimental to our trip, we mull it over. Some of these apps also show the tides and how big they are, which can be crucial. So far everything looked okay for our trip, so off we go on 27 October at 0630hrs. The first night was rough, and Ellen got sick. Yes, I did. The **PPM** was not working. But I have learned to get it over with and adjust and it gets better. The second night, we sailed. Yay! Oddly, as I'm sure you've noticed, so many times on this trip we have not been able to really sail. The weather calmed a bit, and we had a nice sail the next day, too. The third night, we had a thunderstorm. The kind of storm of which we wondered if we should turn around and go back or continue on. Our amazing radar system showed us the whole storm and if there had been a chance to go around it somehow, we would have. But it was pretty much all over the radar. We are more than halfway there. We are going to continue on. There was not much sleeping that night. I sat in the cockpit with Randy and took my turn at the helm when my turn was up. When it was my time to rest, I sat close, under the dodger and stroked Kwanesum, telling her how proud I was of her. The worry was not being damaged physically, but it was worry about being hit by lightning and losing all our electronics. We kept an extra GPS and our computers in our oven for such times. Always when we sailed, we put those in our oven like a Faraday Cage in the hope that they would be safe there. If we were to be hit by lightning, maybe they would be ok and we could use them should all electronics be damaged. But that did not happen. We went on, Kwanesum kept us safe and we arrived at Puesta de Sol Marina in Nicaragua at 0700hrs on 30 October. We carefully entered Estero Aserrodores to get to the marina through the directions we had learned from our research. We were advised that it's best to go into the entrance at high slack tide to avoid any ebbing tidal current coming from the channel. We proceeded in with no problem; 382 nautical miles traveled in those 3 days.

Puesta de Sol Marina was really nice! Even a beautiful hotel is attached. We found a berth in the marina per our instructions when we contacted them. Nice to have the amenities that go with being in a marina. We hadn't been hooked up in a while. Then we took a walk around the grounds. It was a pretty, sunny day and it smelled wonderfully of wood and flowers. We checked in to the country there in the marina when the office opened and they filled us in on what all there was to do around there. Then we meandered to their palapa and had ceviche and cervezas with a perfect view of the water. Now, a nice long nap.

While in Nicaragua, we just stuck close to the marina. We didn't feel like renting a car and exploring. The closest town was over an hour away. We just wanted to enjoy this nice spot. We took a walk down to another large palapa down at the beach. There was really no one there but us and another boat in the marina, John, a single hander from Nebraska. At the palapa, they had beer and wonderful scenery. I swear I saw fireflies on our walk there. I loved the fireflies we had in Virginia when we lived there and I noticed little sparkles here and there on our walk at dusk. It made it even more magical. Mario was there at the palapa serving us beer. He works for the hotel and marina. He speaks no English, but he was adorable. I had found some pods on our walk and he told us, via my very limited Spanish understanding, that they are used to make maracas!

Nicaragua is definitely beautiful and the days there were perfect. My long-time school friend Julia told me her son and his surfing friends bought some property not far from where we were. Nicaragua is a big surfing spot. And we could certainly see why when we walked down the beach to find Hotel Chancletas, which means flip-flops. It's a surfer's paradise and Julia's son Jeff's property is adjacent. It was really so neat there! Lots of grass, and the ocean and surf were amazing. They are very simple buildings, but very accommodating for the kids who want to surf and don't have a lot of money. Groups of young people stay there from all over for surfing. That's it. To eat, sleep, and surf...and drink, and enjoy, and surf. We, of course, found their funky bar at the back of a wonderfully green lawn of grass and, ordered a beer and chatted away with some of the surfers there and the barkeep. I can see why this would charm many a young man or girl who loved surfing. It was a superb walk along the beach there. The surf was definitely surfable. And they were out there. We took our time walking back to the boat, enjoying our barefoot walk in the sand on a beautiful day and watching all the surfing.

We got acquainted with our berth neighbor, John from Nebraska. He suggested one day that we join him for dinner in the neighborhood behind the hotel/marina. Of course! That would be great. We walk past the guarded gates and down the dirt road to the spot John suggested to eat. He had eaten there a few times before and sang high praises. Very simple, sort of primitive buildings... pigs walking along the roads with us. An interesting evening walk to dinner. Handmade signs written on wooden arrows advertising rooms to rent: "Nicaragua Escape No. 2", "Houses, Beds, Tel 867887798". Pretty much all renting to young people who want to surf. We come to our spot, "Joe's Place". "Posada de Joe Portunica" behind a chain link fence. OK! We are up for anything. We go inside the fence to see hammocks, several hammocks, music playing, grass thatched roof, and find a table with a plastic flowered cloth and plastic patio chairs and make ourselves comfortable. Your choice for dinner is this or that. Fish or chicken, with rice and beans and pico de Gallo. Snapper! I love snapper, so that's what I ordered. And the beer of Nicaragua, Toña. We are chatting away, enjoying our delicious homemade dinner, made by Joe's wife, and watching the kids that are there. So relaxed and having fun. You can bring your own booze in, too, so many have done that. Talking about their day, I suppose, having dinner, drinking rum and Pepsi and playing cribbage.

A man approaches our table and John introduces us to Joe, the owner. He and his wife own the restaurant and rooms to rent. We asked Joe about his background, and he told us he has a sailboat anchored out in the marina area and has been there for years. He sailed all around the world and decided to stop there. Having a dairy was mentioned in the conversation and Randy spoke up, saying I had lived and raised my kids on a dairy in California with my first husband. "Oh! Where was your dairy in California?" "In a really small town in Central California called Gustine." "I was born and raised on a dairy in Gustine!" You have got to be kidding me! Here we are, having sailed all this way, and now in Nicaragua, and this guy was born and raised in the small...I'm talking 5,000 people population...town of Gustine?! What are the chances? I was blown away. And, of course, he knew my ex-father-in-law and the family. It was crazy! His name was Joe Fontes and his family's dairy was on Highway 33 near Santa Nella. Not only were we enjoying this wonderful dinner made by his wife, in this funking surfing oasis in Nicaragua, but we found a true connection to the owner! How fun is that? Needless to say, we made that trek back to Joe's Place one more time before we left. This time having perch for our meal. Such a small world. Truly.

As we stayed there a week, a group of 4 boats came in from the south, Bahia del Sol, El Salvador, which is actually where we were going next. It was nice to have their company and learn about our next destination. Robert, who owns the marina here, organized an outing out to the large palapa on the beach for all of us, for wine and snacks and a sunset. He got vans to take us out there instead of having to walk. What a fun night that was. Nice people, good conversation. We really liked Nicaragua, though we didn't see that much of it, but give us nice oceanfront, and we are good. And there can't be much better oceanfront than living on your boat in the ocean.

Why do we love the sea? It is because it has some potent power to make us think things we like to think.

- Robert Henri.

This is so true. One of my favorite parts about traveling from port to port was watching the sea and letting my mind wander.

Now, it's time to head to El Salvador. We always tell ourselves that if the seas are good, the weather is good, we are feeling good, we will continue on to the next port without stopping. But so far, we have really only done that a couple of times. Stopping replenishes us. We need to stop in El Salvador because we have a big crossing after that to get into Mexico and we need to replenish ourselves well and be ready. This leg should just be an overnighter.

Getting into Bahia del Sol, El Salvador, is a bit tricky, we heard and read. We need to time our arrival for the right tide. There is a bar you have to cross, which means waves are breaking on it and that can be tricky. We will be surfing in and it's important to have control of your boat on the way. We got to the entrance of Bahia del Sol very early in the morning on 11 November. We researched, our standard operating procedure, on the best place to stop in El Salvador before tackling the Gulf of Tehuantepec passage, and Bahia del Sol was it. Also, valuable information was gleaned from the boats that came into Nicaragua while we were there, which gave us a big heads up and head start on knowing what to expect.

We are outside the entrance to Estero Jaltepeque, the gateway into Bahia del Sol. We need to wait for slack tide and to be able to contact the harbor master to send someone out to guide us in. That is their standard operating procedure for entrance. While we are out here dancing around in circles biding our time, we see the usual small fishing boats bobbing around in the area too close to the entrance, in our opinion, but not for us to say. We actually were not biding our time because we were told, in no uncertain terms, to make sure everything on the boat was secure. Tightly. When going on in, over the bar

331

and surfing the waves, things might fly. So while we were circling, we did a glanced inventory of possible flying objects, stowed some things below, and made everything else squared away for surfing in.

Finally, around 0800hrs, we were able to hail the harbor master and made a time for Rogelio to drive out and lead us in. This is a must, as you need to not only go in at a high slack tide but follow a distinct path in, to not run into shoals created by the waves that we had to maneuver through. Maneuvering a boat, controlling, steering a boat, is sort of like ice skating. You'd like to think you are constantly in control but actually, the sea (or ice) is in control. Your finest skills are called upon in such instances. My extraordinary skills, or lack thereof, have been challenged many a time on this trip, so it will be our Captain Ran that will man the helm for this jaw clenching ride in.

We are told by the harbor master exactly where to position ourselves to wait for Rogelio. He zooms out on his jet ski and pulls up to Kwanesum to give us the low down and the procedure in. "Stay on my ass!" he says. "Do not let too much distance come between us. Follow directly behind me. Go as fast as you can, keep the petal to the metal and stay right on my ass. Don't worry about running over me." OK. Yikes! Our hearts are thumping, but we are ready. We are determined to stay on Rogelio's ass. We know he knows what he's doing. He's done it a million times, I'm sure. Randy handles Kwanesum like a champ. "All ahead, flank!" I'm hanging on, watching for possible flying objects we may have missed. And...we are surfing! That is a very cool thing to do on a sailboat. Particularly a boat of our size. Woo hoo! We follow Rogelio the rest of the way in and he points out our appointed berth. Ah....we are here. "Only people that have crossed a bar can possibly understand just how terrifying it is." - a quote from another sailor. We tackled the entrance we had read and heard so much about and we made it safe and sound. Time for a safe arrival beer.

As we were celebrating our safe arrival, we were approached by one of the small fishing pangas we saw outside the entrance. Apparently, they told us, we snagged their fishing line at some point while we were outside there. Really…we were not that close to any of the boats. Interesting. "You must pay for our fishing line!" Really… even though you do not have any proof of said incident. And, oddly… we did not have any malfunction of our prop that would have been very self-evident and distressing as we were motoring in over the waves. Hmmmm… We are patient… pretty patient… well, mostly patient… but always an understanding couple of people, and this welcome into Bahia del Sol was unexpected and a bit distressing. But we are tired, we are glad to be here safe and sound, and we really have no evidence that we did not snag their line, so what can we do? We do not have much cash, and we had not yet checked into the country or even gotten off the boat except to tie up to the dock. But we offered them some money, and they took it. Not much option there.

Now we must check into the country. It's a nice spot. We are berthed at Bahia del Sol Hotel and Marina, as previously noted. It's very nice. As we walked to the office, we passed the nice bar and lovely pool. My legs are weird. I'm wobbly and unsteady! By George, I think I have land sickness or vertigo or something! Geez! It must be from all the rocking and rolling we did on the trip here plus the surfing in. This is the first time this has happened to me on this adventure. Interesting. I just went slowly with a wall close at hand.

We had a simple, gratefully easy check-in process, paid our fees and had another beer at the really nice bar near the pool. This is going to be great for a few days. This is country #20 for us! Seriously! I finally started counting back and it's #20. Twenty times checking in and out of a country. Mind you, so many of the islands are different countries. So, the process is done over and over. Only one more country to go before the USofA. For that...I am ready.

Chapter 29
To Tehuantepec or Not To Tehuantepec?

That is the Question

Most cruisers here came in from Mexico. Going South. We are the contrary ones, going North. We met some fun cruisers here in El Salvador. Shared information is always valuable, and cruisers, being the most friendly and thoughtful bunch you can run into, are always ready to share all information, info we needed to head across the Tehuantepec and information they needed from us going South. And you talk about boats and dinghies and provisioning and family and all things boat-related. It's a fun, friendly time. And they taught me how to play Baja Rummy. Cards and Mexican Train Dominoes are prevalent in the cruiser community.

It's pretty in here and peaceful. We took the next day to walk up the road to a restaurant to try the local fare. Along with a few cows along the road, apparently. We were pointed to a recommended restaurant, and a *tienda* (store) where we could do a bit of provisioning. Restaurant *Mar y Sol*. Our goal at the restaurant…*pupusas*, masa flour pouches filled with beans, cheese, and/or meat, a most traditional local fare in El Salvador. Oh, my goodness. Those are really, really good.

Now it's time to hit the road, skedaddle, head on out, get a move on, surf the seas, go like the wind… We check out with the office and line Rogelio up to lead us out again. And, again, we must *"stay on his ass"*. This time, we are heading against the waves breaking on the shoal, which is actually easier to maneuver than surfing in. We are lined up to head out at 1200hrs on 19 November. Another boat, *Indian Summer*, is heading out with us, so we will all stick very close in tandem together: Rogelio, *Kwanesum* and *Indian Summer*. *Indian Summer* is heading south, and we are heading north. We had been constantly checking our weather sources to find a decent window to tackle the Gulf of Tehuantepec and now is the time. And now it's high slack tide so we are ready. We made it through just fine, sticking close to Rogelio, though we did have to slow a bit behind him to wait for some breakers. Glad for our pilot leading us safely out. Glad for my most capable Captain at the helm. Tehuantepec, here we come.

Our destination now is Huatulco, Mexico. They tell of two ways to cross this gulf, our last difficult crossing. Remember I said we are contrary. Pretty much every source we checked about this difficult crossing talked of boats going south. We are going north. Against the grain. This trip and this part of the Pacific, *Golfo de Tehuantepec*, is renowned for big winds, big seas, and possibly hazardous conditions. Not for the faint of heart. But we have traveled over 5,000 nautical miles in *Kwanesum* and have had some very difficult passages that actually turned out to be not too bad! So, with that knowledge and our sea legs, and our sea smarts, our sea spirits, and our positive attitude tucked in our heads, we are ready to trust our intrepid *Kwanesum,* I am trusting my favorite captain, and my captain is trusting his favorite co-captain, and we are ready to choose our path across. Many go along, hugging the shore. In fact, I think most go along the shore. But it takes a lot longer that way. But, we decided to start out hugging the shore. Our weather window looks good. The seas are calm. But by the second day, Randy says "Let's go for it, El! Let's head across the quickest route and not cling to the shoreline anymore." Instead of stopping at Chiapas, Mexico's most southern port, we will head straight to Huatulco. "Roger that, Ran! Let's hit it!" We are always ready to trust our instincts based on our trust of our boat and each other. We're still that way.

Itchy feet.

Sometimes the anticipation and worry of any situation is a lot worse than the actual experience. In fact, I do think that happens more often than not. Cue my peak worry when we went through the Panama Canal. Needless worry but worry none the less. This went well. Our passage went about as well as it ever could have. The weather gods, the sea gods were on our side. We had a great trip!

Captain log 19 November, 2010, 1200hrs: Departed Bahia del Sol, El Salvador. Followed pilot out to the bar for crossing with *Indian Summer*, Christie and John who are going south.

Captain log 20 November, 2010, 1230hrs: Lat/Long 13°41.069N/90°46.390W Off Cape Quetzal, Guatemala. Clear, flat seas. No wind.

Captain log 21 November, 2010, 1150hrs: Lat/Long 14°29.442N/92°28.587W Clear, flat seas. No wind. 12 miles off Puerto Madero.

Captain log 23 November, 2010, 0900hrs: Arrived Marina Chahue, Huatulco, Mexico! A great trip. Weather and seas were perfect. Saw lots of turtles. 4 nights at sea. 467 nautical miles.

We're in Mexico! We've arrived! This is a huge milestone, and our trip was uneventful. It was the longest leg we've done so far, and for the most part, we had sunny days and smooth seas. We can now put in the logbook that our last challenging passage went great. We contacted Marina Chahuè for our berth location. As we pulled in, a group of guys were there waiting for us to help us dock. Always a nice welcome for tired sailors. Safe arrival beer is now in order: a Pilsener Beer from El Salvador for the Captain and an Imperial Beer from Costa Rica for me. Cheers! Thank you, *Kwanesum*, for another safe passage.

Time to go through the process of checking in to the country. The procedure here is to get to immigration down where the cruise ships come in and find the Port Captain. The customs officers will come to our boat first, along with an agriculture officer to check our food aboard. In the proactive stance of making sure things go swimmingly, I made chocolate chip cookies. Yes, I did. It is actually a pretty good idea that is recommended by many, to set the atmosphere for the drudgery of paperwork to follow. Our customs people were terrific and they loved my cookies. Making the boat smell great, too, made everyone happy! They printed our Temporary Import Permit, so we didn't have to take a cab to the airport, which apparently happens. They also gave us a ride to the bank. In some countries you have to go to the bank, pay the fees there, and then take the receipt back to the agent. It can be a pain, but they made it very easy for us. Thankfully, the agriculture inspector didn't feel the need to inspect our galley and refrigerator for any fruits or foods that wouldn't pass muster. That was a relief. Now we are all checked in, the yellow quarantine flag came down, the Mexico courtesy flag is flying on our mast, and we are hungry!

Across the street from the marina, there just happens to be a great pub. Senor Pucks! We ventured over there for breakfast in their patio, and it's fantastic; fresh-squeezed orange juice, great coffee, perfect eggs, bacon, sausage, potatoes, tortillas – whatever you want. It was amazing and just what we needed. We found out that the pub was owned by Randy and Karen, a pair of friendly ex-pat Canadians who were the nicest people! We had some good conversations with them. Excellent breakfasts, burgers and terrific hospitality were gratefully enjoyed by we two salty sailors. We actually went to Senor Pucks for Thanksgiving, too. We watched football that day (soccer to Canadians). It was a perfect spot for us.

We spent two weeks in Huatulco, relaxing, exploring the area, and provisioning for our continued trip up the coast to California. Huatulco is a tourist development centered around the town of La Crucecita in the Mexican state of Oaxaca. We walked to La Crucecita many times, enjoying the beautiful parks with water ways streaming through, and we meandered down where the cruise ships dock. Immigration was down there, so we had to visit there anyway to provide them with our bank receipt when we first checked in.

When cruise ships arrive and disgorge thousands of shoppers, ready to spend their money, we skedaddle out of there. Too many people in a small space all at once. We don't have room for a lot of purchases, so we just tried their ice cream and made tracks back to the boat.

Huatulco is situated where the foothills of the Sierra Madre mountains meet the Pacific Ocean, making it a region rich in history related to Spanish explorers and conquistadors. After the Spanish conquest, Huatulco thrived as a port under Cortés' control and served as a vantage point for Spanish galleons. Legends of famous figures like Sir Francis Drake and Thomas Cavendish also left their mark on the region's history, and these legends live on today. We took advantage of the proximity to the Sierra Madres and arranged a tour of a coffee plantation called *Finca la Gloria*. This plantation is known for its butterfly sanctuary called *Mariposorio Dain Biguid*, where dozens of species of butterflies can be seen. It's also home to the *Cascadas de Llano Grande* (Llano Falls), and the *Rio Copalitilla* originates from there.

We met a small van and three other couples at the park in La Crucecita and drove the 90 minutes up the hills. We stopped on the way for our driver to pick up some tasty, sugary, cocoa tortillas from a charming, small casita for us to munch on for the rest of the trip. Oh, my! These tortillas were delightful and left us wanting more – we even vowed to buy some on our way back! The driver assured us that we would make a stop at the casita when we returned.

Our destination, Finca la Gloria (Finca means estate), welcomed us with open arms. We piled out of the van and were treated to a delightful tea made from Jamaica plants, hibiscus, which was both refreshing and medicinal, along with some wonderful little cookies. We then stretched our legs on a hike to Lliano Fallsto enjoy the cool water and long reat with the sound of the waterfall. It's beautiful there. Now, we hiked back to the coffee plantation to learn about the growth and processing of coffee beans. But wait! That is not all! We were served a sumptuous meal, which was an unexpected surprise. The meal included rice, pork, chicken molé, black beans, *nopales* (cactus pads), and freshly made tortillas – incredibly delicious! And the surprises didn't end there; we also had a mezcal tasting. For those who wanted to partake, including my captain and me, it was a unique experience. Fernando, our guide for the tasting, explained that in this region, they prefer mezcal over tequila. While mezcal and tequila are similar, there is a distinction: tequila can only be made from the blue weber agave plant, found in Jalisco, while mezcal can be produced from any agave plant, including those in Oaxaca. We sampled several varieties, and one had a worm in it, which was not my favorite.

However, *Crema Maguey Azul* was my favorite; it had a liqueur-like quality, and many others were equally ver, very good.

We left Finca la Gloria with some mezcal, the delicious cookies we had enjoyed with tea, and, of course, coffee beans. We said farewell to our gracious hosts, and we climbed back into the van for the journey downhill. On our way back, we made another stop at the little casita-like store, this time for hot chocolate to complement our delectable sugary chocolate tortillas, as well as some other sweets known as *regañadas*, a type of hard and delightful bread cake. These sweet treats were heavenly, and we couldn't resist taking some back to the boat. It was indeed a special and memorable day, and we were grateful for this unique experience.

The remainder of our time in Huatulco was filled with leisurely walks, fantastic meals (those freshly squeezed orange juices!), and enjoyable moments at Señor Frogs. Now it's time to plan our next steps as we continue our journey up the coast.

Itchy feet.

Since we plan to stay in Mexico for an extended period, we do not need to check out of the country. So, at 0955hrs on 7 December, we set our course for our next destination: Puerto Angel. We planned to anchor there for the night and then head to our primary destination, Ixtapa, the following day. Puerto Angel is a charming area with grass-topped umbrellas lining the beach and pangas dotting the shore. Although we experienced beautiful weather when we departed the next morning, we had challenging seas due to steep waves. We've consistently seen a lot of turtles in the Pacific waters. We spent a rolly night at anchor, which didn't make for restful sleep, but we were up and ready to depart at 0800hrs the next day. The journey to Ixtapa, over 300 nautical miles away, would take us a couple of days to complete.

Chapter 30
Begin the Bash!

Huatulco to Ixtapa

"We need to hurry up, Ran! We need to get into Ixtapa before dark." We are sweating it a bit as we don't like to go into new ports after dark and it's almost 1700hrs. And we don't want to fiddle fart outside here because that is not pleasant. But we made it. At 1705hrs on 10 December, we pulled into Marina Ixtapa.

The sail from Huatulco to Ixtapa was a line of beaches with hills behind. Pretty much the same scenery the whole way. Ah! But we did go by Acapulco at night. It was beautiful from our vantage point, like sparkling pavé diamonds on the hills. It is, however, a big shipping port. Acapulco is located on a deep, semicircular bay and has been a port since the early colonial period of Mexico's history. It is a port of call for shipping as well as cruise lines running between Panama and San Francisco. So…very busy. And who happened to be at the helm when we passed the entrance? That's right, co-captain Ellen. We are motor sailing along some smooth seas, because of lack of winds, but we had the stay sail and the main sail up to pick up any wind that might push along a little faster. I was watching the chart plotter as we neared the entrance to Acapulco. I approached the port, and I couldn't help but notice a ship inside that seemed to be in motion or preparing to move. Thanks to our AIS system, which is a real lifesaver, all the ships in the vicinity are displayed as little triangles on our screen. If that triangle shape is moving, swaying, or dancing on the screen, it means the ship is getting ready to move and will be headed in the direction of the point on the triangle. Clicking on the triangle gives us all the information about that ship: its name, country of origin, destination, how fast it's going, and the closest point of approach between the ship and our yacht. These ships move VERY fast. I learned that mostly from my experience sailing with Randy in the San Francisco Bay. As co-captain manning the helm while my captain is sleeping, it is my job to judge whether I need to hail the ship to let him know I'm out there. I hailed the ship, "Omar Maru, Omar Maru, this is the sailing vessel Kwanesum, over." "This is the Omar Maru. Over" (I was so thankful he answered right away.) "Captain, I am due to cross the entrance of the Port of Acapulco at just about the time you will be exiting. I want you to be aware I am out here. Over." "Roger that, Captain, I see you, and I will be passing you on your starboard side. Over." "Thank you, Captain, I appreciate that. Over." I was so proud of myself!! I was very calm. I saw the movement of the ship on the chart plotter and judged the timing with our spectacular, don't leave home without it, AIS system, and all went well. The Omar Maru (fictional name as I can't remember the ship's name) came out, passed me on my starboard side and all was well. And on we go to Ixtapa. Leaving sparkly Acapulco behind.

We had called Marina Ixtapa to make arrangements before we left Huatulco, so now we just needed to hail them on the radio to let them know we were arriving in the nick of time. The marina weaves back into a nice, quiet area with restaurants and shops along the docks and one alligator. Yep! One large alligator apparently lives in the marina and we spotted him a few times. OK. Good deal. We are here. Tie up, safe arrival beer, and again, toast to *Kwanesum* for keeping us safe. Now we change our clothes, spruce up a bit, and go to one of the really nice restaurants on the dock for dinner. A well-deserved dinner.

While in Ixtapa, we had a few goals. Randy and I were last in Ixtapa in October 2003. That was right before I moved back to DC to join Randy, who was already there working for Homeland Security. And we had so much fun while we were here. It was so neat and different coming in here to Ixtapa by boat this time and seeing what had changed and what had not.

Goal 1: We need to find the hotel where we stayed at that time. We had to look at a few before we spotted it. The name had been changed. But we found it!

Goal 2: We need to find the restaurant where I first tasted chilaquiles for breakfast. We found it and you bet I had chilaquiles for breakfast again with fresh squeezed orange juice. Soooo good. Wonderful coffee, too.

Goal 3: We need to find Franks Sports Bar. We had the best time there in 2003, and we found it! And it's the same! Oh my gosh, and Frank is still there! We had to roam around a bit with our memory banks at peak level, trying to find it in the Plaza, but we did find it, and we found Frank! Last time we were here with our friends Robin and Liston and, we had our last night's meal and final, final drinks at Frank's Sports Bar. This time, we were there during the day and had cervezas and ceviches. So great to see Frank is still here and still going strong.

Goal 4: We had to get to Zihuatanejo. A big sailing town. All sailors out here on the Pacific want to get to Zihua at some time or other. There's a great bay to anchor in, but we chose to go into the marina in Ixtapa as we wanted to find the spots we frequented there before. Zihua is a more happening town than Ixtapa. As luck would have it, we met a fellow sailor berthed in Ixtapa that was actually from the town of Manteca in California, very close to where I lived at one time. His name is Pete and he has a car. Perfect. We need Pete and his car. Pete leaves his boat in Ixtapa and travels back and forth from California. So we had a ride to Zihua! We arrived and immediately found Zorro's for some beers and some football. Then we headed to a spot by the water overlooking the anchorage in the harbor that happened to have huge margaritas, and by golly, some of Pete's friends were there. Margaritas are my favorite. A fun afternoon was had by all. To round off the day, we had a perfect dinner of *nacatamales* (tamales cooked in banana leaves) at *Tamales y Atoles Any Restaurant* (*Tamale Anys*). Soooo good. After enjoying the delicious *nacatamales* in La Crucecita, we were eager for more. Zihua lived up to its reputation as a happening place that night, but we had to drive back to Ixtapa. Nevertheless, it had been a fantastic day.

Four fun-packed days in Ixtapa, and we are ready to pound ahead north. Because we are the contrary ones, going north, we will be pounding with the *wind on the nose*, as they say. Does not make for the most pleasant of trips, but with good weather and seas, and a little luck, we hoped for smooth sailing, or at least smooth motor sailing.

We filled *Kwanesum* up at the fuel dock with 230 liters of diesel. That's about 61 gallons. *Kwanesum's* fuel tank holds 75 gallons. That totaled a little over $265. I fried some chicken and boiled some eggs for this leg – easy-to-grab don't require much galley time. Spending too much time below deck while underway isn't my favorite, so having easy/peasy food on hand is a must.

At 1000hrs on 14 December, we pointed the bow north and headed up the Pacific. Destination: Banderas Bay and Marina Riviera Nayarit in the little fishing town of La Cruz de Huanacaxtle. Movin' on up!

Itchy feet.

It was a tough bash up. A long 3.5 days. *Kwanesum* was a champ. She was her usual intrepid self, keeping us safe and getting us to our destination. This leg was a challenge of strong headwinds and pretty big seas. We are tired. But we are here. Saw lots of whales along the way. They were playing and cheering us on when it got really rough. Of course, they loved the rough water. We, on the other hand, did not. We had dolphins playing alongside, too. Good entertainment as you bash away. It actually got a bit chilly at night on this trip. We weren't expecting that. We had to kind of bundle up on our night watches with sweatshirts and blankets. We did our usual 3 hours on/3 hours off which has worked really well for this whole adventure. I've learned to find my spot below, leave all my gear on, including my life jacket, and just lean back and tuck my arms into my sides and sleep. I learned to fall asleep pretty quickly that way, oddly enough.

We arrived at La Cruz de Huanacaxtle at 0930hrs on 17 December. There is a good anchorage here at La Cruz that many take advantage of, but it can be a bit rolly. We are going to stay a good long while, so we wanted to take advantage of being in a marina. We researched the area, as we are wont to do each stop, and this little town and really nice marina were highly recommended. La Cruz de Huanacaxtle is in the Banderas Bay on its north peninsula, kind of cattywampus across the bay from Puerto Vallarta. We are stopping to smell the roses for a while. Found the berth we were assigned, Dock 9 Slip A8, popped open two cervezas, and toasted to *Kwanesum* for our safe arrival and planned to have tequila at 5 o'clock...somewhere.

Chapter 31
La Cruz de Huanacaxtle

If You Can Pronounce It, You Win!

It took us a few tries with a few different people saying the name of this little village out loud to learn how to correctly pronounce La Cruz de Huanacaxtle, let alone how to spell it. But that was fun for me because I love the Spanish language and trying to use it. And trying to spell it. And ...we love this little town and our marina and...there ya go! A perfect haven.

There were more than several great things about our stay here, but top among them was meeting some fabulous people. Life-long friends, actually. Marinas are the best for that especially if you stay a spell. Which we are. As *live aboards* finding information from fellow sailors on the dock is part of the job description. We soon realized that among our new friends on Dock 9, was Scott the Wonder Mechanic!! Yay! And his fun wife Teri and their doggo Bosun. You will remember, Dear Reader, our tales of *Bob* the dinghy and his worthless engine?!! Continually worthless engine! Well, Captain Ran started a conversation with Scott, whose sailboat was berthed down from us. Scott knows how to fix things! And fix *Bob's*

349

engine, he did! Yay! Huge! Huge fix for us. Now we can depend on that engine instead of holding our breath when we use it.

The staff at the marina was fabulous and became good friends. The people in the office, the bartenders, the dock helpers, the waiters/waitresses, the activities staff. A BBQ was prepared on the beach for all of us in the marina, which was super fun. Even included s'mores over a fire at sunset. Pretty darned perfect. They had movies at night outside in a concrete stadium once a week with a bar and popcorn. The President of Mexico even made a stop at the marina. I think he was promoting tourism in the area, but it was pretty exciting seeing him. Marina Riviera Nayarit was fairly new in the area and sorely needed. In our opinion, they did a magnificent job of establishing it with all the needs being met for those that come in on their boats. The Mexican President was there to put his stamp of approval on the project, I'm sure. Kinda fun watching all the goings on that come with such a visit.

The little town was the epitome of a small Mexican fishing village. Cobblestone streets with small food stands here and there, some behind a chain link fence or two, with maybe a horse and a cow in there while you eat made-on-the-premises tortillas, rice, beans and some chicken or fish they just caught, dispatched, and put on the BBQ, while sitting at whatever make-do tables and chairs we found. "Go buy your drinks next door and bring them on over to your table", we were told, and we promptly did that. Loved it! Just delicious. Along with the outside market stands full of trinkets and colorful clothing, magnificent rugs and serapes, and housewares of all kinds, there were huge cast iron pots of something I did not recognize boiling on fire and large buckets of lard in the background waiting to be used. The *tiendas* had big crates and cardboard boxes full of colorful fruits and vegetables lined up along the walls and on the floor. Lettuce, cabbage, potatoes, bananas, limes, tomatoes, onions, most anything you need, and very fresh. My favorite, though, was finding the little tortilla place. Small spot tucked in between other stores, but there they were…my favorite corn tortillas. Fresh made while you wait, if you want, or bags of chips (arghhh!!! Tortilla chips to die for!) Or stacks of fresh tortillas to take back to the boat. Mexican food is my very favorite, so this was the place for me to be sure!!

The markets and restaurants we frequented were quite traditional as you might imagine they would be. Some special cruiser haunts were tucked in amongst all the little stores. Philo's was the hangout for the cruising community, with sailors abundant. Great music, great food, and lots of cervezas and margaritas. Oddly and quite shockingly, we ran into Theo and Marion (sans their wonder dog Skye, who was back at their boat) whom you will recognize from the beginning of our adventure when we met them on the Dismal Swamp in Virginia! At that time, they were sailing in their boat, *Double Dutch*. They told us they now have a new boat, the *Marionetto*! A very fitting name, I should say! Well, here they were at Philo's having lunch when we wandered in! We pretty much all screamed and hugged and caught up on all that transpired since we last saw them. It's such a small world and it makes the world so much fun. We also ran into a friend from our old yacht club in Alameda, Ballena Bay Yacht Club, Jane Fleming! She has a house in Paradise Village around the corner in Banderas Bay and she was at Philo's helping organize a sailing race. We certainly felt right at home here with new friends and now some old friends popping up. Even on Christmas Day, we all filed over to Philo's with a dish we had prepared to add to the chicken and beans that the restaurant had ready. What a special day that was. Christmas Eve, the marina had a really nice event, so we had our holiday away from family plentifully covered with activities and friends.

A very special day was had when we were contacted by our long-time friends, Mary Ann and Bryan, whom you will remember we also saw in Wilmington, NC, when we were coming down the ICW and who were now staying in Puerto Vallarta!! "Come over and meet us for breakfast and spend the day with us!" They did not have to say that more than once. We made a date and Ran and I hiked to the town of Bucerias to catch a bus into Puerto Vallarta, about a 25-minute bus ride. That was quite the experience, but fun. Lots of interesting people on the bus and even a guy who got on at one of the stops with his guitar to serenade us for donations! It's actually a really great way to experience life there, using the bus. We loved it.

We found our rendezvous spot at one of the beautiful churches to meet Mary Ann and Bryan. So good to see them. We then walked to a quaint restaurant for breakfast, sitting outside along some beautiful water. After our leisurely breakfast with great conversation, we proceeded to do a quick tour of Puerto Vallarta with all the colorful wares and beautiful churches with our goal of finding some good tequila, which we did. *Tesoro de Don Felipe Posado*. Perfect. We walked down to the beach and weaved around a hive of umbrellas and pretty people, past lots of vendors selling yummy bbq'd meat on long sticks, or fish on sticks, and found a semi-secluded spot where we sat on the rocks, watched the ocean, and passed the bottle of tequila around. Exceptional conversation and raucous laughter came from that bottle and created such a fun afternoon. That had to be one of the best times ever. We then walked up to the casita Mary Ann and Bryan were renting and up on the roof to watch the sunset. Alas, it was nightfall and time to head back to *Kwanesum*. We were not comfortable with the idea of taking a bus back at that hour so we hailed a cab for the ride back. This day was a day to remember for sure.

La Cruz was fabulous and it treated us so well: music, friends, amazing food, great conversations. But what do we do from here? What is our plan? Big conversations were had. One thought at the time was to take *Kwanesum* up to California and sail her under the Golden Gate Bridge with the flags from all the countries we visited flying on lines from the mast, some forward, some aft. Then pull into a slip at the Oakland Yacht Club, our home port when we were in California, and live aboard there. Dreamers, we are. Another was leaving the boat here in La Cruz, buy a house in California, since the prices were unbelievably good at the time, and doing six months here and six months there. Dreamers, we are 2.0.

It's nice to have choices! We chose the wise financial option to buy a house. We flew back to CA, looked, looked, looked for homes and found one that checked all the boxes. Excellent. That box is checked. But do we want to leave *Kwanesum* here in Mexico? That was heavy on our minds. The almighty dollar always plays a big factor in decisions and paying for the slip here in La Cruz and flights back and forth, and also paying for a house payment, was a bit much. "Let's take her up to California, Ran, and have her there nearer to us."

That decision was made. In the meantime, as I, the resident money manager, calculated how all this would work, it was decided that I would fly back to the house and get a job substituting in the local schools to subsidize our sailing addiction, and Randy would find a crew to bring the boat up to California. This decision bothered me, and it bothered Ran, because we had always done this trip, our retirement adventure, together. We were a team. We knew how the other worked, what the other was thinking, what the other could tolerate; our sailing rhythm was in sync. We could depend on each other to know what to do in any situation that might come up. I was nervous at the thought of Randy sailing up without me. And I hated the fact that I wouldn't be part of that trip. But reason seemed to tell us that this was the best decision.

I flew to our new home, set up the household, and got a job substituting. Ran flew with me, and we took a trip up to Oakland Yacht Club to talk to three of our long-time yacht club friends about being crew on the *'Baja Bash'*, which is the aptly named, trip up to California. The plan was to bring *Kwanesum* up to San Diego. It felt weird. After living on our boat for 4 years with my captain, what was I doing leaving him for this leg of the trip? These guys were *"me hearty and hardy pirates"*, so I was not worried about the crew, I just knew that I was supposed to be the crew. That was an emotional decision for me, and it was hard for Randy, too.

Itchy feet.

Chapter 32
Bashing Baja

The Tale of The Pirates of Kwanesum

This is Captain Ran speaking.

It's time to sail *Kwanesum* back to the States.

To recap, we thought about keeping her in Mexico so we could explore the Sea of Cortez. In reality, however, maintaining our new home in California and *Kwanesum* in Mexico would be cost-prohibitive. So the decision was made. Now for the logistics. Ellen obtained the job she wanted as a substitute teacher back in California to help build our coffers. Although she dearly wanted to make the trip up from Mexico with me on *Kwanesum*, it felt best to stay and funnel that money into said coffers. Throughout our travels, we remained members of the Oakland Yacht Club. There were friends there who we thought might be willing to crew, so we headed up to see if we had any volunteers. And that we did.

Brian Cooley: Distinguished Commodore of the Oakland Yacht Club, a long time dear friend, and sailor extraordinaire. Brian and his wife Mary lived aboard their beautiful Wauquiez, s/v *Mers Douces*. Brian was the first to volunteer. **Bob Martin (Motor Boat Bob)**: Distinguished mechanic and power boater extraordinaire. Also, a member of the Oakland Yacht Club who thought he might like a sailboat cruise up the coast.

Harry Reppert: Distinguished traveler, sailor and onboard cook extraordinaire. Another Oakland Yacht Club experienced sailing member.

The new Pirate Crew of *Kwanesum* was set, with all having extensive experience on the waters of San Francisco Bay. If you can sail the SFBay, you're a good sailor by default. It teaches you a lot.

Dates were set and transportation south to *Kwanesum* was arranged. The plan was for me to go down a week or two before the crew to get things ship-shape and start provisioning. The crew arrived on time and boat familiarization of systems began. Safety and watch schedules were discussed and agreed to. I paid our bill at Marina Riviera Nayarit and said fond farewells to all in the office, in the restaurant, on the dock... everybody. Fond, fond farewells.

Captain log 17 March, 2012, 0830: Left La Cruz de Huanacaxtle, Marina Riviera Nayarit, Dock 9 Slip A8. We are on our way up. Let the bash begin.

Brian put a fishing pole out immediately and caught a small mahi mahi. Dinner! Ceviche! Now, about the winds. Ugh. Winds, of course, were right on our bow. We had the main sail up to steady the boat and were now on our way to bash up to Cabo San Lucas, our next stop. After 300 hard-fought nautical miles, we arrived, three nights on a rough ocean. We were exhausted but glad to be there. The hearty pirate crew of the sailing vessel *Kwanesum* pulled into the Cabo San Lucas marina at 0130hrs, which is not the standard operating procedure, but it was so well lit we had no problem confidently heading in.

Our mission in Cabo was to top off the water and fuel and check out of the country.

Our hard sail to Cabo did not set well with Motor Boat Bob. We had big waves and seas on the nose. Not very comfortable, not very fast. This ride and the three nights at sea were too much for him. Bob had not experienced traveling on the seas in the dark of night and admitted this was too much for him and requested permission to bail out in Cabo and fly home. Of course, he didn't need permission, but it was totally understandable and very smart of him to realize that this would not work for him. You do not want crew aboard that don't want to be there and be able to pull their weight. We were sad to see Bob go.

Some things you learn the hard way. This was my first experience selecting and directing a crew. In retrospect, it might have been better to have clearly vetted the guys about what they expected from this trip and situations that might come from bashing up from Mexico. Except for Brian, who is an exceptional and experienced, intrepid sailor, I should have made sure Harry and Bob understood what their roles would be and what to expect. But as yacht club pirates, we drank a brew or two, they volunteered and all was agreed to.

The first sail plan I voiced to my crew was to tack out toward Hawaii from Mexico, farther away from, and losing sight of, the shore. This would have been a smoother ride in the shipping lanes. Then, we could head back into the San Francisco Bay from that vantage point. But this crew was unsure of losing sight of land. Taking this route close to shore would be a much rougher ride. But my crew wanted to stay within sight of land.

I wanted a happy crew, so I agreed. It made me realize that it was so much easier just sailing with Ellen, as we were always on the same wavelength. Brian was always a person I'd want to sail with, as we had often sailed together on the San Francisco Bay. I knew Ellen would have agreed to go offshore and sail outside. But, then, she was used to that. We had done that often on this voyage. This crew had not. They weren't sure what to expect in taking that course away from the sight of shore.

In Cabo, Motor Boat Bob departed and flew home. The rest of the pirates, Brian, Harry and I, completed the provisioning and checked out of the country. We departed Cabo, made the right turn up the coast, and began the bash up Baja.

As was expected, wind and waves on the nose were the rule and not the exception, unfortunately. Sometimes sailors get lucky going this direction up the coast and have good seas and good weather. We were certainly hoping that would be our situation, but it wasn't. Harry decided he didn't want to stand watches but would tend to the cooking and cleaning. While that was a nice offer, we weren't expecting any cleaning, at all, as we needed to watch our water consumption. And cleaning usually involves the use of water. Who cleans much when you're at sea anyway? Our cooking was supposed to be pretty simple, as our focus was just to get the heck up to San Diego and each stand a watch along the way. Peanut butter and jelly sandwiches are fine, right? I needed a crew on watch, not on the stove or mop. But, I also needed to keep my crew happy. This situation now left the watches and times at the helm to just Brian and me. Thank heaven for Brian. Ellen and I did watches with just the two of us, so that's how this was going to have to go. It was just disappointing not to have that extra downtime that another man on watch would give. This was a rougher trip than Ellen and I had ever done so it was exhausting not having that extra man at the helm to count on.

Before leaving on our Baja Bash, I secured what I thought was a good weather service that I could count on to monitor our trip and give us advice along the way. He came highly recommended, so I felt this was a good decision. Ellen also monitored the weather from home via the Passage Weather app and the Magic Seaweed app. These apps showed the wave height and direction of the waves, the wind direction and speed, as well as the overall weather. All are very important for sailors. She kept us informed via emails I was able to get through our Pactor modem on my Single Side Band radio. As long as a ham operator picked up my request to send an email, this worked well. Sometimes, there's no one out there, or no one can read my signal, but this close to Mexico, I didn't have a problem sending emails. This is another good technical piece of equipment that keeps me in touch. All were very helpful. However, our weather guy turned out to be a dud! He was wrong 90% of the time! I kid you not. I would check with him and then check with Ellen and she would come back saying, "Ran, I'm not seeing that at all!!"

Then she would tell me what her apps were saying and even check a couple of other ones to be sure. This is how we did our weather the whole way on our sailing adventure. We always checked two or three weather sources. The stupid thing was, I was paying this incompetent person, who shall remain nameless, for his expertise! Eventually, we didn't hear from him at all. (We found out later he had a heart attack and died! Well, no wonder we didn't hear from him!) Sorry about that, but it kind of left us hanging out there. We also later heard he had a lot of other troubles of the alcohol kind. Guess I didn't research that one enough.

This wasn't the trip I expected. It was a really tough one. The weather was crappy on this leg of the trip, so we decided to tuck into Magdalena Bay for respite. We were bushed. This is a sheltered anchorage and we could avoid some bad weather in there for a bit. We came in at night and started to anchor in a spot that turned out to be too close to the surf line. We needed to move further away from the surf for a good, solid anchorage.

Brian, in his infinite wisdom had brought night vision goggles with him, but do you think we thought about using them that night trying to find a good anchorage in the dark? Nope. We both forgot completely about having them aboard. We were so tired, though, that it didn't even occur to us.

The next stop would be Turtle Bay, or Bahia Tortuga. After a much-needed night of rest, we poked our head out again and headed on up. More winds on the nose and bashing against waves. By the time we arrived at Turtle Bay, we were wiped out. After two days of ridiculous progress, we pulled in. Such slow going in this direction through these seas and winds. Big, slow. We needed to rest. We were tired, and it was getting cold at night out there. We were about 300-plus miles from San Diego. The weather still wasn't great. We needed to stop. We had a little company here. Other boats came in and hunkered down. Most were going south, waiting for weather, and oddly enough, one boat was going north. A family of 4. No plundering or pillaging in the village by these pirates. Just rest and checking the weather. It was nice to have a couple of days to regroup and visit with everyone there. And to top off with water. Very important water.

A couple of days turned into a week. The weather was not cooperating. As much as we wanted to get home, we needed to wait. We need at least halfway decent weather. Finally, the time came. A short break appeared and we finally headed out on 2 April. Still constantly checking weather, it became necessary to pull into San Quintin to rest. That was a two-day trip up. This journey is not for the faint of heart. Not if you want to be constantly in sight of land. As our luck on this leg seemed to go, bigger weather was appearing on the apps, so we sat there for a couple of days. We were so close to the final leg of this voyage, AKA the BIG Baja Bash. Bash being the operative word.

Heed that knowledge, fellow sailors, if you ever find yourselves going north up Baja.

Finally, we were off and running with San Diego on our minds. The weather looked good for what ended up being a two-day trip. We did get some winds coming from a favorable direction and were able to finally, completely sail *Kwanesum* like the champ she was. What a great relief to be sailing. Now into San Diego and check into our own US of A. When we pulled in, it was mid-afternoon and we had a berth already assigned to us, so we hailed Cabrillo Isle Marina to tell them we were coming in. It was odd, though, as we had heard tales of other boats coming in from Mexico having to go through a big check-in process when back in the US. But that didn't happen to us and we were grateful for that, to be sure. We just hailed them and said "Hey, we're here!" They pretty much said, "Roger that, thank you, Captain," and that was it! They very likely already had our check out information from Mexico on their computers.

Now, celebratory drinks and dinner at Fiddler's Green Restaurant completed the Bash. We crashed for the night and made sure *Kwanesum* was tucked in well the next morning. Harry had his car there in San Diego from when they drove down from Alameda to fly to Cabo. We piled in that car and headed up the I-5 highway at breakneck speed, as Harry put it, to drop me off in Gustine. The remaining two pirates then sped on up to Alameda.

Avast, me pirate hearties! The Bash was done!

Chapter 33
California!

Not All Who Wander Are Lost

A week was relished at home in Gustine to rest. We are nearing the end of our adventure. That reality was becoming more apparent. And the emotions that go with that realization.

Ellen returned with me to San Diego to bring *Kwanesum* up the coast. It was so good to be back on *Kwanesum* with Ellen, my co-captain. It was definitely hard to leave sunshiny San Diego but off we must go, bringing our boat up. We had perfect weather and seas. Our weather sites determined it would be good and we were awfully glad it held true. Our destination was Avalon on Santa Catalina Island for some R&R.

Rest and relaxation in Avalon on *Kwanesum* was wonderful Now on to Ventura. The original plan was to complete the voyage by heading up to the San Francisco Bay and our berth waiting for us at the Oakland Yacht Club. We got to Ventura and loved it there. The weather was great and the Channel Islands made for good sailing. Maybe we will keep the boat here! That thought crossed our minds. What a great place this was. We had a really good slip in the marina and we had friends here with their boats. Excellent restaurants. Just a really nice area. I wonder if we should stay here….

Sadly, we keep realizing…we are on the last leg of our trip…our adventure… our life these last four years. We decided on a permanent slip in Ventura, but… we made the angst-ridden decision to put our beloved *Kwanesum* up for sale. The time had come, it seemed, to let someone else love *Kwanesum*. There is so much emotion at this point I can hardly bear to write it down. The people, places, and adventures we experienced were so unbelievable.

The reality hits hard. Our adventure on *Kwanesum* had come to an end. It may sound like our *itchy feet* are silenced/quieted.

Does this mean we no longer have *itchy feet*? Not by a long shot, but that's another story.

A yacht club friend once said, "I may be Finnish, but I'm not finished yet!"

I would rather be ashes than dust!

I would rather that my spark should burn out in a brilliant blaze than it should be stifled by dry-rot.

I would rather be a superb meteor, every atom of me in a magnificent glow, than a sleepy and permanent planet.

The function of man is to live, not to exist.

I shall not waste my days trying to prolong them. I shall use my time.

- Jack London

Made in the USA
Las Vegas, NV
25 May 2024

90362600R00215